Computer Communications and Networks

For other titles published in this series, go to
www.springer.com/series/4198

The **Computer Communications and Networks** series is a range of textbooks, monographs and handbooks. It sets out to provide students, researchers and non-specialists alike with a sure grounding in current knowledge, together with comprehensible access to the latest developments in computer communications and networking.

Emphasis is placed on clear and explanatory styles that support a tutorial approach, so that even the most complex of topics is presented in a lucid and intelligible manner.

Alan Holt · Chi-Yu Huang

802.11 Wireless Networks

Security and Analysis

Dr. Alan Holt
IP Performance
1-3 Merietts Court
Long Ashton Business Park
Long Ashton
Bristol BS41 9LW
UK

Dr. Chi-Yu Huang
Tata Technologies Ltd
6 Monarch Court
Emerald Park
Emersons Green
Bristol BS16 7FH
UK

Series Editor
Professor A.J. Sammes, BSc, MPhil, PhD, FBCS, CEng
Centre for Forensic Computing
Cranfield University
DCMT, Shrivenham
Swindon SN6 8LA
UK

ISBN 978-1-4471-2575-4   ISBN 978-1-84996-275-9 (eBook)
DOI 10.1007/978-1-84996-275-9
Springer London Dordrecht Heidelberg New York

British Library Cataloguing in Publication Data
A catalogue record for this book is available from the British Library

Cover design: VTEX, Vilnius

Printed on acid-free paper

Springer is part of Springer Science+Business Media (www.springer.com)

Auntie Kath

Preface

This book is about wireless local area networks (WLANs) based upon the IEEE 802.11 standards. It has three primary objectives:

- To introduce the principles of 802.11 wireless networks and show how to configure equipment in order to implement various network solutions.
- To provide an understanding of the security implications of wireless networks and demonstrate how vulnerabilities can be mitigated.
- To introduce the underlying 802.11 protocols and build mathematical models in order to analyse performance in a WLAN environment.

The book is aimed at industry professionals as well as undergraduate and graduate level students. It is intended as a companion for a university course on wireless networking.

A practical approach is adopted in this book; examples are provided throughout, supported by detailed instructions. We cover a number of wireless vendors; namely, Cisco's Aironet, Alactel-Lucent's Omniaccess and Meru Networks. While separate vendors, all three systems have a Cisco IOS-like command-line interface.

The GNU/Linux operating system is used extensively throughout this book. GNU/Linux systems have gained considerable popularity in the server and embedded system market (indeed, both Alcatel-Lucent and Meru Network's wireless equipment are based upon GNU/Linux). As well as the core GNU/Linux software we also use a number of open source applications. Wireless equipment does not operate in isolation. There are times when other network services are required, such as RADIUS. FreeRADIUS, in conjunction with a MySQL database server, is used to demonstrate an enterprise secutity WLAN. For convenience, the Xen virtualisation application is employed to emulate a multi-server environment. We show how to build and configure these systems.

There are many GNU/Linux *distributions* available. In this book, we use Debian and its derivative, Ubuntu. Debian and Debian like distributions have APT, a powerful package management application that greatly simplifies software installation and maintenance. Other distributions will have their advocates and supporters and if you wish to replicate the examples in this book we suggest you use the distribution with which you are most familiar. However, you will have to *translate* the instructions to suit your distribution where they differ from Ubuntu/Debian.

We present a number of mathematical models in this book for analysing the performance of 802.11. We show how to build these models using the commercial application computer algebra, Maple. The examples presented in this book were developed on Maple version 11, but all the examples should work on older versions.

Acknowledgments

The authors would like to thank the following people for the valuable contribution they made to this book: Dr Adrian Davies, Dr Sue Casson (Leeds University), Michael Dewsnip (DL Consulting), Wayne Look (IP Performance), and Damien Parker (IP Performance).

Thanks also to Simon Rees of Spinger for all his support in helping us through this process.

Bristol, UK   Alan Holt
Hamilton, New Zealand   Chi-Yu Huang

Contents

1 Introduction 1
    1.1 IEEE 802 2
    1.2 Wireless LANs 3
    1.3 A Brief History of 802.11 7
    1.4 The RF Environment 8
    1.5 Book Outline 12
    1.6 Summary 13

2 Radio Frequencies 15
    2.1 The Electromagnetic Spectrum 15
    2.2 Radio Waves 17
        2.2.1 Direct Path 19
        2.2.2 Absorption 22
        2.2.3 Reflection 22
        2.2.4 Diffraction 24
        2.2.5 Refraction 25
        2.2.6 Scattering 25
        2.2.7 Multi-path 25
    2.3 Radio Frequency Regulation 27
    2.4 Spectrum Management 32
    2.5 Summary 34

3 Medium Access Control 35
    3.1 802.11 Services 36
    3.2 MAC Frame Format 38
    3.3 Distributed Coordination Function 39
        3.3.1 Carrier Sensing 40
        3.3.2 Transmission Methods 40
        3.3.3 Inter-frame Spacing 41
        3.3.4 Random Back-Off Algorithm 43
        3.3.5 Fragmentation 43

	3.3.6	Fairness	44
3.4		Point Coordination Function	45
3.5		Hybrid Coordination Function	45
	3.5.1	Enhanced Distributed Channel Access	46
	3.5.2	HCF Controlled Channel Access	48
3.6		Summary	50

4 Physical Layer 51

4.1	Frequency Hopping Spread Spectrum	51
4.2	Direct Sequence Spread Spectrum	54
4.3	High-Rate Direct Sequence Spread Spectrum	56
4.4	Orthogonal Frequency Division Multiplexing	58
4.5	Extended Rate PHY	60
4.6	MIMO-OFDM	62
4.7	Beamforming	66
4.8	Summary	71

5 Cryptography 73

5.1	Ciphers	73
	5.1.1 Symmetric Key Cryptography	74
	5.1.2 Asymmetric Key Cryptography	76
5.2	Encryption	78
	5.2.1 RC4	79
	5.2.2 DES and Triple-DES	80
	5.2.3 AES	80
5.3	Message Digests	81
5.4	Digital Signatures	83
5.5	Digital Certificates	84
5.6	Generating Digital Certificates	86
	5.6.1 Generating a Certificate Authority	87
	5.6.2 Generating Certificates	90
	5.6.3 Testing the Certificates	95
5.7	Summary	97

6 Wireless Security 99

6.1	Pre-RSNA	99
	6.1.1 Authentication	100
	6.1.2 Encryption and Integrity	101
6.2	RSNA	101
	6.2.1 Authentication	102
	6.2.2 Key Management	105
	6.2.3 Encryption and Integrity	105
6.3	Summary	108

7 Configuring Wireless Networks 111

| 7.1 | Ad-hoc Network | 112 |

7.2   WEP 114
7.3   WPA with Pre-shared Key 115
7.4   Multiple SSIDs 119
7.5   Wireless Distribution System 121
7.6   Wireless Bridge 123
7.7   Build an Open Source Access-Point 126
       7.7.1   Root Filesystem 126
       7.7.2   Administration 127
       7.7.3   Configuring the Access-Point 129
       7.7.4   Installing Grub 130
       7.7.5   Compile the Kernel 130
       7.7.6   Install Root Directory Structure onto Compact Flash 132
7.8   Summary 134

8   Robust Security Network 135
8.1   Installing FreeRadius 136
8.2   Configuring FreeRadius 138
8.3   Configure FreeRadius to use MySQL 140
8.4   Testing 144
8.5   Configure EAP 146
8.6   Configure TLS 148
8.7   NAS Configuration 149
8.8   Wireless Client 150
8.9   Summary 154

9   MAC Layer Performance Analysis 155
9.1   Fragmentation 155
9.2   Analysis of Multiple Hops 156
9.3   Throughput 158
9.4   Summary 166

10 Link Rate Adaptation 167
10.1   Walffish-Ikegami Model 167
10.2   Berg Model 168
10.3   802.11b Link Rate Adaptation 171
10.4   Link Rate Adaptation in an Urban Area 176
10.5   802.11a Link Rate Adaptation 178
10.6   Link Rate Experiments 182
10.7   Summary 184

A   Build a Xen Server 185
A.1   Install Xen 185
A.2   DomU Configuration 187
       A.2.1   RADIUS Server 187
       A.2.2   MySQL Server 188
       A.2.3   DHCP Server 189

A.2.4 Test Client 190

B   Initial Configuration of Access-Point Controllers 193
     B.1 Alcalel-Lucent Omniaccess Controller 193
     B.2 Meru Controller 194

References 201

Futher Reading 205

Index 207

Abbreviations

AAD	Additional authentication data
ADSL	Asynchronous digital subscriber line
AES	Advanced encryption standard
ANSI	American National Standards Institute
AS	Authentication server
BSS	Basic service set
BSSID	Basic service set Identifier
CBC	Cipher-block chaining
CBC-MAC	Cipher-block chaining with message authentication code
CCK	Complimentary code keying
CCM	Counter mode and cipher-block chaining with message authentication code
CCMP	Counter mode and cipher-block chaining with message authentication code protocol
CFB	Cipher feedback
CFP	Contention free period
CP	Contention period
CRC	Cyclic redundancy check.
CSMA/CA	Carrier sense multiple access with collision avoidance
CTR	Counter mode
CTS	Clear-to-send
DAB	Digital audio broadcasting
DES	Cata encryption system
DHCP	Dynamic host configuration protocol
DN	Distinguished name
DNS	Domain name system
DPSK	Differentiated phase shift keying
DBPSK	Differentiated binary phase shift keying
DQPSK	Differentiated quadrature phase shift keying
DSA	Digital signature algorithm
DVB	Digital video broadcasting

DSSS	Direct sequence spread spectrum
EAP	Extensible authentication protocol
EAPOL	Extensible authentication protocol over local area network
ECB	Electronic codebook
ERP-OFDM	Extended rate PHY, orthogonal frequency division multiplexing
FHSS	Frequency hopping spread spectrum
FFT	Fast fourier transform
FSK	Frequency shift keying
GI	Guard interval
GMK	Group master key
HCF	Hybrid coordination function
HCCA	HCF controlled channel access
HR/DSSS	High rate direct sequence spread spectrum
IBSS	Independent basic service set
IEEE	Institute of Electrical and Electronics Engineers
ICMP	Internet control message protocol
IFFT	Inverse fast fourier transform
IP	Internet protocol
ISM	Industrial, scientific and medical
IR	Infrared
LAN	Local area network
KCK	EAPOL-key confirmation key
KEK	EAPOL-key kncryption key
LEAP	Lightweight EAP
MAC	Medium access control
MAC	Message Authentication Code
MIC	Message integrity code
MD5	Message digest 5
MIMO	Multiple-input multiple-output
MISO	Multiple-input single-output
MRC	Maximum ratio combining
OFB	Output feedback
OFDM	Orthogonal frequency division multiplexing
PBCC	Packet binary convolution coding
PEAP	Protected EAP
PING	Packet internet groper
PLCP	Physical layer convergence procedure
PSK	Pre-shared key
PSK	Phase shift keying
PTK	Pairwise temporal key
PMD	Physical medium dependent
PMK	Pairwise master key
PN	Packet number
PSDU	PLCP service data unit
PPDU	PLCP protocol data unit

QAM	Quadrature amplitude modulation
QPSK	Quadrature phase shift keying
RADIUS	Remote authentication dial in user service
RSA	RSA
RSN	Robust security network
RSNA	Robust security network association
RTS	Request-to-send
SHA	Secure hash algorithm
SISO	Single-input, single-output
SIMO	Single-input, multiple-output
SNMP	Simple network management protocol
SSID	Service set identifier
SSL	Secure socket layer
TCP	Transmission control protocol
TKIP	Temporal key integrity protocol
TLS	Transport layer security
UDP	User datagram protocol
VoIP	Voice over IP
WEP	Wired equivalent privacy
WPA	Wi-Fi protected access

List of Figures

1.1   The IEEE 802 reference model   2
1.2   Performance of Aloha and CSMA schemes   5
1.3   WLANs detected by Kismet Application   9
1.4   Spectrum analysis of 2.4 GHz band   10
1.5   Shannon limit   11
1.6   BER of BPSK modulation   12

2.1   Electric and magnetic field directions   16
2.2   Electric circuit   18
2.3   A half-wavelength Di-pole antenna   18
2.4   Wave components   19
2.5   Refracted radio wave   19
2.6   Free-space loss   22
2.7   Fresnel zone   23
2.8   Diffraction   24
2.9   Diffraction loss   25
2.10 Rayleigh probability density function   27
2.11 Ricean probability density function   28
2.12 802.11 channel allocation in the 2.4 GHz band   30
2.13 U-NII lower and middle   31
2.14 U-NII upper   32

3.1   802.11 reference model   36
3.2   802.11 Infrastructure Network   37
3.3   Authentication/association state machine   37
3.4   MAC header   38
3.5   Frame control field   38
3.6   Channel access with the basic DCF transmission method   41
3.7   Channel access using RTS/CTS and setting the NAV   41
3.8   Fragmentation of a MSDU into MPDUs   44
3.9   MSDU sent as multiple fragments under the RTS/CTS method   . . .   44
3.10 PCF access   46

3.11   Prioritisation in EDCA   48
3.12   The four access categories (ACs) for ECDA   49

4.1   PPDU encapsulation   52
4.2   Frequency hopping spread spectrum   52
4.3   The PLCP frame format for FHSS   54
4.4   Direct sequence spread spectrum   55
4.5   Long preamble   56
4.6   Polyphase complementary codes   57
4.7   PBCC convolutional encoder   58
4.8   Short preamble   58
4.9   The PLCP frame format for OFDM in 802.11a   59
4.10   Cyclic prefix   61
4.11   MIMO Communication system   62
4.12   Space-time coding   63
4.13   Diversity gain for N replica input streams   63
4.14   Spatial multiplexing   64
4.15   Capacity of a MIMO system   65
4.16   Capacity of Tx/Rx diversity   65
4.17   Gain of a simple beamformer   67
4.18   Gain of a simple beamformer (polarplot)   68
4.19   Uniform linear array (ULA)   69
4.20   Gain of a beamformer with a boresight of $0°$ 70
4.21   Gain of a beamformer with a boresight of $45°$ 71
4.22   Beamformer for various boresight angles (polar plot)   72

5.1   ECB encryption   74
5.2   An illustration of the problems related to ECB Encryption   76

6.1   Summary of 802.11i security   100
6.2   Assembly of a WEP frame   102
6.3   802.1X   103
6.4   EAP over LAN (EAPOL)   104
6.5   802.11i key hierarchy   105
6.6   TKIP frame   106
6.7   TKIP encapsulation   107
6.8   Expanded CCMP frame   108
6.9   CCMP header   108
6.10   CCMP encapsulation process   109
6.11   CCMP decapsulation process   109

7.1   An Aironet AP running dual SSIDs   119
7.2   Wireless distribution system   121
7.3   A wireless bridge topology   124
7.4   Output of make menuconfig command   131

8.1   RSN architecture   136

9.1   Probability of MSDU transmission failure.   156
9.2   Probability of MSDU transmission failure.   157
9.3   Successful transmission probaility for multiple links   157
9.4   File transfer times   166

10.1   Walfish-Ikegami model path loss   169
10.2   Street plan   169
10.3   Signal loss in an urban area (Berg model)   172
10.4   802.11b Link rate adaptation versus SNR (dB)   174
10.5   802.11b Link adaptation $NOISE = -90$ dB.   175
10.6   802.11b Link adaptation $NOISE = -87$ dB.   176
10.7   Link adaptation of 802.11b in an urban area ($\phi = 90°$).   177
10.8   Link adaptation of 802.11b in an urban area ($\phi = 55°$).   178
10.9   Walfish-Ikegami model link rate adaptation for BER 10^{-4}   178
10.10   802.11a link rate adaptation versus SNR   180
10.11   Link rate versus distance for 802.11a   181
10.12   Retransmissions versus link rate   183

List of Tables

1.1 Some of the IEEE 802 standards 3

2.1 The electromagnetic spectrum 17
2.2 Signal losses caused by material 23
2.3 ISM bands 29
2.4 Channel allocation in the 2.4 GHz band 30
2.5 5 GHz unlicensed bands 31

3.1 SIFS and aSlotTime values 42
3.2 Contention windows values 43
3.3 Mapping of user priority to access category 47
3.4 Default values of the EDCA parameter set 48

4.1 Details of modulation methods in 802.11 52
4.2 DBPSK encoding 55
4.3 DQPSK encoding 55
4.4 Details of modulation methods in 802.11b 57
4.5 Details of modulation schemes for the 802.11a PHY 59
4.6 802.11g PHYs 61

5.1 Performance of AES 80
5.2 Performance comparison of RC4, DES and AES 81

7.1 Summary of wireless equipment manufacturers 112
7.2 Summary of laptops used to form an ad-hoc network 112

8.1 IP addresses 136

10.1 Modulation techniques supported by 802.11b 172
10.2 802.11a Link rate adaptation (empirical data) 179
10.3 Retransmissions 183

Chapter 1
Introduction

Communication systems that rely on cabling are inherently faster, more reliable, and more secure than wireless systems. Installing a cabling infrastructure can be expensive. Furthermore, if the network traverses public highways, it is subject to regulation and requires the services of a licensed operator. Wireless communication has the advantage of mobility and obviates the need for cabling, but the radio frequency spectrum is also heavily regulated. Nevertheless, the allocation of unlicensed parts of the spectrum has facilitated the growth in wireless local area networks (WLANs).

The European Telecommunications Standards Institute (ETSI) published the first WLAN standard, HiperLAN/1, finalised in 1995, and followed by HiperLAN/2 in 2000. However, it is the IEEE 802.11 WLAN standard that has become the most widely accepted. Portable devices such as laptops, personal digital assistants (PDAs) and even mobile phones have 802.11 chipsets built in as standard. Furthermore, wireless infrastructure equipment (access-points) is relatively inexpensive.

WLAN technology has progressed at a rapid pace. The original IEEE 802.11 standard supported data rates up to 2 Mb/s. At the time of writing this book, devices capable of 54 Mb/s are commonplace. Furthermore, devices that utilise MIMO (multiple input, multiple output) technology, which can support up to 300 Mb/s, are growing in popularity. The 802.11 standard has been very successful in incorporating advances in modulation techniques while maintaining interoperability with legacy schemes. New modulation schemes, however, do not replace subsequent schemes. 802.11 can select any scheme from the current set of modulation schemes in order to optimise frame transmission. In this way, wireless devices can *link rate adapt* according to the channel conditions.

802.11 has not been without its problems, especially with regard to security. WLANs are particularly vulnerable to eavesdropping, unauthorised access and denial of service due to their broadcast nature. The original 802.11 standard had no security provisions at all, neither authentication, encryption or data integrity. Some access-point vendors offered authentication of the client's physical address. The standard was amended in 1999 to support a basic protection mechanism. Wired

A. Holt, C.-Y. Huang, *802.11 Wireless Networks,*
Computer Communications and Networks,
DOI 10.1007/978-1-84996-275-9_1, © Springer-Verlag London Limited 2010

equivalent privacy (WEP) used cryptographic methods for authentication and encryption. The security flaws in WEP, however, have given rise to a complete research field. In 2001, Fluhrer, Mantin, and Shamir showed that the WEP key could be obtained within a couple hours with just a consumer computer [11]. The authors highlighted a weakness in RC4's key scheduling algorithm and showed that it was possible to derive the key merely by collecting encrypted frames and analysing them. Since then, more sophisticated WEP attacks have been developed. Along with advances in computing power, the WEP key can be recovered in seconds. A further vulnerability with WEP is that the pre-shared key is common to all users on the same SSID. Any user associated with an SSID, therefore, can decrypt packets of other users on the same SSID.

These problems have largely been resolved with the deprecation of WEP and the introduction of enhanced security methods. As with the introduction of new modulation techniques, interoperability is an issue. The current security methods rely on modern cryptography techniques which are only available on new devices. On legacy devices, interim solutions have been adopted.

1.1 IEEE 802

The Institute of Electrical and Electronic Engineers (IEEE) is a large non-profit, professional society concerned with technological research and development. Its standards board oversees the development of IEEE standards and is accredited by the American National Standards Institute (ANSI). Project 802 was initiated in 1980 with the aim of defining a set of standards for local area network (LAN) technology. The standards cover the data link and physical layers of the International Organization for Standardization (ISO) open system interconnection (OSI) seven layer reference model [32]. The data link layer is concerned with the reliable transfer of data frames over the physical channel. It implements various forms of error control, flow control and synchronisation. In the 802 reference model, the data link layer comprises two sub-layers, the logical link control (LLC) sub-layer and the medium access control (MAC) sub-layer. Figure 1.1 shows the 802 reference model.

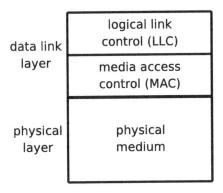

Fig. 1.1 The IEEE 802 reference model

Table 1.1 Some of the IEEE 802 standards

Number	Standard	Comment
802.1	Bridging	
802.2	Logical link control (LLC)	
802.3	CSMA/CD	Ethernet-like LAN
802.4	Token bus	Disbanded
802.5	Token ring	Inactive
802.11	Wireless LANs	Wi-Fi
802.15	Wireless PANs	Bluetooth and Zigbee
802.16	Wireless MANs	WiMAX

LLC is defined in the IEEE 802.2 standard. Its primary function is to provide an interface between the MAC layer and the higher layers (network layer). It performs multiplexing functions in order to support multiple upper layer protocols. Furthermore, it is responsible for flow control and error control. Both connectionless and connection-orientated frame delivery schemes are supported. LLC is unconcerned with the specific details of the LAN medium itself. That is the responsibility of the MAC sub-layer which is primarily concerned with managing access to the physical channel. The physical layer of 802 is responsible for the transmission and reception of bits, encoding and decoding of signals and synchronisation (preamble processing). The physical layer hides the specifics of the medium from the MAC sub-layer.

The first 802 standards were wired LANs. Carrier sense multiple access with collision detect (CSMA/CD) based LANs (802.3) are the most widely used. Token bus (802.4), token ring (802.5) and fibre distributed data interface (FDDI) were also defined.

Wireless network standards emerged in the 1990s. IEEE 802.11 defined a wireless LAN technology that operates in license free bands. 802.11 is commonly referred to as *Wi-Fi*. 802.11 employs a CSMA protocol similar to 802.3 (and Ethernet). However, instead of using collision detection, it uses collision avoidance.

Wireless personal area networks (PANs) are covered by 802.15, where 802.15.1 specifies the Bluetooth standard and 802.15.4 defines Zigbee. IEEE 802.16 is a wireless metropolitan area network (MAN) also known as WiMAX. Table 1.1 shows a summary of some of the 802 standards.

1.2 Wireless LANs

The IEEE 802.11 standard has its roots in *WaveLAN* [37], which was a proprietary wireless LAN system from NCR that pre-dates 802.11. NCR, however, submitted the design of WaveLAN to the IEEE 802.11 committee. The IEEE 802.11 standard was first released in 1997 and ratified in 1999. It was capable of 1 or 2 Mb/s transmission rates (depending upon the wireless channel conditions). It operated in the infrared band and unlicensed radio frequency band. The Federal Communications Commission (FCC), in the US, allocated the 2.4 GHz industrial scientific medical (ISM) band for wireless LANs in 1985. Pre-802.11 and early 802.11 WLANs also used the 900 MHz ISM band. The original 802.11 standard has been superceded by a number of amendments released by the IEEE.

A competitor to the IEEE 802.11 WLAN is the ETSI high performance radio local area network 1 (HiperLAN/1), which uses a CSMA/CA methods similar to 802.11. HiperLAN/2 is similar to 802.11a, however, instead of using CSMA/CA, medium access is dynamic time division multiple access (TDMA). When it was released in 2000, HiperLAN/2 outperformed 802.11. Despite this, 802.11 devices quickly gained market dominance.

802.11 is one of a number of *multi-access* LAN technologies. In general, multi-access protocols fall into two categories: active and passive. Active systems allow users to transmit whenever they have something to send. Various methods are used to avoid collisions. These methods vary in their sophistication, complexity and effectiveness. Passive systems rely on a central controller which grants access to the communication channel by *polling* devices in turn.

802.11 controls channel access through a number of coordination functions. Both contention based (active) and contention free (passive) access techniques are specified in the standard. Contention based access is provided by the distributed coordination function (DCF). DCF is a mandatory component of 802.11. The point coordination function (PCF) supports contention free access and is an optional component of 802.11. The 802.11e amendment supports differentiated services for both contention-based and contention-free access methods.

One of the first active multi-access wireless systems was Aloha [1]. Abramson conceived the Aloha system in 1970 for a packet radio network at the University of Hawaii campus. Packet radio devices communicate over a common frequency band using a random access method.

The first Aloha access scheme (commonly referred to as pure Aloha) is relatively straightforward. A device transmits whenever it has data to send. The device verifies that a packet has been sent successfully (or not) by monitoring the broadcast channel during transmission. If a collision occurs, the packet is retransmitted. Repeated collisions are avoided by employing an exponential back-off algorithm whereby retransmissions are deferred for a random period. While simple, the pure Aloha scheme is inefficient with regards to channel utilisation. The throughput of pure Aloha $S_{\text{pureAloha}}$ is expressed as a function of offered traffic load G, thus:

$$S_{\text{pureAloha}} = Ge^{-2G} \tag{1.1}$$

A slotted version of the Aloha protocol improved throughput efficiency. With the slotted-Aloha scheme, packet transmissions are synchronised to discrete time slots. This has the effect of reducing collision times. While slotted-Aloha is an improvement over pure-Aloha, the channel efficiency is far from ideal. The throughput for slotted Aloha $S_{\text{slottedAloha}}$ is given by:

$$S_{\text{slottedAloha}} = Ge^{-G} \tag{1.2}$$

Fig. 1.2 Performance of
Aloha and CSMA schemes

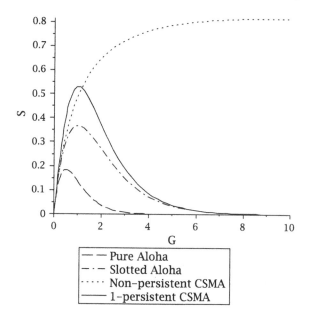

From the graph in Fig. 1.2, it can be seen that slotted Aloha performs better than pure Aloha. The maximum throughput achieved by pure Aloha is only 18 percent, compared to 37 percent for slotted Aloha.

A number of variations of the Aloha protocol have been researched. Half duplex Aloha (Aloha-HD) implements a limited form of carrier sensing. A device defers any transmission (according to its back-off algorithm) if it detects a packet for which it is the recipient. If it detects a packet for which it is not the recipient then it behaves like pure Aloha. Note that this sensing function is only effective if it is able to capture the packet header. If the "sensing" begins after the transmission of the header it is impossible to extract the destination address and determine the recipient. Again, in this case, the device resorts to the pure Aloha protocol. Carrier sense Aloha (Aloha-CS) is a variant of Aloha-HD. It extends the carrier sensing function to include all packets regardless of whether the sensing device is the recipient or not.

Aloha is the predecessor to carrier sense multiple access (CSMA) systems used in many broadcast networks today (both wired and wireless). There is a variety of CSMA protocols:

- non-persistent
- 1-persistent
- p-persistent

With non-persistent CSMA, the device senses the channel prior to transmission. The device initiates the packet transmission if the channel is idle, however, if the channel is busy the device executes a back-off algorithm and reschedules packet transmission to some time in the future (chosen at random). The problem with non-persistence is that even if a number of devices have data to send the channel will, after completion of the current transmission, remain idle until the first back-off timer expires. The problem of channel idle time is overcome by 1-persistent CSMA. A device transmits if it senses the channel to be idle (just like non-persistent CSMA). If the channel is busy, the device continues to sense the channel. When the channel becomes free, transmission begins immediately, while this overcomes the "idle channel" problem. A collision is inevitable, however, once the channel becomes idle if two or more devices had previously deferred transmission when the channel was busy. The throughput of non-persistent CSMA is given by:

$$S_{\text{np-CSMA}} = \frac{Ge^{-aG}}{G(1+2a) + e^{-aG}} \tag{1.3}$$

The throughout of 1-persistent CSMA is:

$$S_{\text{1p-CSMA}} = \frac{G[1 + G + aG(1 + G + aG/s)]e^{-G(1+2a)}}{G(1+2a) - (1 - e^{-aG}) + (1+aG)e^{-G(1+a)}} \tag{1.4}$$

where a is ratio of propagation delay and packet transmission time. The throughput of non-persistent and 1-persistent CSMA is shown in Fig. 1.2. For the purpose of illustration, a value of $a = 0.001$ is used.

With p-persistence, a device sensing the transition of a busy channel to an idle channel, will initiate transmission with a probability p. It defers transmission with a probability $1 - p$, in which case, it performs its back-off algorithm. Ethernet (and its IEEE equivalent, 802.3), though not a wireless LAN, is worth mentioning here as it adopts a 1-persistent CSMA scheme. In all three CSMA schemes, (non/1/p-persistent), the device performs back-off when a collision is detected. However, back-off cannot begin until the end of the packet transmission, even though it is corrupted by the collision with another packet. Collision detection (CSMA/CD) reduces this wasted capacity by ceasing transmission and generating a short jamming signal to ensure that other transmitting devices are aware of the collision. Back-off is performed after transmitting the jamming signal. This scheme is referred to as *listen-while-talk. Ethernet. IEEE 802.3.*

Collision detection, however, is not conducive to wireless networks. Firstly, transmitting a packet and listening for collisions simultaneously would require two radios. This would make wireless devices prohibitively expensive. Secondly, signals in free space suffer greater attenuation than signals transmitted over a wire. While the strength of an interference signal may be sufficiently strong to corrupt a frame at the receiving device, it could have faded beyond detection by the time it reached the distant sending device. This is commonly known as the *hidden node* problem [28]. A related problem is the *exposed* terminal scenario. An *exposed* device must defer to a neighbouring device that is transmitting to some other device which is out of range of the exposed device. The exposed device will not interfere with the signal at the (out-of-range) receiver, yet it is prevented from transmitting. For the reasons described above, 802.11 uses a CSMA scheme based on *collision avoidance* (CSMA/CA) for contention based channel access. 802.11's coordination functions (both contention based and contention free) are discussed in more detail in Chap. 3.

Tobagi and Kleinrock [34] proposed the busy tone multiple access (BTMA) protocol as a solution to the hidden/exposed terminal problem. BTMA uses a data channel and control channel. A device emits a "busy-tone" signal on the control channel when it is receiving on the data channel. Neighbouring devices defer transmission for the duration of the busy-tone.

Split-channel reservation multiple access (SRMA) proposed a handshake between the sender and receiver. This represents a power saving over BTMA which must transmit a continuous signal throughout reception. Like BTMA, SRMA uses a data channel for transmitting data and a separate control channel for exchanging handshakes.

Multiple access collision avoidance (MACA) [23] was the first CSMA/CA-like protocol. It uses an RTS/CTS mechanism influenced by the Appletalk protocol. The transmission of a data frame is preceded by a ready-to-send (RTS) and a clear-to-send (CTS) exchange between the sender and receiver. Unlike SRMA, RTS and CTS frames are sent over the same channel as data frames. The surrounding neighbours in range of the RTS *or* CTS frames defer any pending transmissions. MACAW (MACA for Wireless) [4] is an enhancement of MACA which addresses some of the fairness issues inherent within the protocol.

1.3 A Brief History of 802.11

In 1985, the Federal Communications Commission (FCC) opened up the industrial, scientific and medical (ISM) frequency band for wireless LANs [36]. The first wireless technologies appeared in 1990 and operated in the 900 MHz frequency band with speeds of 1 Mb/s (much slower than wired LANs which, at the time, were capable of 10 Mb/s). Furthermore, the implementations were non-standard. Products that operated in the 2.4 GHz ISM band appeared in 1992. Data rates were still relatively low and based on proprietary solutions.

The IEEE 802.11 project began in 1990 and was approved in 1997. The aim of 802.11 was to develop medium access control (MAC) and physical (PHY) layer standards for fixed, portable and mobile wireless devices.

The original 802.11 specification is seen as the *root* standard. Devices that implement the original 802.11 standard, however, are rare nowadays. Since its publication, the 802.11 working group has introduced a number of enhancements, primarily (but not exclusively) to address performance and security issues. These enhancements to the standard are published as amendments designated by a lower case letter. A few of the more notable amendments are discussed in this section.

The 802.11a and 802.11b amendments appeared in 1999, specifying improved modulation schemes which yielded higher transmission rates. 802.11b wireless LAN equipment quickly became popular. 802.11b devices operated in the same frequency band as the legacy 802.11 specification. Whereas the original 802.11 standard was limited to data rates of 1 and 2 Mb/s, 802.11b supported data rates of 5.5 and 11 Mb/s. As well as improved data rates, 802.11b also introduced wired equivalent privacy (WEP) which supported cryptographic based security.

The 802.11a amendment was completed in 1999. 802.11a operates in the 5 GHz frequency band, and uses orthogonal frequency-division multiplexing (OFDM). It supports up to 54 Mb/s but can rate adapt down to 48, 36, 24, 18, 12, 9 or 6 Mb/s, according to the channel conditions.

The FCC permitted the use of OFDM in 2001. This gave rise to the 802.11g amendment in 2003. Like 802.11a, 802.11g supports transmission rates of up to 54 Mb/s (and link rate adapts in the same way as 802.11a). As 802.11g shares the same frequency spectrum as 802.11b, 802.11g devices have to be backwards compatible with 802.11b devices. 802.11g, therefore, operates a number of protection mechanisms in order to co-exist with 802.11b devices.

The 802.11n amendment was ratified in 2009. The 802.11n PHY relies heavily on multiple-input multiple-output (MIMO) technology for increased speed and range (over 802.11a/g). 802.11n devices can operate in either the 2.4 GHz or the 5 GHz band. In the same way 802.11g has to co-exist with 802.11b, 802.11n implements protection mechanisms to ensure co-existance with pre-802.11n devices.

Security provisions were first specified in the 802.11b amendment, which adopted WEP for authentication and encryption. As outlined above, WEP had many flaws. WEP could be exploited with minimal effort and know how. Indeed the FMS attack has been incorporated into tools, such as AirSnort and Aircrack. The 802.11i amendment was developed to address the shortcomings of WEP.

802.11 devices suffered from interoperability problems between vendors when they initially came on the market. The Wi-Fi Alliance was formed to address interoperability issues. A number of companies formed the Wi-Fi Alliance in order to test the compliance of 802.11 equipment. Equipment that passes the compliance test is entitled to bear the Wi-Fi certification logo, which is a registered trademark of the Wi-Fi Alliance. Most 802.11 devices display the Wi-Fi logo. For this reason, Wi-Fi and 802.11 devices have become synonymous. When the wired equivalent privacy (WEP) security methods in 802.11b were found to be flawed, the IEEE initiated the 802.11i project to address the problem. The Wi-Fi Alliance also introduced a certification program called Wi-Fi Protected Access (WPA) which was based upon a draft version of the amendment. When 802.11i was fully ratified, the Wi-Fi Alliance issued the WPA2 certification programme.

1.4 The RF Environment

802.11 devices operate in unlicensed radio frequency (RF) bands. While these frequency bands are unlicensed, they are not unregulated. Both Wi-Fi and non-Wi-Fi devices must adhere to strict power limits (depending upon region and frequency band) and methods of modulation. No user can claim exclusive access rights to unlicensed bands (unlike licensed bands). Therefore, the radio spectrum at these frequencies are shared resources. For this reason, devices must observe certain codes of etiquette in order to use an unlicensed frequency band. The Federal Communications Commission (FCC) outlines three basic principles for operating in an unlicensed band [10]:

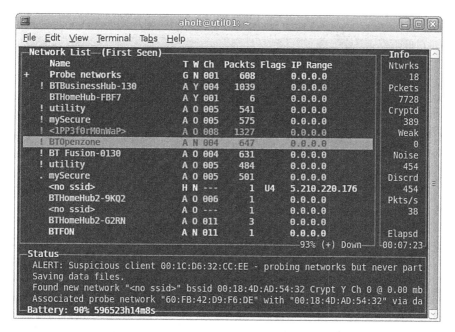

Fig. 1.3 WLANs detected by Kismet Application

i. Listen before talk
ii. When talking, make frequent pauses and listen again
iii. Don't talk too loud

In general, devices operating in these bands must not cause harmful interference to neighbouring devices. However, devices must accept interference that may have "undesirable" effects on their ability to operate. Congestion is one of the undesirable effects brought about by the popularity of 802.11. Figure 1.3 shows a screen shot of the Wi-Fi analyser Kismet. This shows the number of WLANs operating in the vicinity of one of the authors. The location of this wireless scan was a small rural town in Wiltshire, UK. It shows a number of wireless networks distributed across the 2.4 GHz frequency band. Yet, This town is not a densely populated metropolitan city. If we may be allowed to submit somewhat more anecdotal evidence, a few miles away, in the city centre of Bristol, the iPhone of one of the authors detected more that 100 wireless hotspots in its new shopping complex!

These unlicensed bands are not solely reserved for 802.11 devices. For example, the 2.4 GHz band, often called the industrial, scientific and medical (ISM) band, is also open to other communication devices, such as cordless telephones (DECT), baby monitors and Bluetooth devices. Even dumb, non-telecommunications emitters, like microwave ovens, operate at these frequencies. The images in Fig. 1.4 shows a spectral analysis of the 2.4 GHz band (using a WiSpy 2.4× spectrum analyser [27]). The top image shows 802.11 wireless networks denoted by the blue "humps" occupying discrete channels. The bottom image shows the "interference" received from a domestic microwave oven in operation.

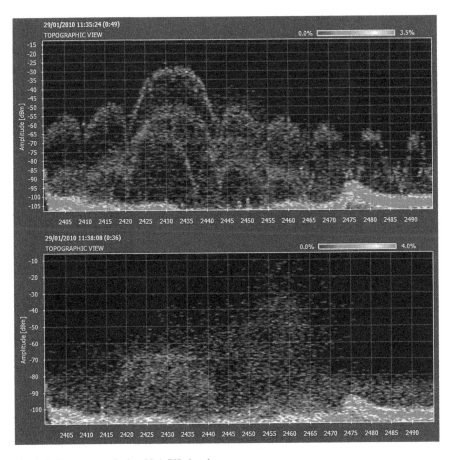

Fig. 1.4 Spectrum analysis of 2.4 GHz band

The range, performance and reliability of wireless communications is governed by signal strength and noise level (amongst other things). Shannon's theorem [31] gives us some insights into the upper bound of a channel's capacity:

$$C = B \times \log_2(1 + \text{SNR}) \tag{1.5}$$

where C (bits/s) is the channel capacity, B (Hz) is the channel bandwidth and SNR is the signal-to-noise ratio. The graph in Fig. 1.5 shows maximum transmission speed as a function of SNR for a channel bandwidth of $W = 20$ MHz.

The spectral density of radio signals (or any electromagnetic radiation, for that matter) diminishes with distance, resulting in a reduced signal strength at the receiver. Obstructions in the signal path compound the problem further by absorbing and scattering radio signals. Radio signals can be reflected by physical objects resulting in multiple signal paths between the transmission end-points. Reflected/refracted signals arrive at the receiver out of phase with the direct path signal and combine destructively. This causes *multipath fading*.

Fig. 1.5 Shannon limit

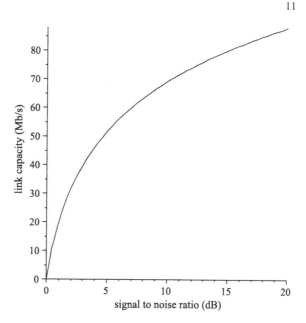

The receiver power level requirements for a particular wireless interface card, are referred to as the *receive sensitivity* P_{rx}:

$$P_{rx} = \text{noise floor} + \text{SNR} \tag{1.6}$$

The electronics that comprise the receiver, generate internal thermal noise. For an ideal receiver the thermal noise N can be calculated by the expression:

$$N = kTB \tag{1.7}$$

where $k = 1.38 \times 10^{-23}$ J/K is the Boltzmann constant, T is the temperature (typically 290 K) and B (Hz) is the bandwidth of the channel. The level of internal noise is referred to as the *noise floor*. A real receiver, however, will incur losses. Equation 1.8 could underestimate the noise floor by as much as 15 dB, thus:

$$\text{noise floor} = N + 15 \text{ dB} \tag{1.8}$$

In addition to the internal thermal noise of the wireless interface card, there are also external sources of thermal and electromagnetic noise in the environment. This is expressed as the SNR:

$$\text{SNR} = \frac{E_b}{N_0} \times \frac{R}{B_T} \tag{1.9}$$

where E_b is the energy per bit, N_0 is the noise per 1 Hz, R is the system rate and B_T is the system bandwidth. In general, the bit error rates (BER) of wireless systems diminish with increased SNR (though BER is also dependent upon the modulation scheme used). The graph in Fig. 1.6 shows the BER for binary phase shift key (BPSK). Typically, BER results are plotted against E_b/N_0 rather than SNR. We adopt this convention here.

Fig. 1.6 BER of BPSK
modulation

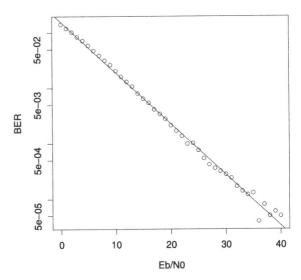

A link budget analysis of a wireless communication system yields the transmission power requirements P_{tx} given the end-to-end gains and losses:

$$P_{tx} = P_{rx} + 2L_c - G_{tx} - G_{rx} + \text{FSPL} + \text{fade margin} \qquad (1.10)$$

G_{tx} and G_{rx} are the gains of the transmitting and receiving antenna respectively. L_c is the loss introduced by the antenna cable and connectors. For simplicity, we assume that the cable loss is the same at each end. FSPL is the free-space loss. We will discuss free-space loss in more detail in Chap. 2. The fade margin accounts for the losses experienced due to multi-path fading. This fade margin can be anything up to 30 dB.

1.5 Book Outline

The organisation of the book is outlined as follows:

Chapter 2: Radio Frequencies. We introduce the basic principles of the electromagnetic spectrum with respect to radio frequencies (RF). We focus on the part of the spectrum where WLANs operate; namely, microwave frequencies. Radio wave propagation methods are discussed in detail. RF regulation with respect to WLANs is also covered in this chapter.

Chapter 3: Medium Access Control. The MAC sub-layer is introduced in this chapter. The MAC layer implements a number of coordination functions, which are responsible for controlling wireless channel access. The distributed coordination function (DCF) and point coordination function (PCF) are covered. We also cover the hybrid coordination function (HCF) from the 802.11e ammendent which addresses quality of service issues within 802.11 WLANs.

Chapter 4: The Physical layer. The primary focus is the physical sub-layers of 802.11; namely, the PLCP and PMD. Modulation techniques are discussed in detail together with associated amendments in which they appeared appear. We close the chapter with a review of MIMO and beamforming.

Chapter 5: Cryptography. The 802.11 standard makes extensive use of cryptographic methods for security. Cryptographic concepts are introduced in this chapter. It covers encryption, message digests, digital signatures and digital certificates. We use applications such as OpenSSL to demonstrate the concepts presented. In Chap. 8 we describe how to build a WLAN based on the RSN (robust security network) framework. EAP-TLS is used as the authentication method and requires, therefore, digital certificates. This chapter describes how to generate X.509 digital certificates using OpenSSL.

Chapter 6: Wireless Security. An overview of the 802.11e ammendment is presented in this chapter. We discuss RSNA (robust security network association) and pre-RSNA security methods. We cover authentication, encryption and message integrity within 802.11.

Chapter 7: Configuring Wireless Networks. In this chapter, we show how to implement a number of wireless network solutions. We show examples using Cisco, Alcatel-Lucent and Meru equipment. We also show how to implement an open source access-point.

Chapter 8: Enterprise Security. In this chapter, we give a detailed description of how to implement a wireless network with enterprise security. Enterprise security requires a RADIUS server for authentication. We show how to configure the open source RADIUS package, Freeradius.

Chapter 9: MAC Layer Performance Analysis. Models of the 802.11 MAC sublayer are developed and analysed. We show the effects of the RTS/CTS mechanism and fragmentation on performance.

Chapter 10: Link rate adaptation. 802.11 devices select modulation techniques (and consequently link speeds) according to the RF environment. In this chapter we develop a number of signal loss models and use them to analyse link rate adaptation.

1.6 Summary

Wireless communication systems present a set of challenges which are distinct from those of wired based systems. This book is aimed at addressing the performance and security issues associated with 802.11 WLANs.

The book presents configuration examples of various wireless network solutions across a number of different vendor platforms. We also rely heavily on open source (such as GNU/Linux) for building the supporting infrastructure required for enterprise level WLAN security.

Chapter 2
Radio Frequencies

The range and performance of wireless communication systems are governed by signal strength and noise level (expressed as the signal-to-noise ratio). 802.11 wireless devices adjust their transmission rate according to the channel conditions. Radio signals weaken with distance. Obstructions in the signal path compound the problem further by absorbing and scattering radio signals. Radio signals can also be reflected by physical objects, resulting in multiple paths between the transmission end-points. Reflected signals arrive at the receiver out of phase with the line-of-sight signal and combine destructively. This is known as multi-path fading.

Systems operating in open or unlicensed bands have to contend with radio devices in co- and adjacent channels. Undesired signals with frequencies in or near the receiver's bandpass get processed by the same circuitry as desired signals. Interference can also result from undesired signals that are far outside the receiver's bandpass frequencies. If the signal levels are high enough, local oscillator harmonics can produce anomalies in the receiver.

This chapter introduces radio frequency (RF) waves and RF wave propagation. We introduce radio regulation with respect to WLANs and discuss spectrum management methods adopted by 802.11.

2.1 The Electromagnetic Spectrum

Radio waves are a form of electromagnetic radiation. Electromagnetic radiation is energy radiated by a charged particle as a result of acceleration. James Clark Maxwell derived a mathematical framework based upon Faraday's empirical data on magnetic lines of force. Maxwell's equations describe how electromagnetic waves propagate. Electric and magnetic fields propagate as sinusoids at right angles to each other. Figure 2.1 shows the direction of an electric field (E) and magnetic field (H) relative to the direction of the wave propagation. The wave propagates out in all directions, creating a spherical wave front. For a given source emitting RF energy at a power level P_{tx}, the power density S is given by:

$$S = \frac{P_{tx}}{4\pi d^2} \quad \text{W/m}^2 \tag{2.1}$$

A. Holt, C.-Y. Huang, *802.11 Wireless Networks,*
Computer Communications and Networks,
DOI 10.1007/978-1-84996-275-9_2, © Springer-Verlag London Limited 2010

Fig. 2.1 Directions of electric and magnetic fields relative to the direction of propagation

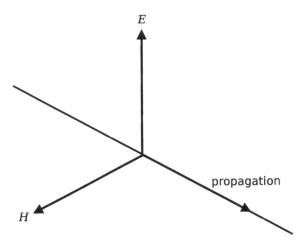

where d is the distance between the radiator and the wave front (radius of the sphere).

The frequency range of electromagnetic waves form the electromagnetic spectrum and range from extremely low frequencies of a few Hertz to Gamma rays at 100s of Exa-Hertz. The wavelength λ of a electromagnetic wave is related to its frequency f by the relationship:

$$c = \lambda f \tag{2.2}$$

where the speed of light in free-space is $c \approx 3 \times 10^8$ m/s. Wavelengths, therefore, range from many thousands of kilometers for frequencies at the lower end of the electromagnetic spectrum, to picometers at the upper end.

All radiation in the electromagnetic spectrum has common properties. The electromagnetic spectrum is continuous over the entire frequency range. However, the way in which electromagnetic radiation interacts with matter varies according to the frequency. For this reason, the spectrum is divided into different types of radiation. Table 2.1 shows the classification of electromagnetic radiation.

Visible light occupies a very narrow band in the range of 430 to 790 THz. Above the visible light range lies ultraviolet, X-ray and Gamma rays. For the current purpose, however, we are mostly interested in radiation with frequencies below that of visible light; namely, radio waves. The original 802.11 standard specified a PHY based on infrared (which lies just below the visible light range). 802.11 infrared devices, however, did not achieve much commercial success, so we will confine our attention to radio wave frequencies. Radio wave frequencies range from a few hertz to 300 GHz. Wireless LAN communication systems operate within a range of frequencies commonly known as *microwaves*. Microwaves are a subset of radio waves that cover the EHF, SHF and UHF bands.

Table 2.1 The electromagnetic spectrum

Acronym	Band name	Wavelength (m)		Frequency	
		Upper	Lower	Lower	Upper
ELF	Extremely low frequency	10^8	10^7	3 Hz	30 Hz
SLF	Super low frequency	10^7	10^6	30 Hz	300 Hz
ULF	Ultra low frequency	10^6	10^5	300 Hz	3 kHz
VLF	Very low frequency	10^5	10^4	3 kHz	30 kHz
LF	Low frequency	10^4	10^3	30 kHz	300 kHz
MF	Medium frequency	10^3	10^2	300 kHz	3 MHz
HF	High frequency	10^2	10	3 MHz	30 MHz
VHF	Very high frequency	10	1	30 MHz	300 MHz
UHF	Ultra high frequency	1	10^{-1}	300 MHz	3 GHz
SHF	Super high frequency	10^{-1}	10^{-2}	3 GHz	30 GHz
EHF	Extremely high frequency	10^{-2}	10^{-3}	30 GHz	300 GHz
FIR	Far infrared	10^{-3}	10^{-4}	300 GHz	3 THz
MIR	Mid infrared	10^{-4}	10^{-5}	3 THz	30 THz
NIR	Near infrared	10^{-5}	10^{-6}	30 THz	300 THz
NUV	Near ultraviolet	10^{-6}	10^{-7}	300 THz	3 PHz
FUV	Far ultraviolet	10^{-7}	10^{-8}	3 PHz	30 PHz
EUV	Extreme ultraviolet	10^{-8}	10^{-9}	30 PHz	300 PHz
SX	Soft X-rays	10^{-9}	10^{-10}	300 PHz	3 EHz
HX	Hard X-rays	10^{-10}	10^{-11}	3 EHz	30 EHz
Y	Gamma	10^{-11}	10^{-12}	30 EHz	300 EHz

2.2 Radio Waves

All electronic circuits radiate RF energy. Consider the circuit in Fig. 2.2, connecting an RF source to a load by a transmission line. If the conducting wires are close together, the transmission line acts as a wave guide and the RF energy emitted by the source is delivered to the load along the conductors of the circuit. The RF energy will radiate out from the two conducting wires of the transmission line into the environment. However, as the wires are close together, the electromagnetic waves will effectively cancel each other out. As the distance between the conducting wires increases, RF energy is emitted into the surrounding environment. Furthermore, the wavelength of the emitted energy is in the order of the distance between the wires. The energy radiates away from the transmission line in the form of free-space electromagnetic waves. Radio antennas can be thought of as transmission lines that have been configured for the purpose of efficiently transmitting energy from the conductors into free-space (see Fig. 2.3).

The propagation of radio waves is governed by frequency. Below 2 MHz, radio waves propagate as *ground* waves. Ground waves follow the contours of the Earth. For frequencies between 2 and 30 MHz, *sky wave* propagation is the dominant mode. Radio signals are refracted by the ionosphere. Long range coverage can be achieved; however, the range is dependent upon frequency, time of day and the season.

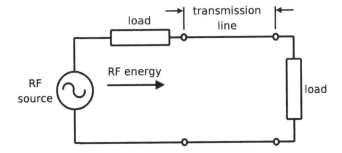

Fig. 2.2 Electric circuit

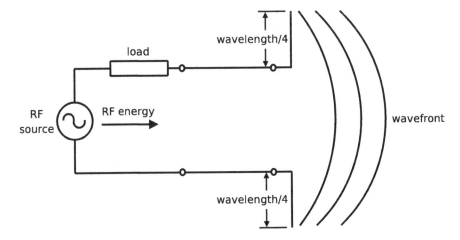

Fig. 2.3 A half-wavelength Di-pole antenna

At frequencies above 30 MHz, signals propagate between transmitter and receiver along a direct line-of-sight path. The range of these signals is limited by the
curvature of the Earth, amongst other things. Radio waves at these frequencies are
subject to very little refraction by the ionosphere; rather, they tend to propagate
through it (making them ideal for satellite communications). As 802.11 WLANs
operate at microwave frequencies, we are not concerned with ground or sky wave
propagation modes here.

Radio waves are affected by the environment and objects within that environment. The means by which radio wave propagate are given by:

- Direct path
- Absorption
- Reflection
- Refraction
- Diffraction
- Scattering

Fig. 2.4 Wave components

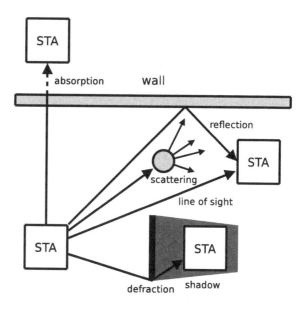

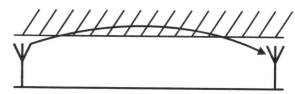

Fig. 2.5 Refracted radio wave

Figure 2.4 illustrates direct path, absorption, reflection, diffraction and scattering. Refraction tends to be an outdoor phenomenon and is illustrated in Fig. 2.5.

2.2.1 Direct Path

When a line of sight exists between a transmitter and receiver, signals arrive at the receiver along a direct path. As the wave front emanates from the transmitter, the RF energy *spreads* as it propagates into the surrounding area. The nature of the spreading depends upon the antenna. An isotropic antenna produces a spherical wave front whereby RF energy spreads equally in all directions. This spreading of the wave front causes the power density to diminish. It can be seen from (2.1) that the power density S diminishes according to an inverse square law (with respect to distance). Furthermore, only a small proportion of the wave is incident to the receive antenna. The *effective aperture* of the receive antenna determines how much energy the receiver captures. The level of power received is the product of the power density S and the effective aperture A_e:

$$P_{rx} = SA_e \qquad\qquad (2.3)$$

The size of the effective aperture A_e is given by;

$$A_e = \frac{\lambda^2}{4\pi} \qquad (2.4)$$

Combining (2.1), (2.3) and (2.4), gives:

$$P_{rx} = \frac{P_{tx}\lambda^2}{(4\pi d)^2} \qquad (2.5)$$

The loss L due to the spreading of the wave front as it propagates through free-space is the ratio of the transmission power over the receive power, thus:

$$L = \frac{P_{tx}}{P_{rx}} = \left(\frac{4\pi d}{\lambda}\right)^2 \qquad (2.6)$$

Sometimes it is practical to express the free-space loss equation in decibels:

$$\text{FSPL} = 10\log_{10} L \qquad (2.7)$$

Rearranging yields:

$$\text{FSPL} = 10\log_{10}\left(\frac{4\pi d}{\lambda}\right)^2 = 20\log_{10}\left(\frac{4\pi f d}{c}\right)$$
$$= 20\log_{10}(d) + 20\log_{10}(f) + 20\log_{10}\left(\frac{4\pi}{c}\right) \qquad (2.8)$$

We developed this model using Maple. For convenience we define a constant for the speed-of-light ($c = 2.99792458 \times 10^8$ m/s):

```
> c := 2.99792458e8:
```

Below is the Maple function for the free-space loss model in (2.8):

```
> FSPL := (f,d,K) -> 20*log10(f) + 20*log10(d) + K;
```

$$\text{FSPL} := (f, d, K) \rightarrow 20\log_{10}(f) + 20\log_{10}(d) + K$$

The constant K in the Maple function determines the units for frequency and distance. As c is in meters per second, then the distance d is in meters and f is in Hz:

```
> K1 := 20*log10(4*Pi/c);
```

$$K1 := \frac{20\ln(1.334256381 \times 10^{-8}\pi)}{\ln(10)}$$

Whenever possible, Maple returns results in *exact* form. In the example above, $K1$ is expressed as a rational number. To return a result in (inexact) floating point format:

```
> evalf(K1);
```

$$K1 := -147.5522168$$

We can calculate the free-space loss for $f = 2.412 \times 10^9$ Hz and $d = 1000$ m, which is approximately 100 dB:

```
> evalf(FSPL(2.412*10^9,1000,K1));
```

$$100.0953293$$

If we want to pass the frequency and distance parameters to the function in units of GHz and km respectively, then we compute the constant (K2) thus:

```
> K2 := 20*log10(4*Pi*GHz*1000/c): evalf(K2);
```

$$K2 := 92.44778326$$

For f in MHz and d in miles, the constant is:

```
> K3 := 20*log10(4*Pi*MHz*1609.344/c): evalf(K3);
```

$$K3 := 36.58076092$$

In the examples below, we show how to compute the free-space loss for different units. The Maple expression below gives the free-space loss for 1 km at a frequency of 2.412 GHz:

```
> evalf(FSPL(2.412,1,K2));
```

$$100.0953293$$

The expression below shows the free-space loss for 1 mile. We use the same frequency as the example, except we express it in units of MHz:

```
> evalf(FSPL(2412,1,K3));
```

$$104.2283070$$

We define graph objects of the free-space loss for frequencies 2.437 and 5.24 (GHz):

```
> G1 := plot(FSPL(2.412,i,K2), i=0..1,
  labels=["distance (m)", "loss (dB)"],
  labeldirections=["horizontal", "vertical"],
  legend=["2.412 GHz"], color=black, linestyle=DASH):
> G2 := plot(FSPL(5.24,i,K2), i=0..1,
  labels=["distance (m)", "loss (dB)"],
  labeldirections=["horizontal", "vertical"],
  legend=["5.24 GHz"], color=black, linestyle=SOLID):
```

The statement below generates the graph in Fig 2.6. It can be seen that the losses are greater in the 5 GHz band than the 2.4 GHz band but this is due to the effective aperture of the antenna rather than the frequency of the signal itself.

```
> display(G1,G2);
```

Fig. 2.6 Free-space loss

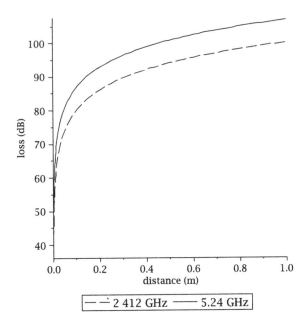

The free-space loss equation(s) discussed above are for isotropic antennas. Isotropic antennas, however, are merely theoretical and do not exist in practice. Actual antennas exhibit some form of directionality. The isotropic antenna is merely used as a reference point when comparing the gain from using real antennas.

2.2.2 Absorption

When radio waves encounter an obstacle, some of the energy is absorbed (and converted into some other kind of energy, such as heat). The energy that is not absorbed will continue to propagate through the medium; however, the signal that finally reaches the receiver will be attenuated. The amount of energy absorption, and consequently the degree of attenuation, is dependent upon the material from which the obstruction is composed. Table 2.2 shows the losses for a selection of building materials.

2.2.3 Reflection

Radio waves reflect off the surfaces of objects that are large relative to the signal's wavelength. The object material governs the amount of signal that is reflected. Obstacles *near* the line-of-sight can reflect the wave causing duplication at the receiver. These reflections may interfere, either constructively or destructively, depending

Table 2.2 Signal losses caused by material

Material	Loss (dB)
Brick (3.5/7/10.5 cm)	3.5/5/7
Wooden wall	8
Door (wood/metal)	4/12
Glass (0.25/0.5 cm)	0.8/2
Glass (security)	9
Roof (dry/wet)	5/7
Flat Roof (metal)	12
Concrete	12

Fig. 2.7 Fresnel zone

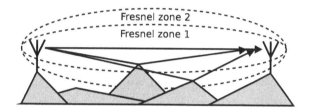

upon whether they are in or out of phase with the signal travelling along the direct path.

Fresnel zones provide a means of analysing the interference due to obstacles near to the line-of-sight. If a transmitted wave reflects off the obstacle, such that it arrives at the receiver 180° out-of-phase with the wave direct path, then the obstacle is located on the radius of the first Fresnel zone. As the point of reflection (causing the 180° phase shift) moves between the antennas, an ellipsoid is formed (first Fresnel zone). The radius of the second Fresnel is formed by points where the reflected waves arrive at the receiver in-phase with the direct path signal. Obstacles within the first Fresnel cause destructive interference with the wave on the direct path, whereas obstacles in the second Fresnel zone cause reflected waves to interfere constructively. As a general rule of thumb, losses are equivalent to free-space, provided that 80% of the first Fresnel zone is clear. Figure 2.7 shows the first and second Fresnel zone and how a wave is reflected by obstacles that impinge on the zones. There are, theoretically, an infinite number of Fresnel zones. Odd and even numbered zones result in destructive and constructive interference respectively. However, the degree of interference diminishes as the zone numbers increase. The Fresnel zones can be calculated:

$$F_n = \frac{\sqrt{n\lambda d_{tx}(d_{\text{path}} - d_{tx})}}{d_{\text{path}}} \quad (2.9)$$

where d_{path} is the distance between the transmitter and receiver and d_{tx} is the distance between the transmitter and the obstacle.

Fig. 2.8 Diffraction

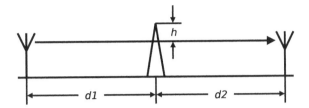

2.2.4 Diffraction

Radio waves can penetrate the shadow of an object by means of diffraction. Diffraction occurs when a radio wave encounters the edge of an object that is large compared to the wavelength. Part of the wave's energy is *bent* around the object, causing a change in direction relative to the line-of-sight path. Non line-of-sight devices located in the shadow of an object are able to receive signals, albeit attenuated. The more deeply the receiver is located in the shadow, the greater the attenuation of the diffracted signal. The diffraction loss L_{diff} is given by:

$$L_{\text{diff}} = 6.9 + 20\log(\sqrt{(v - 0.1)^2 + 1} + v + 0.1) \tag{2.10}$$

where v is Fresnel parameter:

$$v = h\sqrt{\frac{2}{\lambda}\left(\frac{1}{d_1} + \frac{1}{d_2}\right)} \tag{2.11}$$

The parameter h is the height of the object above the direct line of the signal and d_1 and d_2 are the respective distances between the two devices and the obstacle (see Fig. 2.8).

Define the Fresnel parameter v in Maple:

```
> v := (h,d1,d2) -> h * sqrt((2/lambda) * i
        ((1/d1)+(1/d2)));
```

$$v := (h, d1, d2) \rightarrow h\sqrt{\frac{2(\frac{1}{d_1} + \frac{1}{d_2})}{\lambda}}$$

The Maple function for the diffraction loss (L_{diff}) is:

```
> diffloss := (h,d1,d2) -> 6.9 + 20 * log10(sqrt(1 +
              (v(h,d1,d2) - 0.1)^2) + v(h,d1,d2) - 0.1);
```

$$\text{diffloss} := (h, d1, d2) \rightarrow 6.9 + 20\log_{10}(\sqrt{(v(h, d1, d2) - 0.1)^2 + 1} + v(h, d1, d2) + 0.1)$$

The 3D surface graph in Fig. 2.9 shows the diffraction loss between two devices 1000 m apart. An object obstructs the direct signal path and is located $100 \le d_1 \le 900$ meters from one device (and $d_2 = 1000 - d_1$ meters from the other). The height of the obstruction above the line-of-sight between the antennas is given by h. The graph in Fig. 2.9 is produced by the command:

Fig. 2.9 Diffraction loss

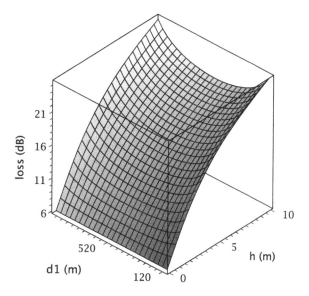

```
> plot3d(diffloss(h,d1,1000-d1), h=0..10, d1=100..900,
  font=[TIMES,ROMAN,12], axes=BOXED,
  labels=["h (m)", "d1 (m)", "loss (dB)"],
  labeldirections=[HORIZONTAL, HORIZONTAL, VERTICAL]);
```

2.2.5 Refraction

When a wavefront passes out of one media into another with a different propagation velocity, the wave is bent. This *redirection* of the wave is called refraction. Figure 2.5 shows a refracted wave.

2.2.6 Scattering

A wave is scattered when it encounters an irregular object which is of a similar size relative to the wavelength. The energy distribution of the wave undergoes random changes in direction, phase and polarisation.

2.2.7 Multi-path

Multi-path fading can be modeled using statistical models. Two popular models are the Rayleigh distribution and the Rice distribution. Signal propagation through the troposphere and ionosphere exhibit properties of Rayleigh fading. The Rayleigh distribution is also appropriate for built-up urban areas when the line-of-sight signal is not dominant. If the line-of-sight signal is dominant, then Ricean fading is a more appropriate model. The probability distribution function for Rayleigh fading is given by:

$$f_{\text{rayleigh}}(x, \sigma) = \frac{x}{\sigma^2} e^{-x^2/2\sigma^2} \tag{2.12}$$

```
> rayleigh := (x,sigma) -> (x/sigma^2) *
              exp(-1*(x^2)/(2 * sigma^2));
```

$$\text{rayleigh} := (x, \sigma) \rightarrow \frac{x e^{-\frac{1}{2}\frac{-x^2}{\sigma^2}}}{\sigma^2}$$

Define a list of values for σ (along with their respective line style):

```
> slist := [[0.5, "dash"], [1,"dot"], [2,"dashdot"],
  [4,"solid"]]:
```

Create a sequence of plots of the probability distribution function (pdf) for each value of σ in the list, `slist`:

```
> raylplots := seq(plot(rayleigh(x,s[1]), x=0..10,
  labeldirections=["horizontal", "vertical"],
  labels=["X", "pdf"],font=[times,roman,12],
  linestyle=s[2],legend=[s[1]], color=black),
  s in slist):
```

The command below produces the graph in Fig. 2.10:

```
> display(raylplots);
```

The Rice distribution is given by the expression below:

$$f_{\text{rice}}(x, u, \sigma) = \frac{x}{\sigma^2} e^{-(x^2+u^2)/2\sigma^2} I_0(xu/\sigma^2) \tag{2.13}$$

where $I_0(x)$ is the zero order, first kind, modified Bessel function. Note that the Rayleigh distribution is a special case of Rice distribution; that is, when $u = 0$, the Rice distribution reduces to the Rayleigh distribution. Create a Maple function for $I_0(x)$:

```
> I0 := (x) -> BesselI(0,x);
```

$$I0 := x \rightarrow \text{Bessel}I(0, x);$$

Define the pdf for the Rice distribution:

```
> rice := (x,u,sigma) -> (x/sigma^2) *
          exp(-1*(x^2 + u^2)/(2 * sigma^2)) *
          I0((x*u)/sigma^2);
```

Fig. 2.10 Rayleigh
probability density function
for various values of σ

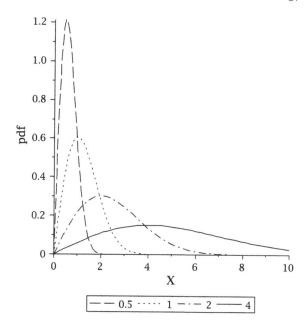

$$\text{rice} := (x, u, \sigma) \rightarrow \frac{xe^{-\frac{1}{2}\frac{(x^2+u^2)}{\sigma^2}} I_0\left(\frac{xu}{\sigma^2}\right)}{\sigma^2}$$

Define a list of values for u:

```
> ulist := [[0, "dash"], [0.5,"dot"], [1,"dashdot"],
           [2,"spacedash"], [4,"solid"]];
```

Create a sequence of plots of the pdf for each value of u in the list `ulist` and $\sigma = 1$:

```
> riceplots := seq(plot(rice(x,u[1],1), x=0..8,
  labels=["X", "pdf"],font=[times,roman,12],
  labeldirections=["horizontal", "vertical"],
  linestyle=u[2],legend=[u[1]],color=black),
  u in ulist):
```

The command below produces the graph in Fig. 2.11:

```
> display(riceplots);
```

2.3 Radio Frequency Regulation

The radio spectrum is a public resource and subject to strict regulation. National regulatory bodies are responsible for controlling radio emissions and frequency use. In the UK, for example, the regulatory body is OFCOM. In the US, regulatory control is divided between the Federal Communications Commission (FCC) for commerce

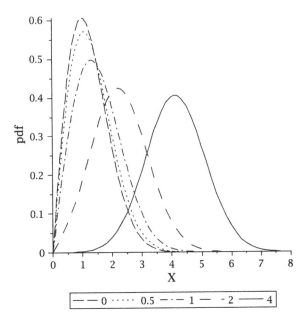

Fig. 2.11 Ricean probability density function, for various values of u and $\sigma = 1$

and the National Telecommunications Information Administration (NTIA) for government.

The radio spectrum is divided into bands and allocated to a particular service, such as broadcasting, radio astronomy, radar or telecommunications. The UK, for example, regulates the radio frequency spectrum from 9 kHz to 275 GHz and publishes the frequency allocation table in [37]. There are three categories of radio band allocation:

- Licensed
- Open
- Unlicensed

For licensed bands, licenses are granted by the regulatory bodies to organisations for exclusive rights to use a particular frequency band. Deciding who has the right to use the spectrum is not straightforward, but regulatory bodies employ a number of methods:

- First come first served
- Lottery
- Administrative process
- Auction

The first come, first served and lottery methods are seldom used. In the past, the regulatory bodies have favoured the administrative process; however, auctions have become popular in recent years. Spectrum auctions were first used in New Zealand in 1990 and have been adopted by many other countries since then. The UK was one of the first to allocate 3G (third generation) licenses in this way. Raising

Table 2.3 ISM bands

Frequency		Comment
Lower	Upper	
6,765 kHz	6,795 kHz	
13,553 kHz	13,567 kHz	
26.957 MHz	27.283 MHz	
40.65 MHz	40.7 MHz	
83.996 MHz	84.04 MHz	
167.992 MHz	168.008 MHz	
443.05 MHz	433.92 MHz	
902 MHz	915 MHz	US Legacy 802.11 and pre-802.11 proprietary devices
2.400 GHz	2.500 GHz	802.11b/g devices
5.725 GHz	5.875 GHz	Overlaps with U-NII band in US
24 GHz	24.25 GHz	
61 GHz	61.5 GHz	
122 GHz	123 GHz	
244 GHz	246 GHz	

considerable capital for the treasury, the radio spectrum is more than just a public resource; it is also a valuable commodity. Not all licensed parts of the spectrum are exclusive; some parts are *shared* in that they are allocated to specific technologies instead of organisations.

Spectrum licensing ensures reliable frequency usage, but has been argued that it is inefficient [7]. When a frequency band is subject to *open* regulation, operating within the band does not require a license.

An open frequency band can be shared by many users, thus achieving greater efficiency. Uncoordinated access to the band, however, could render the frequency band unusable. For this reason, a minimum standard of etiquette is imposed on its usage.

Like open frequency bands, unlicensed bands do not require a license. However, the standards of etiquette and technical conformance are more rigorous. There are a number of unlicensed bands allocated for industrial, medical and scientific (ISM) applications. ISM apparatus is allowed in the UK provided it is operated in accordance with the 1949 Wireless Telegraphy Act. The ISM frequency bands are shown in Table 2.3.

802.11 devices use a number of ISM bands. The first ISM band used for wireless was the 900 MHz band. However, this was primarily in the US. The 2.4 GHz ISM band is used by 802.11b and 802.11g devices. The band is divided into a number of *overlapping* channels. The US specifies 11 channels, while Europe (ETSI) specifies 13. The bandwidth of each channel is 22 MHz, with a 5 MHz separation between the centre of each band. A comparison of the US and European channel allocation

Table 2.4 Channel allocation in the 2.4 GHz band

Channel	Frequency (GHz)		US	Europe
	Lower	Upper		
1	2.401	2.423	Yes	Yes
2	2.406	2.428	Yes	Yes
3	2.411	2.433	Yes	Yes
4	2.416	2.438	Yes	Yes
5	2.421	2.433	Yes	Yes
6	2.426	2.448	Yes	Yes
7	2.431	2.453	Yes	Yes
8	2.436	2.458	Yes	Yes
9	2.441	2.463	Yes	Yes
10	2.446	2.468	Yes	Yes
11	2.451	2.473	Yes	Yes
12	2.456	2.478	No	Yes
13	2.461	2.483	No	Yes

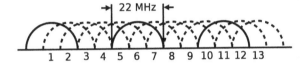

Fig. 2.12 802.11 channel allocation in the 2.4 GHz band

is shown in Table 2.4. Channel frequencies are considered to be non-overlapping if separated by 25 MHz. Any single channel can have up to four neighbouring channels that overlap. Within the frequency band, it is possible to have a maximum of three overlapping channels. For US WLANs, these channels are 1, 6 and 11, whereas in Europe, other combinations are possible. The 802.11 channel arrangement in the 2.4 GHz band is shown in Fig. 2.12, where the solid lines present the three non-overlapping channels 1, 6 and 11. Despite this, it has been reported that, under certain conditions, there are *no* non-overlapping channels. If antennas are sufficiently close together, then no pair of channels are completely interference-free [13].

802.11a devices operate in a number of unlicensed bands in the 5 GHz range. The allocation of the spectrum and operating parameters vary across regions. Table 2.5 contrasts the regulations for the US (FCC) and Europe (ETSI). In the US, these bands are referred to as unlicensed national information infrastructure (U-NII) bands. These frequency bands are not ISM bands; however, the 5.725–5.825 U-NII upper band used in the US overlaps with the ISM 5.725–5.875 GHz band. Figure 2.13 shows channel allocation for the lower and middle U-NII bands and Fig. 2.14 shows channel allocation for the upper band.

5.150–5.250 GHz: 802.11a devices that operate in this band are limited to indoor use. The reason for this is to minimise interference with mobile satellite services (MSS). Devices must perform transmit power control (TPC) and digital frequency

Table 2.5 5 GHz unlicensed bands

Region	No. channels	EIRP			
		(U-NII low)	(U-NII mid)	(U-NII worldwide)	(U-NII high)
		5.15–5.25/GHz	5.26–5.35/GHz	5.470–5.725 GHz	5.726–5.825 GHz
US	12	50 mW	250 mW	Reserved	1 W
Europe	19	200 mW	200 mW	1 W	Reserved

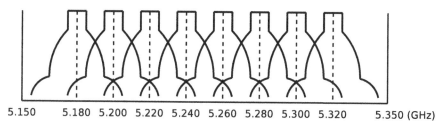

Fig. 2.13 U-NII lower and middle

selection (DFS). EIRP (equivalent isotropically radiated power) is restricted to 200 mW and the maximum mean EIRP spectral density should not exceed 0.25 mW in any 25 kHz band.

5.250–5.350 GHz: In order to minimise interference to Earth exploration satellite services (EESS), 802.11a devices are restricted to indoor use. They must perform TPC and DFS. EIRP is limited to 200 mW and the maximum mean EIRP spectral density must not exceed 10 mW in any 1 MHz.

5.470–5.725 GHz: Devices in this band can operate both indoors and outdoors and must perform TPC and DFS functions. EIRP is restricted to 1 W with a maximum mean EIRP spectral density not exceeding 50 mW in any 1 MHz band.

A summary of the U-NII bands is presented below:

U-NII low (5.15–5.25 GHz): Devices are restricted to indoor use. Regulations require the use of an integrated antenna. EIRP is limited to 50 mW and the maximum mean EIRP spectral density cannot exceed 0.25 mW per 1 MHz. If the directional gain of the antenna exceeds 6 dB, then the EIRP and EIRP spectral density needs to be reduced by an amount corresponding to the antenna gain, less 6 dB. Initially, the FCC Part 15 specified that only integrated antennas could be used. This regulation was lifted in 2004, allowing the use of external antennas [9].

U-NII mid (5.25–5.35 GHz): Devices can operate both indoors and outdoors. EIRP is limited to 50 mW and the maximum mean EIRP spectral density cannot exceed 12.5 mW in any 1 MHz band. If the directional gain of the antenna exceeds 6 dB, then the EIRP and EIRP spectral density needs to be reduced by an amount corresponding to the antenna gain, less 6 dB.

U-NII Worldwide (5.470–5.725 GHz): Devices can operate both outdoors and indoors. Devices must operate (TPC and DFS). EIRP is limited to 250 mW. This

Fig. 2.14 U-NII upper

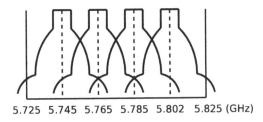

5.725 5.745 5.765 5.785 5.802   5.825 (GHz)

band was introduced by the FCC in 2003 in order to align devices that used the U-NII bands in the US with other parts of the world [9].

U-NII Upper 5.725 to 5.825 GHz): Typically, for devices that operate outdoors. EIRP is limited to 1 W and the maximum mean EIRP spectral density cannot exceed 50 mW per 1 MHz. If the directional gain of the antenna exceeds 6 dB, then the EIRP and EIRP spectral density needs to be reduced by an amount corresponding to the antenna gain, less 6 dB. There are exceptions to this rule for point-to-point links. No reductions in EIRP or EIRP spectral density are required for antennas with gains up to 23 dB. EIRP (and EIRP spectral density) must be reduced by 1 dB per dB gain over 23. This band overlaps with the 5.725–5.725 GHz ISM and is, therefore, sometimes referred to as the U-NII/ISM band.

2.4 Spectrum Management

In unlicensed bands, WLAN devices must observe certain standards of "etiquette" in terms of spectrum usage. In the previous section, we mentioned some of the regulations regarding transmission power output. In addition to transmission power, WLAN devices must use spread spectrum techniques.

Spread spectrum is method of spreading a narrow band signal over a wider frequency band. Spreading communications signals over wider bands makes them more resilient to unintentional interference and jamming. Consequently, spread spectrum is used extensively in military radio applications. Spread spectrum methods employ two modulation stages:

- Modulation of the spreading code
- Modulation of the (spreaded) message

The original 802.11 standard specified two spread spectrum techniques (for devices that operated in radio frequency bands), namely, frequency hopping spread spectrum (FHSS) and direct sequence spread spectrum (DSSS). With FHSS, devices (both transmitter and receiver) hop from channel-to-channel in a pseudo-random sequence. Different transmitter/receiver pairs use a different pseudo-random sequence in an attempt to minimise the collisions within the same channel band. With DSSS, the transmitter and receiver use the same center frequency. The energy of the original signal is spread over a wider band by multiplying it with a pseudo random sequence (called a chipping code). Resilience to interference is due to the spreading of any interference. At the receiver the DSSS signal undergoes *despreading*. Since the original standard, new modulation techniques have been introduced. A high rate DSSS (HR/DSSS) was introduced in the 802.11b amendment and OFDM (orthogonal frequency division multiplexing) in 802.11a (also later used in 802.11g and 802.11n).

802.11 devices, as mentioned in Chap. 1, adjust their modulation scheme, and consequently their link speed, according to RF environment. The 802.11 standard does not specify how link rate adaptation should be performed. It is, therefore, at the discretion of the vendor how link rate adaptation should be implemented.

The 802.11k ammendment [20] was introduced to provide a framework for radio resource measurements. The radio measurements framework enables devices to collect data on the performance of a radio link and disseminate that information throughout the network. A wireless device can either take local measurements or request measurements taken by a neighbouring device. Radio measurement may be used for a number of applications. If we consider a wireless network consisting of multiple access-points, with legacy 802.11, devices associate with access-points based upon the best signal. This can lead to an uneven distribution of devices amongst access-points. Some access-points will be overloaded while others are underutilised. Location awareness will help to distribute the load more evenly across access-points.

As discussed in the previous section, devices operating in the 5 GHz range must perform TPC (transmit power control) and DFS (dynamic frequency selection). The 5 GHz range is already occupied by *primary users*, such as radar and satellite services. The IEEE 802.11h amendment was introduced to meet the European regulatory requirements of WLANs that operate in the 5 GHz range (IEEE 802.11a devices). 802.11h is an enhancement to MAC for TPC and DFS. TPC procedures enable the transmit power of wireless to devices to be controlled. The aim of TPC is to minimise the interference between adjacent wireless networks while optimising frame transmission reliability.

802.11h [19] is responsible for setting both the regulatory and local power levels for the frequency band. The *local maximum transmit power level* is set according to the transmission capabilities of devices and the level of interference. The local maximum transmit power level must not exceed the regulatory power levels. Devices may adjust the power level of any frame transmission, provided that the local maximum transmit power level is not exceeded. Devices associate with access-points based upon their power capabilities.

The local maximum transmit power level is set by the access-point and relayed to devices using beacon, probe response and association response frames. Furthermore, this level is updated dynamically to reflect changes in the channel conditions. 802.11h also specifies a transmit-power reporting function.

The aim of DFS is to minimise interference in other wireless users in the area. In the 5 GHz range the primary users of this band are radar and satellite communication. Wireless devices gather information on the condition of a channel and send it to the access-point. Based on this information, the access-point will then determine if it needs to switch to another channel.

With DFS, the access-point controls communication within the BSS. Devices may not access the channel without authorisation from the access-point (and are, therefore, unable to use active scanning). Prior to authorising any communication, an access-point selects a channel and monitors it for radar signals. If interference is detected, the access-point selects another channel to monitor. When it finds a channel free of interference, it announces it to the network. The access-point continues to monitor the channel. If any interference is detected, the access-point instructs other devices in the BSS to cease transmitting. The access-point then identifies a new channel and informs the devices to switch over to it.

Non-access-point devices are not required to do interference detection, provided they operate under the control of an access-point that does. Devices that do have interference detection capabilities will inform the access-point if it detects a primary user (or another wireless network). The access-point defines quiet periods during which devices may scan the channel.

2.5 Summary

Radio waves belong to the subset of the electromagnetic radiation below infrared. At the upper part of the radio band are microwaves which range from 300 MHz to 300 GHz. 802.11 devices operate in microwave bands. In this chapter, we have discussed how radio waves propagation and their effect of wireless communication systems. We have also discussed spectrum management techniques used in 802.11 WLANs. These techniques are subject to a great deal of research and will, hopefully, lead to more effective use of the radio spectrum.

The radio spectrum is a valuable resource for many sectors, including broadcasting, mobile telephony, aviation, public transport, navigation and defence. Consequently, the radio spectrum has become a commodity; and has had a huge impact on economic welfare. The use of an unlicensed spectrum for WLANs has had a major impact on the growth of WLAN technology. Wireless devices are easy to mass market due to the lack of any licensing procedure, which would, otherwise, significantly contribute to the cost of production. Furthermore, usage is more efficient because the spectrum is shared. Typically, an individual user's needs for channel resources are sporadic. Thus, one user may use a channel while the others are idle.

However, as the number of users increases, so does the amount of interference. Thus, we are faced with a dilemma; strict regulation can lead to under-utilisation, while liberal access can results in a *tragedy of the commons* whereby the spectrum is overgrazed.

Chapter 3
Medium Access Control

Devices operating in a wireless environment have to deal with factors that are not present in wired LANs. Nevertheless, 802.11 must appear as a traditional 802 LAN to the protocol layer above. 802.11 defines a medium access control (MAC) data link sub-layer which provides services to the logical link control (LLC) sub-layer. Below the MAC sub-layer is the physical layer which comprises two sub-layers. The physical layer convergence protocol (PLCP) sub-layer and the physical medium dependent (PMD) sub-layer will be discussed in more detail in Chap. 4. The diagram in Fig. 3.1 shows the 802.11 reference model.

LLC frames are passed to the MAC layer and encapsulated in MAC service data units (MSDUs) by prepending a header and appending a frame check sequence (FCS) to the payload. An MSDU is mapped to one or more MAC protocol data units (MPDUs). MPDUs are passed to the physical layer for transmission.

The 802.11 MAC controls access to the RF channel via a number of logical functions, called the *coordination functions*. Coordination functions determine when a device may transmit frames over the wireless medium. The distributed coordination function (DCF) and the point coordination function (PCF) were defined in the original standard.

DCF is a mandatory component of 802.11 and provides a contention based service. Frame delivery with DCF is best-effort. PCF is an optional component of 802.11 which supports time-bound frame delivery. PCF divides the wireless medium into alternating contention-free periods (CFP) and contention periods (CP). During the contention free periods, access to the RF channel is controlled by a *master* node (typically an access-point) using a polling mechanism. DCF is used for the contention periods.

In addition to DCF and PCF, the 802.11e amendment was introduced to support quality of service. The hybrid coordination function (HCF) is a backwards compatible enhancement to the legacy 802.11 MAC.

This chapter gives an overview of the 802.11 MAC layer services and discusses the coordination functions, DCF, PCF and HCF.

A. Holt, C.-Y. Huang, *802.11 Wireless Networks,*
Computer Communications and Networks,
DOI 10.1007/978-1-84996-275-9_3, © Springer-Verlag London Limited 2010

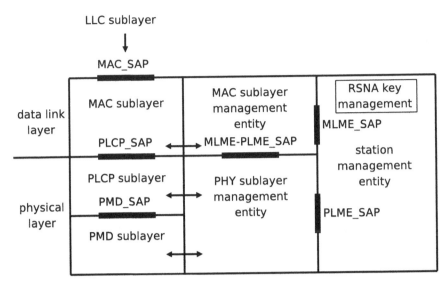

Fig. 3.1 802.11 reference model

3.1 802.11 Services

802.11 defines a number of architectures; namely, the basic service set (BSS), the independent basic service set (IBSS), and the extended service set (ESS). A BSS consists of a number of wireless devices and an access-point. Wireless devices communicate through the access-point. BSS (and ESS) is also known as infrastructure mode. With IBSS, devices associate with each other in an *ad-hoc* manner and can communicate directly without an access-point. A number of BSS can be interconnected through a distribution system (DS) to form an extended service set (ESS). The DS is typically a wired LAN technology, such as Ethernet or IEEE 802.3. Wireless distribution systems (WDS) are also possible and we discuss a proprietary solution in Chap. 7. The diagram in Fig. 3.2 illustrates the BSS, ESS and IBSS architectures.

802.11 provides a number of services. As well as frame delivery, it also offers authentication, re-authentication and privacy functions. These services are available in infrastructure and ad-hoc mode. Additional services are supported in infrastructure mode (by the access-point); for example, association, re-association and disassociation.

A brief description of these services is outlined here. Before a device can send or receive frames over the (BSS/ESS) WLAN, it must make itself known to the access-point by associating with it. When a device moves from one BSS to another, it must undergo a re-association with the new access-point. A device disconnects from BSS by issuing a disassociation request to the access-point. The access-point may in turn, issue a disassociation request to the device.

A device must authenticate itself before it can associate. 802.11 has a number of authentication methods, the simplest of these is open authentication where a device

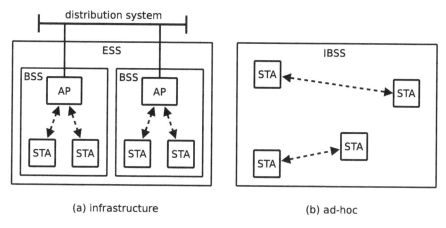

(a) infrastructure
(b) ad-hoc

Fig. 3.2 802.11 Infrastructure Network

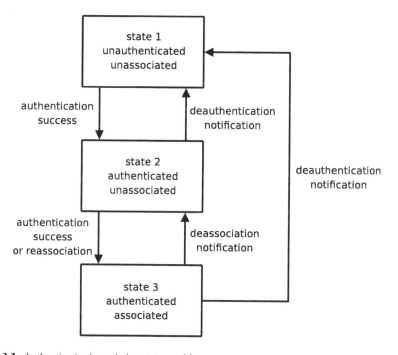

Fig. 3.3 Authentication/association state machine

sends an authentication request to the access-point and the access-point replies with an authentication response (without verifying the authenticity of the device). 802.11 also provides a number of cryptographic-based authentication schemes. These are discussed in later chapters. The authentication/association state machine is shown in the diagram in Fig. 3.3.

Prior to authentication/association, devices must identify any access-points that are within range. Two methods of scanning are available; namely, *passive* and *active*. In passive scanning mode, a device monitors each channel for beacon frames that are broadcast by the access-points in the vicinity. With active scanning, a device sends an explicit probe request. Access-points within range respond with a probe response. The device caches any BSS identifiers (BSSIDs) acquired in the scanning process (either passive or active).

Beacon frames are not just for announcing wireless networks; they are also used to synchronise the clocks on all devices within the BSS. Beacons are transmitted periodically by the access-points. The beacon carries a target beacon transmission time (TBTT) so that devices know when the next beacon is due. Devices in the BSS do not schedule frame transmission when the TBTT is due.

3.2 MAC Frame Format

This section describes the 802.11 MAC frame format. A MAC frame (see Fig. 3.4) consists of a number of fields. A description of each field is provided below:

Frame control: The frame control field comprises a number of sub-fields. The structure of the frame control field is shown in Fig. 3.5. These sub-fields are described below:

- Protocol Version: Identifies the version of the MAC. There is currently only one standard for the MAC and it is assigned the value 0.
- Type: Describes the frame type, either: management, control or data.
- Subtype: The context of these values depends upon the type of field (that is, whether the frame is management, control or data).
- ToDS: Set to 1 if the frame is to the DS.
- FromDS: Set to 1 if the frame is from the DS.
- More frag: If a frame has been fragmented, then all but the last frame has this field set to 1.
- Retry: If the frame is a retransmission, then this bit is set to 1 (and 0 otherwise).
- Power mgmt: If the sending device is in power save mode, this bit is set to 1 (and 0 otherwise).

frame control	duration/ ID	addr 1	addr 2	addr 3	sequence control	addr 4	frame body	FCS

Fig. 3.4 MAC header

protocol version	type	subtype	to DS	from DS	more frag	retry	power mgmt	more data	WEP	other

Fig. 3.5 Frame control field

- More data: When a device is in power save mode, the access-point can buffer the frames destined for it. This bit is set to 1 to indicate that the access-point has one or more frames for a sleeping device.
- WEP: This field is set to 1 to indicate that WEP was used to encrypt the frame body.
- Other: Set to 1 if strict ordering is enabled.

Duration/ID: The duration/ID field specifies the time to transmit the frame and receive an ACK. This is used to set the network allocation vector (NAV) in neighbouring devices.

Sequence control: The sequence control field is a 12-bit sequence number plus a 4-bit fragment number and is used to identify and order the MSDU fragments (MPDUs).

Addresses: The addr fields (1–4) contain 48-bit addresses. The meaning of these addresses depends upon whether the frame is being sent to or from the DS, indicated by the *to DS* and *from DS* sub-field in the frame control field. The interpretation of these four address fields is deferred until the discussion below.

Frame body: The frame body field contains the payload and the FCS (32-bit CRC Code).

The meaning of the address fields in the MAC header are determined by the ToDS and FromDS fields. Here, we provide an explanation of the address fields of the MAC header.

In ad-hoc mode (IBSS), addressing is straight-forward. Addr-1 is the MAC address of the destination; that is, the ultimate recipient of the frame. Addr-2 is the source address of the sender. Addr-3 is set to the BSSID. Addr-4 is not used. In the frame control field, both ToDS and FromDS are set to zero.

In infrastructure mode, addressing is more involved. Consider a device sending frames to another device. Even if both devices are within range, the frame has to be sent via an access-point. For frames sent in the direction of the DS (from a device to an access-point), ToDS = 1 and FromDS = 0. Addr-1 is set to the BSSID, Addr-2 is the source address (that of the sender) and Addr-3 is the address of the destination device. For frames sent from the DS (from an access-point to a device) ToDS = 0 and FromDS = 1 Addr-1 is set to the destination address, Addr-2 is the source address and Addr-3 is the BSSID. In both these cases, Addr-4 is unused.

Now consider a device sending a frame to a device on another BSS. Both devices are associated with different access-points. ToDS = 1 and FromDS = 1 when frames are transmitted between access-points. Addr-1 is set to the MAC address of the receiving access-point and Addr-2 is set to the MAC address of the transmitting access-point. Addr-3 and Addr-4 are set to the destination and source addresses respectively.

3.3 Distributed Coordination Function

The distributed coordination function (DCF) is a mandatory component of 802.11 and is based upon a carrier sense multiple access (CSMA) protocol. DCF may also employ a collision avoidance mechanism which uses a ready-to-send/clear-to-send (RTS/CTS) handshake prior to sending a data frame. The reason for the RTS/CTS mechanism is to resolve the hidden terminal problem (discussed in Chap. 1).

3.3.1 Carrier Sensing

A device must sense the wireless channel before initiating a transmission. 802.11 defines two carrier sensing methods:

- Physical Carrier Sensing (PCS)
- Virtual Carrier Sensing (VCS)

With PCS, carrier-sensing is performed at the physical layer using a clear channel assessment function (CCA). CCA can use either coherent or non-coherent methods of signal detection. Coherent signal detection involves preamble detection whereby the sensing node synchronises with the frame's preamble. With this method, the CCA function must be running continually so that it can detect the preamble on the channel. With the non-coherent method, the received signal strength indicator (RSSI) is compared to some (configurable) threshold. Signal detection can be initiated mid-frame and is, therefore, more energy efficient.

VCS uses a timer called the network allocation vector (NAV) to "reserve" the RF channel. The NAV is specified in the duration field in the MAC header. Each device keeps track of the NAV and "senses" the channel by checking its value. If the NAV is non-zero, then another device is transmitting.

A device senses the wireless channel prior to transmitting a frame for a period specified by the distributed inter-frame space (DIFS). If the channel is free for this period, the device transmits the frame. Inter-frame spaces are discussed in more detail in Sect. 3.3.3 below.

If, however, the device senses that the channel is busy, it defers transmission and continues to sense the channel. Once the channel becomes free, the device senses the channel for the remaining DIFS interval, and then enters a back-off period where the device waits for a (back-off) timer to expire. The timer is frozen if the channel becomes busy and resumes when it becomes free again. The device transmits when the timer reaches zero.

3.3.2 Transmission Methods

DCF supports two transmission methods, basic and RTS/CTS. The latter method supports collision avoidance.

With the basic transmission method, if the device senses the RF channel is idle, it transmits the data frame. All neighbouring devices that detect the frame set their NAV according to the duration field value in the header of the data frame. The duration field value is set to the time to transmit the data frame, the time to transmit

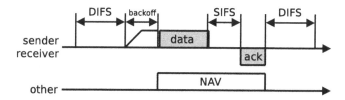

Fig. 3.6   Channel access with the basic DCF transmission method

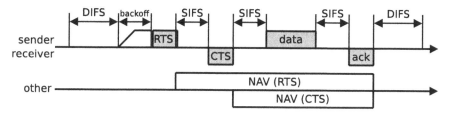

Fig. 3.7   Channel access using RTS/CTS and setting the NAV

the ACK and the SIFS (short inter-frame space) intervals. If the data frame is received correctly, the receiving device responds (after pausing for a SIFS) with an ACK before the NAV expires. The basic DCF transmission method is illustrated in Fig. 3.6.

Sending data under the collision avoidance method involves a four-way frame exchange whereby a device attempts to reserve the RF channel prior to sending data. Communication is initiated with an RTS (ready-to-send) frame (upon sensing the RF channel is idle). When the recipient receives the RTS frame, it waits for a SIFS and then transmits a CTS (clear-to-send). Neighbours of the sender and receiver detect either the RTS or CTS (or both) and set their NAVs to the values in the duration field. The respective duration fields in the RTS and CTS are calculated according to the expressions in (3.1). Figure 3.7 shows the RTS/CTS protocol in operation.

$$\text{RTS: duration\_field} = t_{cts} + t_{data} + t_{ack} + 3 \times \text{SIFS}$$
$$\text{CTS: duration\_field} = t_{data} + t_{ack} + 2 \times \text{SIFS}$$

(3.1)

Once the RTS/CTS exchange has been successfully completed, data and ACK frames are sent in the same way as the basic access method.

3.3.3 Inter-frame Spacing

Devices must wait for a period called an inter-frame space (IFS) before transmitting a frame. The duration of the IFS depends upon the type of frame; thus the 802.11 MAC implements frame prioritisation using IFS intervals of different lengths. The IFS times, defined in the (original) standard, are:

- Short IFS (SIFS).

- PCF IFS (PIFS).
- DCF IFS (DIFS).
- Extended IFS (EIFS).

The IFSes above are listed in order of priority; thus: SIFS < PIFS < DIFS < EIFS. The SIFS precedes the highest priority packets; namely, ACK, CTS and polling response frames. In DCF mode, any new transmission of data must be preceded by a DIFS. Similarly, in PCF mode, a new transmission is preceded by a PIFS. As the DIFS is greater than PIFS, PCF transmissions have greater priority than DCF transmissions. The EIFS is used in DCF mode instead of the DIFS when a frame transmission does not result in a correct sequence. The PIFS and DIFS intervals are calculated according to:

$$PIFS = aSIFSTime + aSlotTime$$
$$DIFS = SIFS + 2 \times aSlotTime \tag{3.2}$$

The SIFS is PHY dependent and given by:

$$SIFS = RxRFDelay + RxPLCPDelay + MacProcessingDelay$$
$$+ RxTxTurnaroundTime \tag{3.3}$$

and the aSlotTime as:

$$aSlotTime = CCATime + RxTxTurnaroundTime + AirPropagationTime$$
$$+ MacProcessingDelay \tag{3.4}$$

Equations (3.3) and (3.4) are dependent upon a number of parameters, which are described below:

CCATime: The minimum time required by the PHY to determine the state of the channel.

RxTxTurnaroundtime: The maximum time the PHY takes to switch between receive and transmit modes.

MacProcessingDelay: Time taken for the MAC to process a frame.

frameTXtime: Frame transmission time.

ackTXtime: Acknowledgment frame transmission time.

RxRFDelay: Time taken to deliver a symbol from the PHY to PLCP.

RxPLCPDelay: Time take to deliver a symbol from the PLCP to the MAC layer.

AirPropagationTime: Propagation delay through the wireless channel.

Table 3.1 shows the slot time and SIFS values for each PHY.

Table 3.1 SIFS and aSlotTime values	PHY	aSlotTime	SIFS
	FHSS	50 μs	28 μs
	DSSS	20 μs	10 μs
	OFDM	9 μs	16 μs

PHY	CW min	CW max
FHSS	15	1023
DSSS	31	1023
OFDM	15	1023

Table 3.2 Contention windows values

3.3.4 Random Back-Off Algorithm

If two (or more) wireless devices sense that the channel is busy, they defer their respective transmissions until it is idle. If both devices transmit when the channel becomes available (after waiting for a DIFS) there will be a collision. To avoid such collisions, transmissions are staggered between devices by using a random back-off algorithm. Each device waits for a random amount of time-slots before transmitting. The device with the shortest back-off timer gains contention of the channel. The back-off timers in the other devices are frozen. Timers resume their countdown once the channel becomes idle again and the procedure is repeated. The length of the timer (in slots) is determined by the binary exponential back-off (BEB) algorithm. The number of slots is selected, uniformly, at random, from the interval $[0, CW - 1]$, where CW is the current size of the contention window. The back-off timer can be calculated using the expression below:

$$\text{backoff} = \lfloor CW \times U(0, 1) \rfloor \times \text{aSlotTime} \qquad (3.5)$$

where $U(0, 1)$ is a uniform random number in the interval $[0, 1]$. The value of CW depends upon the number of collisions and previously successful transmissions. We denote the contention window on the ith failed transmission attempt as CW_i, given by:

$$CW_i = 2^i \times (CW \min + 1) - 1, \quad 0 \leq i \leq m \qquad (3.6)$$

where $m = \log_2 CW \max / CW \min$. On the first transmission attempt, CW_0 is set to $CW_0 = CW \min$. Each time a collision is experienced, the contention window is doubled. W_i never exceeds $CW \max$, where $CW \max = 2^m \times (CW \min + 1) - 1$. The contention window is reset to $CW \min$ when the frame is successfully transmitted. The parameters for the BEB algorithm vary according to the PHY. $CW \min$ and $CW \max$ values are shown in Table 3.2.

3.3.5 Fragmentation

As wireless channels are inherently unreliable, MSDUs over a certain size, may be fragmented and sent as a sequence of smaller MPDUs. Figure 3.8 shows the fragmentation of an MSDU and the encapsulation of MPDUs. The receiving node is responsible for recombining the MPDUs into a MSDU. This process is called *defragmentation*.

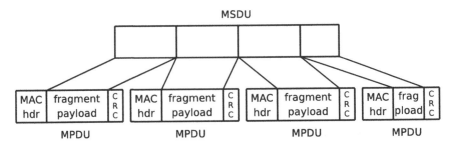

Fig. 3.8 Fragmentation of a MSDU into MPDUs

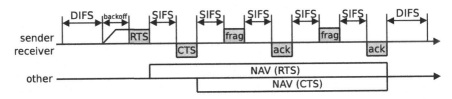

Fig. 3.9 MSDU sent as multiple fragments under the RTS/CTS method

Each MPDU is sent independently and acknowledged separately. Thus, any individual MPDUs, lost in transmission may be retransmitted rather than the whole MSPU. The transmission of an MSDU is successful if all of the MPDUs (or any retransmissions) have been transmitted successfully. Each MPDU is sent as an independent transmission. An automatic repeat request (ARQ) mechanism is used for error control. 802.11 implements a stop-wait, positive acknowledgment ARQ of each MPDU. For each MPDU, an acknowledgment timeout (AckTimeout) is set. The MPDU is retransmitted if the acknowledgment timeout expires. If the maximum number of retransmission attempts of a MPDU is reached, the transmission of the entire MSDU is aborted (that is, the remaining MPDUs in the sequence are discarded). Figure 3.9 shows how a MSDU is sent as multiple fragments (MPDUs) using the RTS/CTS transmission method.

3.3.6 Fairness

DCF suffers from some fairness issues. Devices adapt their bit rate according to the condition of the channel. The frame error rate increases as the channel condition deteriorates (resulting in retransmissions). Under hostile RF conditions, lowering the transmission rate can mitigate the frame error rates (thus reducing retransmissions). Devices transmitting at lower bit rates, however, will occupy the wireless channel for greater periods than those using higher bit rates. This leads to what is known as the *performance anomaly* in 802.11.

In terms of channel access, 802.11 achieves long-term fairness. For a small number of devices, 802.11 is deemed short-term fair. A device with a long contention window will seize control of the channel as its residual back-off interval will eventually expire. Short-term fairness, however, diminishes as the number of devices increases. Devices that suffer collisions will incur long back-off intervals. Devices that merely defer their transmission because they sense the channel through the NAV have preferential access over devices that have suffered collisions.

DCF does suffer from an upstream/downstream unfairness. If there $N - 1$ devices are associated with an access-point, then, all devices, including the access-point, receive a $1/N$ share of the channel capacity. As DCF does not support quality of service, the access-point is the same priority as any other device, even though it initiates all of the downstream flows on the WLAN.

On the whole, DCF is considered fair. 802.3, for example, suffers from the *capture effect* problem, whereby, under high load, a single device can seize control of the channel over consecutive frame transmissions. DCF, however, does lack service differentiation. The coordination functions discussed below facilitate prioritisation and deterministic frame delivery.

3.4 Point Coordination Function

The DCF only supports a best-effort frame delivery service. PCF was introduced to provide support for time-bounded frame delivery. PCF only works in infrastructure mode. A point coordinator (PC) runs on an access-point and sends beacon frames periodically. This divides the channel into a sequence of *superframes* consisting of a contention-free period (CFP) followed by a contention period (CP).

The PC initiates a CFP by gaining control of the channel by sending a beacon frame after a PCF inter-frame space (PIFS). The beacon frame announces the duration of the CFP (specified by the *CFPMaxDuration* Value). All devices that receive the beacon set their NAV to the value of the *CFPMaxDuration*, thereby suspending DCF access. DCF access is resumed when the NAV reaches zero. Stations are granted access to the RF channel under control of the PC.

The PC carries a list of devices which may transmit during the CFP and grants access by polling the devices on its list. The PC awaits a SIFS after the beacon frame and then sends a CF-Poll frame to the first device. The device responds by sending an ACK if it has no frames to send; otherwise it sends a CF-ACK+data. If the device sends a CF-ACK+data, the PC responds with a CF-ACK+CF-Poll frame. The PC, therefore, can simultaneously poll the next device on the list and acknowledge the data from the previous one. The PC can piggy-back the data it needs to send to devices on the CF-Poll, CF-ACK and CF-ACK+CF-Poll frames. At the end of the CFP, CP is resumed and the devices use the DCF transmission method to gain control of the channel. Figure 3.10 shows the PCF access method.

3.5 Hybrid Coordination Function

While PCF was developed for time-bound frame delivery, there are a number of problems. The time between beacons (which signals the start of the CFP) is unpre-

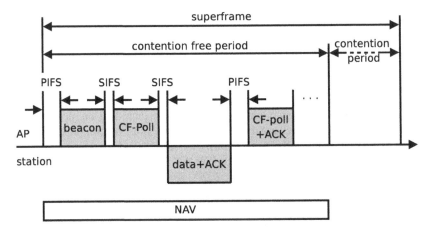

Fig. 3.10 PCF access

dictable. The PC schedules beacons at TBTT, but transmission must wait until the RF channel has been idle for a period up to a PIFS. If the channel is not idle at the end of a superframe, the beacon frame is delayed. This causes the time-bound data frames, due to be sent during the CFP, also to be delayed.

Another problem is the variable length of the data frames sent by the polled devices. The frame lengths can vary according to payloads and physical layer modulation techniques. In order to address the shortcomings of PCF, the IEEE introduced the hybrid coordination function (HCF) in the 802.11e amendment to support quality of service over WLANs.

HCF defines two channel access methods; namely, enhanced distributed channel access (EDCA) and HCF controlled channel access (HCCA). EDCA provides a contention-based access method, whereas a controlled access method is provided by HCCA. HCF's contention-based service is based on the DCF. PCF is supported so that legacy devices can be offered a contention-free service.

A device operating under HCF control transmits a frame during a *transmit opportunity* (TXOP). TXOPs represent bounded time intervals defined by a start time and maximum length. A device is granted a TXOP when it wins contention of the wireless medium. The type of TXOP is dependent upon the channel access method. TXOPs obtained during the contention-based period is called a EDCA-TXOP. Similarly, a TXOP obtained during the contention-free period is called a HCCA-TXOP.

3.5.1 Enhanced Distributed Channel Access

EDCA is an enhancement to the legacy DCF, providing prioritised best-effort frame delivery over the wireless channel. Prioritisation is achieved through a number of coordination function parameters. These parameters control the device's channel sensing period, contention window size, and the amount of time for which it can continuously transmit frames after acquiring the channel.

Table 3.3 Mapping of user priority to access category

Priority	UP	AC	Traffic category
Lowest	1	AC_BK	Background
–	2	AC_BK	Background
–	0	AC_BE	Best-effort
–	3	AC_BE	Best-effort
–	4	AC_VI	Video
–	5	AC_VI	Video
–	6	AC_VO	Voice
Highest	7	AC_VO	Vioce

EDCA frame delivery is based on differentiating user priorities (UPs). UPs are designated integer values of 0–7 and correspond to 802.1D MAC bridge priority tags. 802.11e maps UPs to four access categories (ACs). The mapping of UPs to ACs is shown in Table 3.3.

Four separate back-off entities (one for each AC) operate within each device. The priority of an MSDU is determined by the AC parameters associated with the back-off entity responsible for delivering the MSDU. Each back-off entity contends for a TXOP independently. The channel is sensed for a period called the arbitration inter-frame space (AIFS). The AIFS associated with a particular AC, AIFS[AC], is computed by:

$$\text{AIFS}[AC] = \text{SIFS} + \text{AIFSN}[AC] \times \text{aSlotTime} \tag{3.7}$$

The minimum value of AIFS[AC] is equal to DIFS in the legacy 802.11. The AISF number (AIFSN) is initially set to 2 by the HC. However, the back-off entity can elect to increase the AIFS[AC] by increasing the AIFSN[AC]. An increase in the AISFN[AC] (and consequently the AIFS[AC]) has the effect of reducing the priority of the MSDUs sent by that back-off entity.

The minimum and maximum contention window sizes (CWmin and CWmax respectively) are also determined by the AC. The smaller the values of CWmin and CWmax, the higher the channel access priority. The contention window size for any given back-off stage i is given by:

$$\text{CW}_i[AC] = \min(2^i(\text{CW}\min[AC] + 1) - 1, \text{CW}\max[AC]) \tag{3.8}$$

The diagram in Fig. 3.11 shows that the frames are assigned priorities with ACs according to their AIFS. Once a back-off entity has seized control of the channel, it transmits for the period defined by the TXOP. TXOP limits are defined per AC and the TXOPlimit[AC] determines the back-off entity's share of the channel capacity. Furthermore, 802.11e allows the continuation of an EDCA-TXOP, that is, a back-off entity may deliver multiple MSDUs provided that it does not exceed the TXOPlimit[AC]. The default EDCA parameter set is shown in Table 3.4.

Finally, 802.11e devices maintain two per AC retry counters. QSRC[AC] and QLRC[AC] are the short and long retry counters, respectively. The counters are applied depending upon the length of the MSDU. For AC_VO and AC_VI, the retry

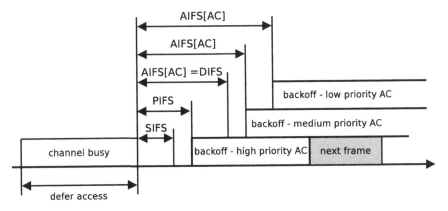

Fig. 3.11 Prioritisation in EDCA

Table 3.4 Default values of
the EDCA parameter set

AC	CWmin	CWmax	AIFSN	TXOP limit (per PHY)	
				DSSS, CCK, PBCC	OFDM, ERP-OFDM, DSSS-OFDM
AC_BK	31	1023	7	0	0
AC_BE	31	1023	3	0	0
AC_VI	15	31	2	6.016 ms	3.008 ms
AC_VO	7	15	2	3.264 ms	1.504 ms

counters are set low because the traffic assigned to these ACs is intolerant to high delays. As AC_BK and AC_BE are less sensitive to delay, the retry counters are set higher. Figure 3.12 shows how frames are mapped to AC queues and their associated EDCA parameters for transmission under control of the coordination function.

3.5.2 HCF Controlled Channel Access

Channel access under HCCA is controlled by the hybrid coordinator (HC) which runs on the access-point. HCCA is similar to PCF in that it divides the channel into CFP (contention-free period) and CP (contention period). During the CFP (like PCF), HCCA uses a polling mechanism. HCCA differs from PCF, in that when a device is polled, it can transmit packets for the duration of the HCCA transmission opportunity (HCCA-TXOP). HCCA initiates CFP by broadcasting a beacon frame after waiting for a PIFS. This silences wireless devices for the duration of the CFP. The HC will allocate HCCA-TXOPs to devices on its polling list using a CF-Poll frame.

A device must send a quality of service reservation request to the HC in order to add itself to the polling list. This sets up a traffic stream (TS) within the HC. Traffic

Fig. 3.12 The four access
categories (ACs) for ECDA

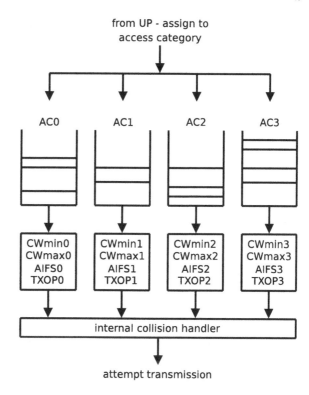

specification (TSPEC) parameters are included in the quality of service management
frame sent by the device. The TSPEC parameters include the mean data rate (ρ) the
MSDU size (σ) for the application ([AC]). If A is a cumulative traffic process, the
traffic is sent in the period $t - s$, where $t > s$, is bounded by:

$$A(t) - A(s) \leq \rho \cdot (t - s) + \sigma \tag{3.9}$$

The HC scheduler performs an admission control function to determine if suffi-
cient resources are available to support the TSPEC request. For any traffic stream k,
the admission control function computes the number of MSDUs that arrive within a
set service interval (SI) at the mean rate:

$$N_k = \left\lceil \frac{\text{SI} \times \rho_k}{\sigma_k} \right\rceil \tag{3.10}$$

SI is taken as the lowest value of the maximum service intervals of all admitted
flows. The transmission opportunity TXOP_k is given by:

$$\text{TXOP}_k = \max \left[\frac{N_k \sigma_k}{R_k} + O, \frac{\sigma_{\max}}{R_i} + O \right] \tag{3.11}$$

R_k is the minimum transmission rate for the PHY, σ_{max} is the maximum MSDU size and O is the overhead. The TS is admitted, if:

$$\frac{\text{TXOP}_{n+1}}{\text{SI}} + \sum_{k=1}^{n} \frac{\text{TXOP}_k}{\text{SI}} \leq \frac{B - T_{CP}}{B} \qquad (3.12)$$

where B is the beacon period and T_{CP} is the time reserved for traffic under the contention-based delivery. A TXOP is allocated to an individual AC (on a device) rather than to the device itself. An AC transmits until it has exhausted its buffer or the TXOP expires. At the end of CFP, or if all of the devices on the polling-list have no more frames to transmit, the HC broadcasts a CF-End frame.

The CF-End frame signals the start of the CP. Devices may contend for EDCA-TXOPs using the contention-based access method. The HCCA, however, continues to operate alongside EDCA during the CP. If the medium becomes idle, the HC can seize control of the channel and issue HCCA-TXOPs.

3.6 Summary

802.11 defines a number of coordination functions for managing the contention of the wireless medium. DCF (distributed coordination function) uses carrier sense, multiple access with collision avoidance (CSMA/CA) and provides a best-effort frame delivery service. DCF suffers from a number of fairness problems.

A coordination function is specified for contention-free access, called PCF (point coordination function). PCF requires centralised control and can, therefore, only operate in infrastructure mode (not ad-hoc mode). With PCF, the access-point divides the channel into contention-free and contention-based (DCF) periods. A contention-free period is initiated by a beacon frame sent by the access-point. The beacon announces the duration of the contention-free period and all clients set their NAV (network allocation vector) accordingly. When the contention-free period has expired, access to the wireless channel is controlled by the DCF. PCF has a number of drawbacks. The centralised polling scheme is inefficient. Transmission times of the polled devices are unknown and contention-free periods lead to unpredictable beacon delays. Furthermore, PCF is an optional part of the standard and is rarely implemented.

The differentiation of frames is not supported in the original 802.11 coordination functions. The 802.11e amendment specifies HCF (hybrid coordination function) for quality of service. Enhanced distributed channel access (EDCA) and HCF controlled channel access (HCCA) provide contention-based and controlled access schemes, respectively.

EDCA implements a priority scheme, whereby higher priority traffic has a greater chance of acquiring the channel than lower priority traffic. Furthermore, each priority level is assigned a greater transmit time, called a Transmit Opportunity (TXOP). The TXOP is a bounded interval during which the sender is free to transmit as many frames as possible. HCCA is similar to legacy PCF; however, instead of alternating contention-free and contention-based access periods between successive beacons, contention-free periods can be initiated at any time.

Chapter 4
Physical Layer

The 802.11 physical layer is divided into two sub-layers; the physical layer convergence procedure (PLCP) sub-layer and the Physical Medium Dependent (PMD) sub-layer. The PLCP sub-layer is responsible for encapsulating MPDUs from the MAC layer into frames which are transmitted by a PMD entity. The PMD sub-layer is responsible for implementing the transmission encoding scheme. MPDUs are mapped to PLCP service data units (PSDUs) which are, in turn, encapsulated in PLCP protocol data units (PPDUs). The PMD specifies a number of PHYs in order to support multiple modulation schemes. The format of PPDUs varies according to the PHY. Figure 4.1 shows the encapsulation of a MPDU/PSDU into a PPDU.

The original 802.11 standard specified three PHYs; frequency hopping spread spectrum (FHSS), direct sequence spread spectrum (DSSS) and infra red (IR). The IR PHY did not achieve commercial success and so will not be discussed here. For more details on IR PHY, refer to [5].

FHSS and DSSS support transmission speeds of 1 and 2 Mb/s. A high rate DSSS (HR/DSSS) was introduced in the 802.11b amendment, supporting speeds of up to 11 Mb/s. Instead of spread spectrum, 802.11a and 802.11g use orthogonal frequency division multiplexing (OFDM) and are capable of speeds of up to 54 Mb/s. The 802.11n combines improved OFDM methods with multiple-input, multiple-output (MIMO) technology. 802.11n can achieve transmission rates of 600 Mb/s. A summary of the PHYs in the 802.11 amendments is shown in Table 4.1.

4.1 Frequency Hopping Spread Spectrum

FHSS uses frequency shift keying (FSK) for the spreading code modulation. Devices transmit/receive on a common frequency for a short period (known as the dwell time), before "hopping" to another channel. Devices (both transmitter and receiver) hop from channel-to-channel in a pseudo-random sequence. Different transmitter/receiver pairs use a different pseudo-random sequence in an attempt to minimise the collisions within the same channel band. In order to avoid narrow band

A. Holt, C.-Y. Huang, *802.11 Wireless Networks,*
Computer Communications and Networks,
DOI 10.1007/978-1-84996-275-9_4, © Springer-Verlag London Limited 2010

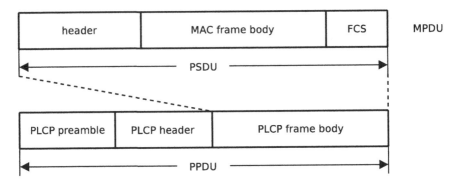

Fig. 4.1 PPDU encapsulation

Table 4.1 Details of modulation methods in 802.11

Standard version	Release date	Data rates (Mbit/s)	Modulation
802.11	1997	1, 2	FHSS, DSSS
802.11b	1999	1, 2, 5.5, 11	DSSS, HR/DSSS
802.11a	1999	up to 54	OFDM
802.11g	2003	up to 54	ERP-OFDM
802.11n	2007-8	up to 600	MIMO-OFDM

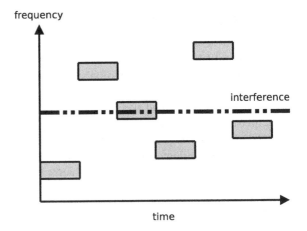

Fig. 4.2 Frequency hopping spread spectrum

interference that affects the current hop, from also affecting the next hop, consecutive hops have a spectral separation of 6 MHz. The diagram in Fig. 4.2 illustrates FHSS.

For a maximum of p channels, the xth channel hopping sequence F_x is defined as:

$$F_x = \{f_x(1), f_x(2), \ldots f_x(p)\} \qquad (4.1)$$

where $f_x(i)$ is the frequency of the ith hop of the xth hopping pattern. The compu-
tation of $f_x(i)$ is regional and is given by the expression below [21].

$$f_x(i) = \begin{cases} (b(i) + x) \bmod (79) + 2 & \text{North America, China, Europe} \\ & \text{(not including France and Spain)} \\ ((i-1) \times x) \bmod (23) + 73 & \text{Japan} \\ (b(i) + x) \bmod (27) + 47 & \text{Spain} \\ (b(i) + x) \bmod (35) + 48 & \text{France} \end{cases} \quad (4.2)$$

The base-hopping sequences $b(i)$ are also regional. For North America, China
and Europe, the base-hopping frequencies are shown in Tables 14–15 of [21]. For
Spain and France, the base-hopping frequencies shown in Tables 14–16 and 14–17
of [21] respectively. Using Maple, we demonstrate how the $f_x(i)$ is calculated.

For North America, China and Europe, assign the base-hopping sequence B:

```
> B :=    [0,  23, 62,   8, 43, 16, 71, 47, 19, 61, 76, 29,
          59, 22, 52, 63, 26, 77, 31,  2, 18, 11, 36, 71,
          54, 69, 21,  3, 37, 10, 34, 66,  7, 68, 75,  4,
          60, 27, 12, 25, 14, 57, 41, 74, 32, 70,  9, 58,
          78, 45, 20, 73, 64, 39, 13, 33, 65, 50, 56, 42,
          48, 15,  5, 17,  6, 67, 49, 40,  1, 28, 55, 35,
          53, 24, 44, 51, 38, 30, 46]:
```

Define the function for computing $f_x(i)$ for North America, China and Europe:

```
> f := (i, x) -> (i + x) mod 79 + 2;
```

$$f := (i, x) \rightarrow (i + x) \bmod 79 + 2$$

Calculate the hop sequence for $x = 7$:

```
> seq(f(i,7), i in b);
9,  32, 71, 17, 52, 25, 80, 56, 28, 70,  6, 38, 68, 31,
61, 72, 35,  7, 40, 11, 27, 20, 45, 80, 63, 78, 30, 12,
46, 19, 43, 75, 16, 77,  5, 13, 69, 36, 21, 34, 23, 66,
50,  4, 41, 79, 18, 67,  8, 54, 29,  3, 73, 48, 22, 42,
74, 59, 65, 51, 57, 24, 14, 26, 15, 76, 58, 49, 10, 37,
64, 44, 62, 33, 53, 60, 47, 39, 55
```

Gaussian frequency shift keying (GFSK) is used to encode the resultant spread
code for transmission. The benefits of frequency encoding is that it offer some im-
munity to noise, as noise tends to affect the signal amplitude. GFSK, however, is
not spectral efficient; consequently, the data rates are low.

Figure 4.3 shows the PLCP frame format for FHSS.

The frame fields are described below:

- sync: sequence of alternating ones and zeros.
- SFD: start frame delimiter. Marks the start of a PSDU using the bit pattern:
  0000110010111101.
- PLW: PSDU length word. The length of the PSDU in octets

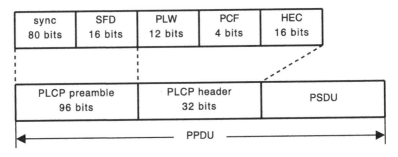

Fig. 4.3 The PLCP frame format for FHSS

- PSF: PLCP signalling field. Specifies the transmission rate of the PSDU.
- HEc: header check error. The value of the frame check sequence from the transmitter.

4.2 Direct Sequence Spread Spectrum

DSSS uses phase shift keying for both the spreading code and message modulation. The spreading code is a pseudo-random "noise" sequence called a *chip* sequence. The chip sequence is XORed to each data bit prior to transmission. Figure 4.4 shows how a narrowband signal is *spread* over a wider frequency band using DSSS. 802.11 uses an 11-bit *Barker* code as a spreading code[1]:

$$\{+1, -1, +1, +1, -1, +1, +1, +1, -1, -1, -1\}$$

As the symbols in the chip occur at a much higher frequency than the data bits, the energy of the original signal is spread over a wider frequency band.

The resultant spread spectrum signal is then modulated for transmission using phase shift keying techniques. Two-level phase shift keying is the simplest form of PSK. Otherwise known as binary PSK (BPSK), the modulator modifies the phase of a carrier signal f_c to reflect a binary 0 or 1:

$$s(t) = \begin{cases} A\cos(2\pi f_c t) & 0 \\ A\cos(2\pi f_c t + \pi) & 1 \end{cases} \tag{4.3}$$

---

[1] In 802.11, $+1$ is represented by a 1 and -1 by a 0.

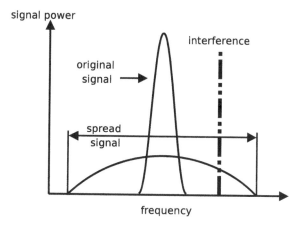

Fig. 4.4 Direct sequence spread spectrum

Table 4.2 DBPSK encoding

Phase change (radians)	Value
0	0
π	1

Table 4.3 DQPSK encoding

Phase change (radians)	Value
0	00
$\pi/2$	01
π	10
$4\pi/3$	11

A four-level PSK utilises the channel bandwidth more effectively. Quadrature phase shift keying uses four phase shifts, for example:

$$s(t) = \begin{cases} A\cos(2\pi f_c t + \frac{\pi}{4}) & 11 \\ A\cos(2\pi f_c t + \frac{3\pi}{4}) & 01 \\ A\cos(2\pi f_c t - \frac{3\pi}{4}) & 00 \\ A\cos(2\pi f_c t - \frac{\pi}{4}) & 10 \end{cases} \qquad (4.4)$$

802.11b actually uses differentiated phase shift keying (DPSK) methods; namely, differential binary phase shift keying (DBPSK) and differential quadrature phase shift keying (DQPSK). Unlike PSK, where the phase is set according to the input, DPSK changes the phase relative to the last input value. The phase changes for DBPSK and DQPSK are shown in Tables 4.2 and 4.3, respectively.

A DSSS PPDU comprises a DSSS PLCP preamble, DSSS PLCP header followed by the frame payload (MPDU) and the MPDU. In future amendments, the

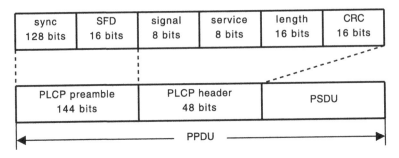

sync 128 bits	SFD 16 bits	signal 8 bits	service 8 bits	length 16 bits	CRC 16 bits

Fig. 4.5 Long preamble

DSSS PLCP preamble and header is referred to as the *long* preamble and header, to distinguish it from the *short* preamble and header, introduced in 802.11b (discussed below). The frame format is shown in Fig. 4.5. The fields are described below:

- Sync: sequence of alternating one's and zero's.
- SFD: Start frame delimiter. This field signals the beginning of the PHY-dependent parameters within the preamble.
- Signal: Specifies the modulation technique used. For 1 Mb/s DBPSK, this field is 10, and for 2 Mb/s DQPSK, it is 20. In 802.11b, where higher data rates are supported, this field is set to 55 or 110 for 5.5 Mb/s and 11 Mb/s respectively.
- Service: Reserved.
- Length: The transmission time of MPDU in microseconds.
- CRC: Cyclic-redundancy-check. Uses CRC-16 as a frame check sequence.

4.3 High-Rate Direct Sequence Spread Spectrum

The 802.11b amendment introduced a "Higher-Speed Physical Layer Extension in the 2.4 GHz Band". The high-rate direct sequence spread spectrum (HR/DSSS) technique produced improved transmission rates.

- Complementary code keying (CCK)
- Packet binary convolution coding (PBCC)

Both CCK and PBCC yield data rates of 5.5 and 11 Mb/s. CCK is a block code, where the symbols are divided into fixed blocks and used as code words. The CCK modulation is based on the use of polyphase complementary codes. CCK codes are (nearly) orthogonal; that is, autocorrelations are negligible for lags greater than zero. The polyphase complementary codes are complex rather than binary. The diagram in Fig. 4.6 shows an example of a polyphase code with the real and imaginary components represented on the horizontal and vertical planes, respectively.

The subset of allowed code words is less than the possible total number of code words. Complementary codes are symbols with desirable correlation features. The received code word is compared to the set of valid code words. If the received code

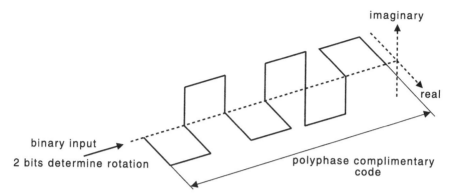

Fig. 4.6 Polyphase complementary codes

Table 4.4 Details of modulation methods in 802.11b

Link rate	Code	Code length	Modulation	System	Symbol rate (MS/s)	Bits per symbol
1 Mb/s	Barker code	11	DBPSK	DSSS	1	1
2 Mb/s	Barker code	11	DQPSK	DSSS	1	2
5.5 Mb/s	CCK	4	DQPSK	HR/DSSS	1.375	4
11 Mb/s	CCK	8	DQPSK	HR/DSSS	1.375	8

word is *close* to a particular valid code word, then that code word is selected as the transmitted code word. In this way, an errored code word can be recovered at the receiver. CCK uses a symbol length of 8 complex chips and the codeword C is derived from the expression below [30]:

$$C = \{e^{j(\phi_1+\phi_2+\phi_3+\phi_4)}, e^{j(\phi_1+\phi_3+\phi_4)}, e^{j(\phi_1+\phi_2+\phi_4)},$$
$$e^{j(\phi_1+\phi_4)}, e^{j(\phi_1+\phi_2+\phi_4)}, e^{j(\phi_1+\phi_3)}, e^{j(\phi_1+\phi_2)}, e^{j(\phi_1)}\} \qquad (4.5)$$

The terms ϕ_1, ϕ_2, ϕ_3 and ϕ_4 are selected according to the data rate (5.5 or 11 Mb/s). Six bits (of the 8) are used to encode the polyphase complementary key code. The code word is then rotated by 0, $/\pi/2$, π or $3\pi/4$ according to the remaining two bits of the byte.

If the channel conditions cannot support high data rates, then the a device can drop its transmission speed to 1 or 2 Mb/s by using the DSSS PHY from legacy 802.11 [15].

PBCC is based upon convolution codes. Each input bit is processed by a series of shift registers and modulo-2 addition operations. The coder produces two output bits from an input bit and the bits are then stored in the shift registers. Figure 4.7 shows the convolution encoder for PBCC.

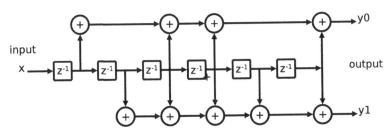

Fig. 4.7 PBCC convolutional encoder

short sync 56 bits	short SFD 16 bits	signal 8 bits	service 8 bits	length 16 bits	CRC 16 bits

short PLCP preamble 72 bits (1 Mb/s)	short PLCP header 48 bits (2 Mb/s)	PSDU (2,5.5 or 11 Mb/s)

◄─────────────────────── PPDU ───────────────────────►

Fig. 4.8 Short preamble

In 802.11b, two preamble/header types are supported; namely, *long* and *short*. The long preamble/header is the same as for the 1 and 2 Mb/s DSSS specification, as defined in the original standard (see Fig. 4.5). The format of PPDU using the short preamble header is shown in Fig. 4.8.

4.4 Orthogonal Frequency Division Multiplexing

The IEEE 802.11a PHY specifies orthogonal frequency division multiplexing (OFDM) as its modulation scheme [8, 25, 41]. OFDM is not exclusive to 802.11, but is also used in other wireless technologies, such as HiperLAN/2 and 802.16 (WiMAX). It is also used in digital audio broadcasting (DAB), digital video broadcasting (DVB) and asynchronous digital subscriber line (ADSL) systems.

OFDM transmits a high-speed binary signal over a number of closely-spaced, lower-rate sub-carriers. In 802.11a, there are a total of 52 sub-carriers, 48 of which are data sub-carriers and the remaining 4 are pilot subs-carriers. The PLCP frame format for 802.11a is shown in Fig. 4.9. The (binary) bits of the PPDU are encoded with a convolution code. Furthermore, bits are reordered and bit interleaved, then mapped to a complex number and divided amongst the sub-carriers. The sub-carrier then undergoes an inverse fast Fourier transform (IFFT) and is transmitted.

Sub-carrier signals are modulated using one of four modulation methods; namely, BPSK, QPSK, 16 or 64 state quadrature amplitude modulation (QAM). Convolution codes are used to protect against errors. 802.11a devices can transmit at speeds

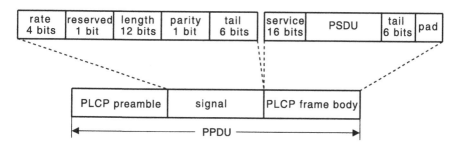

Fig. 4.9 The PLCP frame format for OFDM in 802.11a

Table 4.5 Details of modulation schemes for the 802.11a PHY

Mode	Link rate (Mb/s)	Modulation	Coding rate	Coded bits Bits/carrier	Bits/OFDM sym.	Data bits bits/OFDM sym.
1	6	BPSK	1/2	1	48	24
2	9	BPSK	3/4	1	48	36
3	12	QPSK	1/2	2	96	48
4	18	QPSK	3/4	2	96	72
5	24	16QAM	1/2	4	192	96
6	36	16QAM	3/4	4	192	144
7	48	64QAM	2/3	6	288	192
8	54	64QAM	3/4	6	288	216

of 6, 9, 12, 18, 24, 36, 48 or 54 Mb/s, depending upon the modulation scheme and convolution code; see Table 4.5.

Traditional frequency division multiplexing uses guard bands between channels in order to mitigate against co-channel interference. With OFDM, however, the sub-carriers overlap. The orthogonal properties of the modulated sub-carrier ensures that adjacent signals do not interfere with each other. Two functions, f and g, are orthogonal if their inner product is zero; that is:

$$\langle f, g \rangle = \sum_{-1}^{1} f(x)g(x)dx \tag{4.6}$$

For example, consider the two "orthogonal" functions:

$$f(x) = 2x + 3$$
$$g(x) = 5x^2 + x - 17/9 \tag{4.7}$$

We define the functions f and g in Maple:

```
> f := x -> 2*x + 3;
```

$$f =: x \rightarrow 2x + 3$$

```
> g := x -> 5 * x^2 + x - 17/9;
```

$$g =: x \rightarrow 5x^2 + x - 17/9$$

The inner product, in the interval $[-1, 1]$, yields a result of zero, demonstrating that f and g are orthogonal:

```
> int(f(x)*g(x), x=-1..1);
```

$$0$$

The sub-carriers (sometimes called tones) comprise sinusoidal waveforms that are eigenfunctions of a linear channel. This property ensures that, in the presence of multi-path, orthogonality is preserved between sub-carriers. The OFDM signal $s(t)$, is given by:

$$s(t) = \frac{1}{\sqrt{N}} \sum_{k=0}^{N-1} x_k \phi_k t, \quad 0 < t < NT \tag{4.8}$$

where $\phi_k(t)$ is the kth baseband subcarrier and takes the form:

$$\phi_k(t) = e^{j2\pi f_k t} \tag{4.9}$$

The term NT is the length of the OFDM symbol and x_k is the kth complex data symbol (selected from, for example, a QAM or PSK constellation). The kth sub-carrier frequency, f_k, is given by:

$$f_k = \frac{k}{NT} \tag{4.10}$$

which ensures the orthogonality of the sub-carriers, $\phi_k(t)$. Orthogonality between the sub-carriers can be lost due to the dispersive nature of the channel. This, in turn, causes inter-carrier interference (ICI). Furthermore, channel dispersion can cause ISI between successive OFDM symbols. ISI can be prevented by inserting a silent guard interval (GI) between successive OFDM symbols. This can, however, cause a loss of orthogonality. Adding a cyclic prefix preserves the orthogonality of the sub-carriers and prevents ISI. The cyclic prefix is introduced by extending the symbol period by Δ, thus:

$$s(t) = \frac{1}{\sqrt{N}} \sum_{k=0}^{N-1} x_k \phi_k t, \quad -\Delta < t < NT \tag{4.11}$$

Part of the signal is replicated at the start of the OFDM symbol to create a GI. Figure 4.10 is a graphical representation of the use of the cyclic prefix.

4.5 Extended Rate PHY

802.11g, like 802.11a, supports data rates up to 54 Mb/s using extended rate PHY (ERP). Unlike 802.11a, however, 802.11g operates in the same 2.4 GHz band as

Fig. 4.10 Cyclic prefix

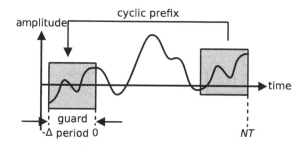

Table 4.6 802.11g PHYs

PHY	Data rate (Mb/s)	Mandatory
ERP-OFDM	≤ 54	Yes
ERP-DSSS/CCK	1, 2, 5.5, 11	Yes
DSSS-OFDM	≤ 54	No
ERP-PBCC	22, 33	No

802.11b. 802.11g devices, therefore, have to co-exist with legacy devices. For this reason, 802.11g defines a number of PHYs. Four PHYs are defined in total, two of which are mandatory and two optional. The four PHYs are summarised in Table 4.6. 802.11g PHYs.

ERP-CCK/DSSS is used when a 802.11g device communicates with an 802.11b device. It uses DSSS for 1 and 2 Mb/s rates and CCK for 5.5 and 11 Mb/s (depending upon the state of the channel). For all intents and purposes, the 802.11g device operates as a 802.11b device.

ERP-OFDM is the same OFDM scheme as 802.11a but modified for the 2.4 GHz range. The PPDU format is the same as for 802.11a (refer back to Fig. 4.9) and supports the date rates. When two 802.11g devices exchange frames, they can use ERP-OFDM. However, in the presence of other 802.11b devices, 802.11g devices must operate a protection mechanism. 802.11b devices cannot detect ERP-OFDM signals and, therefore, cannot determine if a wireless channel is busy during the transmission of an ERP-OFDM frame. For this reason, 802.11g, when using ERP-OFDM, updates the NAV (network access vector) of non-ERP devices by sending RTS/CTS frames (or CTS-to-self frame) using the DSSS or CCK modulation.

802.11g defines two optional PHYs: DSSS-OFDM and ERP-PBCC. DSSS-OFDM is a hybrid modulation scheme whereby DSSS is used to modulate the preamble and frame header and OFDM to modulate the payload. DSSS-OFDM does not need to operate a protection mechanism; therefore, RTS/CTS frames do not need to precede a data frame. ERP-PBCC is a single-carrier modulation scheme that encodes the payload with a 256-state packet binary convolution code. ERP-PBCC achieves data rates of 22 and 33 Mbp/s.

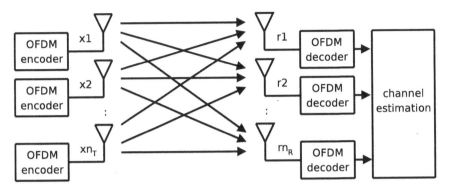

Fig. 4.11 MIMO Communication system

4.6 MIMO-OFDM

The MIMO-OFDM PHY (in 802.11n) supports data rates of up to 300 Mb/s. In addition to the PHY, there are efficiency enhancements to the MAC, such as frame aggregation and block acknowledgements. The 802.11n PHY relies heavily on multiple-input, multiple-output (MIMO) technology for high data rates. MIMO systems consist of multiple antennas and RF chains at the transmitter and receiver (see Fig. 4.11). The number of antennas/RF chains at the transmitter (n_T) need not be the same as the number at the receiver (n_R). MIMO technology is conducive to OFDM systems which transmits signals in multiple narrowband channels. MIMO-OFDM is, therefore, subject to a great deal of research in the quest for high speed wireless systems.

MIMO systems bring about increases in capacity through spatial diversity gains and spatial multiplexing. Spatial diversity exists in both receive and transmit forms. With receive diversity, two or more antennas are spaced apart, so that they receive uncorrelated signals (having travelled along independent paths). In its simplest form, the antenna with the best signal is selected for processing by the RF chain. This is called *switched* diversity. Maximum ratio combining (MRC) is a more advanced receive diversity method. With MRC, advanced digital signal processing (DSP) methods are used to combine the separate signals into a single, higher quality signal for improved gain. Multiple RF chains are required for this method.

Receive diversity methods have been studied and refined over many years. Indeed, receive diversity has been employed by devices running pre-802.11n standards (802.11a/b/g). The advent of transmit diversity is more recent. A simple scheme involves transmitting from the antenna that yields the best signal at the receiver. This involves obtaining feedback from the receiver about the channel environment.

A more sophisticated method of transmit diversity exists which can mitigate the effects of fading by sending multiple signals. The transmit bit stream is encoded in space and time. Space-time codes (STC) are used to send replica signals which can be *constructively* recombined at the receiver. Figure 4.12 shows the concept of STC in MIMO systems.

Fig. 4.12 Space-time coding

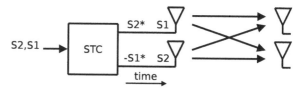

Fig. 4.13 Diversity gain for
N replica input streams

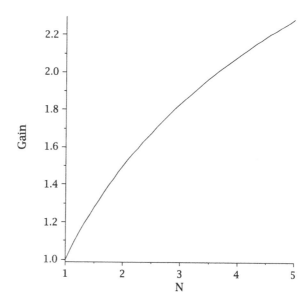

The diversity gain for N independent, Rayleigh distributed input signals, is given by:

$$\text{diversity gain} = \sum_{k=1}^{N} \frac{1}{k} \tag{4.12}$$

We define the diversity gain in Maple:

```
Gdiversity := (N) -> sum(1/k, k=1..N);
```

$$\text{Gdiversity} := N \rightarrow \sum_{k=1}^{N} \frac{1}{k}$$

The statement below produces the graph in Fig. 4.13:

```
> plot(Gdiversity(N), N=1..5, labels=["N", "Gain"],
  labeldirections=[HORIZONTAL, VERTICAL],
  color=black, font=[TIMES,ROMAN,12]);
```

Spatial multiplexing exploits multi-path environments to send parallel data streams. A high rate signal is divided into several lower rate signals which are transmitted simultaneously in the same frequency band. The receiver can decode the

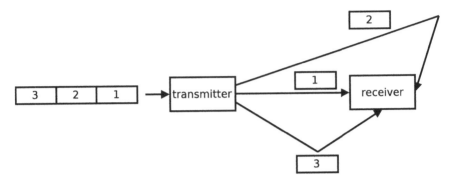

Fig. 4.14 Spatial multiplexing

different signal streams, provided that they arrive at the antenna array with suffi-
cient spatial separation. Figure 4.14 shows how parallel data streams are sent from
multiple antennas over diverse paths.

Here, we examine the performance gains of MIMO systems, comparing them
with the single-input, single-output (SISO), single-input, multiple-output (SIMO),
multiple-input, single-output (MISO) systems. Shannon's formula [29] gives the
theoretical channel capacity for a single-input single-output (SISO) configuration.
The expression for Shannon's channel capacity theorem is given in (1.5) in Chap. 1.
The capacity of a MIMO system increases linearly with the number of antennas, K,
where $K = \min[n_T, n_R]$:

$$C_{\text{mimo}} = K w \log_2(1 + \text{SNR}) \tag{4.13}$$

With SIMO/MISO systems ($1 \times K / K \times 1$), there is a logarithmic increase in
capacity with the number of antennas:

$$C_{tx/rx} = w \log_2(1 + K \cdot \text{SNR}) \tag{4.14}$$

Maple does not have a $\log_2$ function, so, for convenience, we define one:

```
> log2 := (x) -> log10(x)/log10(2):
```

Define C_{mimo} in Maple:

```
> Cmimo := (W,SNR,K) -> K * W * log2 (1 + SNR):
```

Create the 3D plot in Fig. 4.15:

```
> plot3d(Cmimo(20*10^6,snr,k)/10^6, k=1..6, snr=0..20,
  axes=boxed, labels=["k", "SNR (dB)","C (Mb/s)"],
  labeldirections=[HORIZONTAL, HORIZONTAL, VERTICAL],
  font=[TIMES,ROMAN,12]);
```

Define a Maple function for $C_{tx/rx}$:

```
> Ctxrx := (W,SNR,K) -> W * log2 (1 + K * SNR):
```

Fig. 4.15 Capacity of a
MIMO system

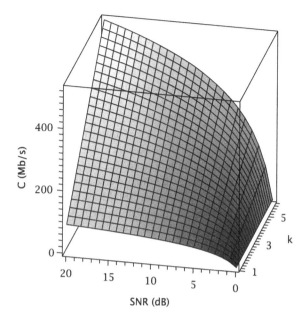

Fig. 4.16 Capacity of Tx/Rx
diversity

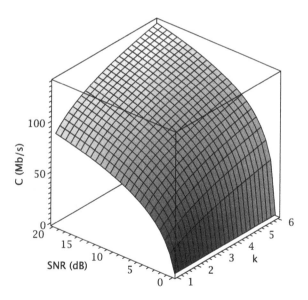

The graph in Fig. 4.16 is generated by the statement:

```
> plot3d(Ctxrx(W,snr,k)/10^6, k=1..6, snr=0..20,
  axes=boxed, labels=["k", "SNR (dB)","C (Mb/s)"],
  labeldirections=[HORIZONTAL, HORIZONTAL, VERTICAL],
  font=[TIMES,ROMAN,12]);
```

While MIMO promises improved coverage, range and performance, there is an associated increase in complexity and cost. Antennas may be inexpensive and DSP costs are decreasing, but Moore's law does not apply to RF components. For this reason, there has been considerable research into hybrid-selection schemes. With hybrid-selection, L out of K antenna signals are chosen for processing. While there is some performance loss over full $K \times K$ systems, significant cost savings are made by reducing RF chains from K to L.

802.11n specifies a number of improvements to OFDM. The number of sub-carriers is increased to 56 (4 or which are used for signalling) which yields a 20% increase in transmission rate over 802.11a/g which uses 52 (minus 4 for signalling) sub-carriers. When channel bonding is used (described below), 114 (6 for signalling) are used. As mentioned above, OFDM uses a guard interval (GI) to protect against inter-symbol interference due to multi-path. With legacy 802.11a/g, the GI is 800 ns, whereas, with 802.11n, the GI is 400 ns. This results in a symbol rate increase of 10%. 802.11n can transmit in a channel of either 20 MHz or 40 MHz bandwidth. The feature that enables 40 MHz channels is called channel bonding. There is a trade-off, however, in terms of the number of overlapping channels that can co-exist. In the 2.4 GHz band, there is only capacity for one (non-overlapping) 40 MHz channel (plus one legacy 20 MHz channel). The 5 GHz band is wider, and can accommodate multiple non-overlapping 40 MHz channels. For this reason, channel bonding is usually reserved for the 5 GHz band.

Just as the 802.11g amendment had to be designed to inter-operate with legacy 802.11b, similar issues arise in 802.11n. As 802.11n operates in both the 2.4 GHz and 5 GHz band, it has to co-exist with 802.11b/g and 802.11a devices. Legacy preambles and headers are used so that 802.11a/b/g devices can detect the presence of 802.11n frames. Under certain circumstances, however, the use of legacy preambles and headers can be a problem. When an 802.11n payload is transmitted, the change in power levels (due to MIMO and beamforming) can cause legacy devices to reset their NAV. For this reason, 802.11n devices usually resort to the RTS/CTS protection mechanism.

4.7 Beamforming

Beamforming is a method for achieving directional signal transmission/reception using sensor arrays combined with signal processing techniques. The receive directionality of the array can be altered by means of analysing the interference patterns formed by "multiple" signals arriving at the array elements. The phase and amplitude of the signal is controlled by the beamformer so that the signal pattern interferes constructively in the direction of the receiver and destructively in other directions. Beamforming is an optional component of 802.11n.

Beamforming cannot be used in conjunction with the MIMO techniques described above. Spatial multiplexing, for example, relies on a rich multiple environment, whereas beamforming produces a single, coherent RF signal beam in the direction of the receiver. In this section we demonstrate the directional radiation

Fig. 4.17 Gain of a simple beamformer, $\theta_b = 30°$ and $\theta_w = 90°$

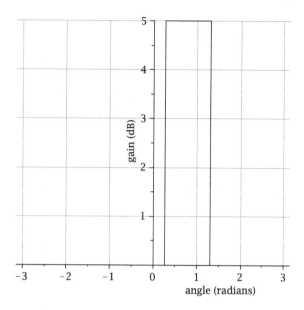

patterns of a beamforming sensor array can be analysed. A simple model of beamforming gain is given by:

$$g(\theta) = \begin{cases} c & \theta_b - \theta_w/2 \leq \theta < \theta_b + \theta_w/2 \\ 0 & \text{otherwise} \end{cases} \tag{4.15}$$

where θ_b is the boresight angle and θ_w is the beam width. Equation (4.15) is implemented as a Maple function:

```
> g := (a,b,c) -> piecewise(a >= b - w/2 and
  a < b + w/2, c, 0);
```

$$g := (a, b, c) \rightarrow \text{piecewise}\left(a \geq b - \frac{w}{2} \text{ and } a < b + \frac{w}{2}, c, 0\right)$$

Set the beamwidth to 90°:

```
> w := Pi/2;
```

$$w := \frac{1}{2}\pi$$

Create a plot of the beamforming gain with a boresight angle of $\theta_b = 30°$:

```
> G6 := plot(g(a, Pi/6, 5), a=-Pi..Pi,color=black):
```

The command below produced the graph in Fig. 4.17:

```
> display(G6, labeldirections=["horizontal","vertical"],
  labels=["angle (radians)", "gain (dB)"],
  gridlines=true, thickness=1, font=[times,roman,12]);
```

Fig. 4.18 Gain of a simple beamformer (polarplot), $\theta_b = 30°$ and $\theta_w = 90°$

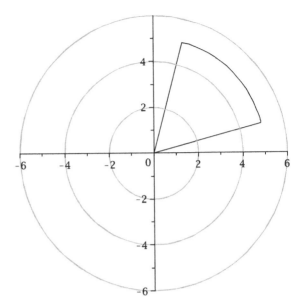

We can represent the gain as a polarplot:

```
> G1 := polarplot(g(a,Pi/6,5), a=-Pi..Pi, color=black):
```

Define a set of concentric circles for scale:

```
> C := polarplot([2,4,6], color=gray):
```

The graph in Fig. 4.18 was produced with the statement:

```
> display(G1, C, scaling=constrained);
```

While simple, the model above is unrealistic. The model below of a uniform linear array is derived from [3]. It consists of a set of elements arranged in a straight line, Δ distance apart (see Fig. 4.19). The directionality of the array is defined by its boresight angle θ_b, which is the angle of maximum radiation intensity:

$$\theta_b = \pm \arccos\left(-\frac{\gamma\lambda}{2\pi\Delta}\right) \tag{4.16}$$

For a beamforming array, the boresight angle is towards the destination node. The gain of the beamformer at angle θ for a given boresight (destination node direction) is given by:

$$g(\theta, \theta_b) = \frac{\left(\frac{\sin(m\psi(\theta,\theta_b))}{\sin(\psi(\theta,\theta_b))}\right)^2}{\frac{1}{2}\int_0^\pi \left(\frac{\sin(m\psi(\theta,\theta_n))}{\sin(\psi(\theta,\theta_b))}\right)^2 \sin\theta\, d\theta} \tag{4.17}$$

where m is the number of elements in the antenna array. The function ψ is given by:

$$\psi(\theta, \theta_b) = \frac{\pi\Delta}{\lambda}(\cos\theta - \cos\theta_b) \tag{4.18}$$

Fig. 4.19 A uniform linear array (ULA). Elements are Δ distance apart

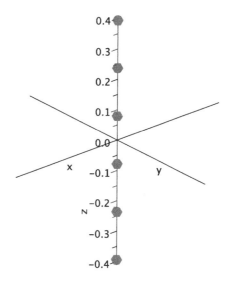

For $\Delta = \lambda/2$, the gain expression in (4.17) reduces to:

$$g(\theta, \theta_b) = \frac{1}{m}\left(\frac{\sin(m\psi(\theta, \theta_b))}{\sin(\psi(\theta, \theta_b))}\right)^2 \tag{4.19}$$

For brevity, we define an intermediate function $(f1)$:

```
> f1 := (a,b) -> (sin(m * psi(a,b))/ sin(psi(a,b)))^2;
```

$$f1 := (a, b) \rightarrow \frac{\sin(m\psi(a, b))^2}{\sin(\psi(a, b))^2}$$

The ψ function is defined as:

```
> psi := (a,b) -> (Pi*Delta/lambda) * (cos(a) - cos(b));
```

$$\psi := (a, b) \rightarrow \frac{\pi\Delta(\cos(a) - \cos(b))}{\lambda}$$

Finally, the gain function is:

```
> g1 := (a,b) ->
  f1(a,b)/(0.5*int(f1(i, b)*sin(i),i=0..Pi));
```

$$g1 := (a, b) \rightarrow \frac{f1(a, b)}{0.5\left(\int_0^\pi f1(i, b)\sin(i)di\right)}$$

We carry out an analysis using this beamforming model. The speed of light c and centre frequency f of the signal are set:

```
> c := 2.99792458e8:
```

```
> f := 2.412e9:
```

From this, we can derive the wavelength λ:

Fig. 4.20 Gain of a
beamformer with a boresight
of 0°

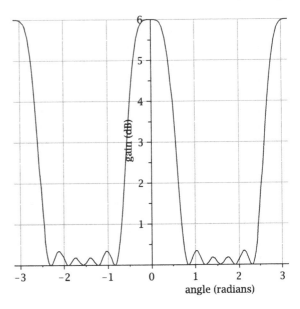

> lambda := c/f;

$$\lambda := 0.1575456053$$

Set the array element spacing Δ to half the wavelength:

> Delta := lambda/2;

$$\Delta := 0.07877280265$$

Set the number of antenna elements in the array:

> m := 6;

$$m := 6$$

Create a plot of the gain for a boresight angle of 0°:

> G2 := plot(g1(a,0), a=-Pi..Pi, color=black):

The graph in Fig. 4.20 was produced with the statement:

> display(G2, labels=["angle (radians)","gain (dB)"],
  labeldirections=["horizontal", "vertical"],
  font=[times,roman,12], gridlines=true);

The graph in Fig. 4.21 shows the gain of the beamformer for a 45° boresight angle. It was produced by the following statements:

> G3 := plot(g1(a, Pi/2), a=-Pi..Pi,color=black):
> display(G3, labels=["angle (radians)","gain (dB)"],
  labeldirections=["horizontal", "vertical"],
  font=[times,roman,12], gridlines=true);

Fig. 4.21 Gain of a beamformer with a boresight of 45°

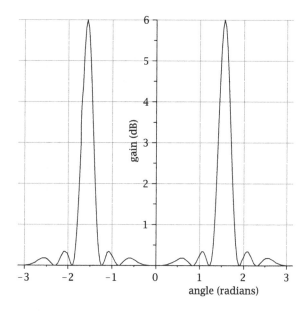

We plot (polar) graphs for various boresight angles ($\theta_b = \{0°, 30°, 90°, 110°\}$):

```
> G4 := polarplot(g1(a,0), a=-Pi..Pi,
  color=black, legend=["0 degrees"], linestyle=dot):
> G5 := polarplot(g1(a,Pi/6), a=-Pi..Pi,
  color=black, legend=["30 degrees"], linestyle=dash):
> G6 := polarplot(g1(a,Pi/2), a=-Pi..Pi,
  color=black, legend=["90 degrees"], linestyle=solid):
> G7 := polarplot(g1(a,Pi*110/180), a=-Pi..Pi,
  color=black, legend=["110 degrees"],
  linestyle=dashdot):
```

The polarplot in Fig. 4.22 was produced by the statement:

```
> display(G4,G5,G6,G7,C,scaling=constrained);
```

4.8 Summary

PHYs in the RF domain use spread spectrum methods. Spread spectrum techniques are designed to reduce the effects of narrowband interference. Typically, spread spectrum methods employ two modulation stages. First, the message is modulated by a *spreading* code. The resultant message is then modulated for transmission over the wireless channel.

The original 802.11 standard specified two spread spectrum technique, FHSS (frequency hopping spread spectrum) and DSSS (direct sequence spread spectrum). Both FHSS and DSSS supported 1 and 2 Mb/s data rates.

Fig. 4.22 Beamformer for various boresight angles (polar plot)

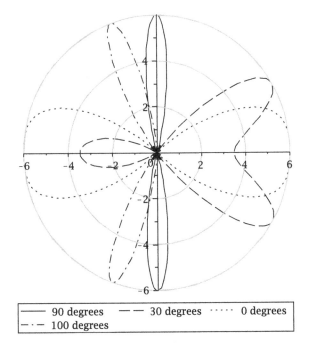

| —— 90 degrees | — — 30 degrees | ····· 0 degrees |
| —·— 100 degrees | | |

HR/DSSS (high-rate DSSS) was introduced in 802.11b, which was capable of speeds of 5.5 and 11 Mb/s. 802.11b operates in the same 2.4 GHz band as legacy 802.11.

The 802.11a amendment was ratified at the same time as 802.11b. It supports rates of up to 54 Mb/s. 802.11a operates in the 5 GHz range and uses OFDM (orthogonal frequency division multiplexing). OFDM is resilient to severe channel conditions, such as narrowband interference and multi-path fading. ISI (inter-symbol interference) is avoided by selecting sub-carrier frequencies which are mathematically *orthogonal*.

Speeds of up to 54 Mb/s in the 2.4 GHz band were realised with the introduction of 802.11g. 802.11g uses OFDM, similar to 802.11a. As 802.11g operates in the same band as 802.11b, 802.11g devices must use certain protection mechanisms in order to co-exist with 802.11b devices.

The 802.11n PHY uses MIMO (multiple-input, multiple-output) techniques to achieve data rates of up to 300 Mb/s. MIMO systems exploit the spatial domain by using multiple antennas and RF chains at both the transmitter and receiver. 802.11n still uses OFDM, but specifies a number of enhancements; for example, more subcarriers, shorter guard intervals and channel bonding.

Beamforming is the technique that combines RF signals from multiple omnidirectional antennas into a directional beam. This has the effect of increasing the gain in the direction of the receiver and reducing interference in other directions in much the same way as a directional antenna. Unlike a directional antenna, however, the beamforming array (sometimes called a smart antenna) is not physically aligned.

Chapter 5
Cryptography

The broadcast nature of WLANs makes them inherently vulnerable, more so then their wired counterparts. Whereas signals transversing a wired network are confined to communication devices (for example, hubs, switches, routers) and the cables that connect them, wireless signals (can) propagate beyond the boundaries of the intended domain of (legitimate) receivers. WLANs, therefore, rely heavily on cryptography for implementing security.

Cryptography is synonymous with encryption.[1] Indeed the subject of cryptography used to be exclusively about the confidentiality of messages. More recently, however, the field has expanded (largely due, one might speculate, to the growth of information technology) to include authentication and message integrity.

In this chapter, we present an overview of cryptography. We avoid a mathematical treatment of the subject, preferring a practical approach instead; see [40] for a rigorous mathematical treatment of cryptographical techniques.

5.1 Ciphers

Ciphers fall into two broad categories; namely, *symmetric key* and *asymmetric key*. Symmetric key cryptography (also known as secret key) uses a shared single secret key for both encryption and decryption processes, whereas, with asymmetric key cryptography (also called public key cryptography), two keys are used; one for encryption and the other for decryption. The two keys are *mathematically* linked, whereby one is designated the *public* key and the other is designated the *private* key. Symmetric and asymmetric key cryptographic methods are discussed in this section.

---

[1]The use of the term "encryption" in this chapter, also refers implicitly to the reverse process "decryption". We use the term *decryption* when we need to distinguish it from the encryption process.

A. Holt, C.-Y. Huang, *802.11 Wireless Networks,*
Computer Communications and Networks,
DOI 10.1007/978-1-84996-275-9_5, © Springer-Verlag London Limited 2010

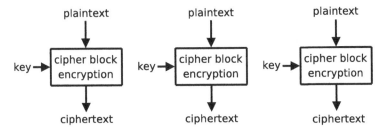

Fig. 5.1 ECB encryption

5.1.1 Symmetric Key Cryptography

There are two types of symmetric key cipher; namely, stream ciphers and block ciphers. With stream ciphers, data is encrypted one digit (bit or byte) at a time. Stream ciphers approximate one-time pad ciphers (also known as Vernam ciphers). With one-time pads, a *keystream* is applied to the plaintext to produce the ciphertext. One-time pads have been proved to be completely secure. However, the keystream can only be used once, otherwise security is compromised. Furthermore, the size of the keystream must be at least the size of the plaintext message. For large messages, therefore, one-time pads are impractical.

Stream ciphers, for convenience, use a smaller key (which are likely to be less than the size of a plaintext message). The cipher uses this initial key to generate a pseudo-random keystream to match (or exceed) the length of the message. The keystream is applied to the plaintext (typically by XORing) to produce the ciphertext.

In contrast, a block cipher processes fixed-length groups of bits. A block of plaintext symbols of size $m > 1$ are encrypted to create a block ciphertext of the same size. For the reverse process (decryption), the ciphertext is decrypted in blocks of size m to produce plaintext blocks of size m. Consequently the cipher key will be of length m. To encrypt messages longer than the block size (m) a *mode of operation* is used. Various modes of operation have been developed, each varying in sophistication. Some of them, effectively, behave as stream ciphers. A detailed discussion of all modes of operation are beyond the scope of this book (see [12] for more information). Some of the common ones are listed below:

- Electronic codebook (ECB)
- Cipher-block chaining (CBC)
- Cipher feedback (CFB)
- Output feedback (OFB)
- Counter (CTR)

The simplest of these modes of operation is ECB. The plaintext message is divided into n-bit blocks and encrypted with a key of that length (illustrated in Fig. 5.1). The problem with this method is that, if a plaintext (n-bit) block appears repeatedly throughout the message, it will result in replica ciphertext blocks. We use a simple example to illustrate this problem. Create a file plain.txt with the command-line below:

```
$ echo -n "0123456789ABCDEF0123456789ABCDEF" >plain.txt
```

It can be seen that the file consists of two, 16 byte (128-bit) repeating sequences: 0-9,A-F. If we examine the file using the command od, we see the "*" character denoting repetitions of the previous line:

```
$ od -X plain.txt
0000000 33323130 37363534 42413938 46454443
*
0000040
```

We encrypt the plain.txt using 128-bit ECB (we redirect the output to od):

```
$ openssl enc -k secret -aes-128-ecb -in plain.txt |
> od -X
Verifying - enter aes-128-ecb encryption password:
0000000 746c6153 5f5f6465 ff081061 1bc14f2c
0000020 6a0e2904 42f71db1 801f410b d8c89430
*
0000060 e93b7afc adacb89c 2eef7448 6d34640e
0000100
```

The encryption process has added a 128-bit block at the beginning and end of the data stream, but for the purpose of this example, we can ignore them. The "*" character on the third line of the hexdecimal output indicates that the second and third line of ciphertext are identical to each other, corresponding to the replica blocks of plaintext. However, if we repeat this experiment using 128-bit CBC, we see that the resulting ciphertext of each 128-bit block is different, even though the plaintext blocks are identical:

```
$ openssl enc -aes-128-cbc -k secret -in plain.txt |
> od -X
0000000 746c6153 5f5f6465 28795aec 955b170c
0000020 d5a2690b 2367cb71 c8ca66b8 0f8a6ca4
0000040 26db9f39 fc7605b4 eba6a3d8 f804ac29
0000060 6cc916d0 edac713b 239e9abc e51f29c9
0000100
```

A more graphical illustration of the problem is shown in Fig. 5.2. Here, we encrypt an image using both ECB and CBC (with the AES cipher). Figure 5.2(a) shows the original (plaintext) image. Figure 5.2(b) shows the image encrypted using ECB mode. It can be seen that some elements of the image are still visible. However, in Fig. 5.2(c) (encrypted using CBC), the resultant "image" resembles noise.

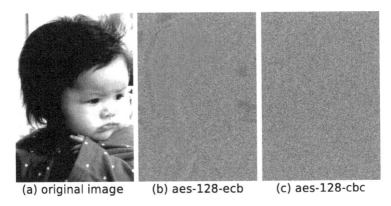

(a) original image   (b) aes-128-ecb   (c) aes-128-cbc

Fig. 5.2 An illustration of the problems related to ECB Encryption

5.1.2 Asymmetric Key Cryptography

The problem with symmetric key cryptography is that the shared key needs to be exchanged in a secure manner. If the key is intercepted, then security is compromised. Given that encryption is used for the purpose of transmitting data over an insecure channel, it would be unwise to send the key over the channel itself. Asymmetric key cryptography was conceived to overcome this problem.

Asymmetric key cryptography uses a pair of keys. One key is called the *public key* and the other (corresponding) key is called the *private key*. The public key (as the name suggests) is made publically available and the private key, is kept secret. When used for confidentiality, the public key is used to encrypt the message. Only the private key can decrypt it. For authentication purposes, the private-key is used to encrypt the message. While the message can be decrypted by anyone with the public key, the receiver can be confident that the message is from the sender who holds the corresponding private key.

Here, we present an example (albeit non-wireless) of the use of asymmetric key ciphers. Consider two hosts, a local *client* and a remote *server*.[2] Commands can be issued from the client host to the server using the secure shell (SSH) application. By default, authentication is password based, for example:

```
client$ ssh server "/bin/uname -n"
user@host's password:
server
```

An alternative method of authentication is public/private key. Generate both the public and private keys on the client host:

```
client$ ssh-keygen -t rsa
```

---

[2]The command-line prompts "client$" and "server$" are used to indicate the client and server hosts, respectively.

```
Generating public/private rsa key pair.
Enter file in which to save the key (/home/aholt/.ssh/
id_rsa):
Created directory '/home/users/aholt/.ssh'.
Enter passphrase (empty for no passphrase):
Enter same passphrase again:
Your identification has been saved in /home/aholt/.ssh/
id_rsa.
Your public key has been saved in /home/aholt/.ssh/
id_rsa.pub.
The key fingerprint is:
d9:94:30:20:6e:18:99:0e:41:93:b1:90:67:b1:4d:6b
aholt@client
```

Do not supply a passphrase, when prompted; just hit return. This creates two files in the directory *.ssh*, *id_rsa* and *id_rsa.pub*:

```
client$ ls .ssh/id_*
.ssh/id_rsa   .ssh/id_rsa.pub
```

The file *id_rsa* contains the private key and *id_rsa.pub* the public key. Copy the public key file *id_rsa.pub* to the server. We can do this securely with the scp command:

```
client$ scp .ssh/id_rsa.pub server:.ssh/
aholt@server's password:
id_rsa.pub          100%   394       0.4KB/s    00:00
```

Log on to the server and change the permissions of the *.ssh* directory so that it is readable and executable by *other* (and *group*):

```
server$ chmod 755 .ssh
```

Append the client's public key to the server's *authorized_keys2* file:

```
server$ cat .ssh/ id_rsa.pub >> .ssh/authorized_keys2
```

Now we can SSH from the client to the server without having to supply a password:

```
client$ ssh server "/bin/uname -n"
server
```

Asymmetric key ciphers are more computationally expensive than symmetric key ciphers. For this reason, asymmetric key ciphers are seldom used for the encryption of large messages. Symmetric key ciphers are more appropriate for this application. Asymmetric key ciphers are used in conjunction with symmetric key ciphers; that is, shared keys (symmetric keys) are encrypted with a public key so that they can be transmitted securely to the party with the associated private key. Once both parties are in possession of the shared key, they can use it to encrypt messages.

Other applications of asymmetric key ciphers are digital signatures and digital certificates. These concepts are discussed in detail below.

5.2 Encryption

We have used the terms *plaintext* and *ciphertext* above. We provide an explantion of these terms here, though we accept that the reader may have already deduced their meaning. Messages that can be readily understood are called *plainext* (or sometimes *cleartext*). Encryption is a method, whereby plaintext is converted into a corresponding unintelligible form called *ciphertext* so that it can be sent over (or stored on) an insecure medium. The process of converting the ciphertext back to plaintext is called decryption. Only the intended recipient should have the knowledge to decrypt the message. If the (encrypted) message is intercepted, then the confidentiality of the plaintext message is ensured.

Consider the simple substitution cipher *ROT13*, a version of the Caesar cipher developed in ancient Rome. ROT13 "scrambles" plaintext messages by rotating the ascii value of each character thirteen places. As there are 26 characters in the alphabet, the "decryption" process is merely a matter of rotating the ascii values another thirteen places. A version of the ROT13 "cipher", written in Python, is given below:

```python
#!/usr/bin/env python

import sys

rotate = lambda c,k: (ord(c) - k - 13) % 26 + k

def rot13(msg):
    newmsg = []
    for c in msg:
        if c.islower():
            newmsg.append("%c" % (rotate(c,97)))
        elif c.isupper():
            newmsg.append("%c" % (rotate(c,65)))
        else:
            newmsg.append(c)
    return(''.join(newmsg))

if __name__=='__main__':

    for line in sys.stdin.readlines():
        print rot13(line.strip())
```

The plaintext message "Julius Caesar" can be scrambled with the command line:

```
$ echo Julius Caesar | ./rot13.py
Whyvhf Pnrfne
```

Similarly, the ciphertext can be unscrambled:

```
$ echo Whyvhf Pnrfne | ./rot13.py
Julius Caesar
```

ROT13 is mainly used to hide offensive statements, of for solutions to puzzles and joke punchlines on on-line forums. It is not a serious cryptographic application. In fact, encryption systems deemed to be weak are criticised by comparing their effectiveness to that of ROT13. In the following sub-sections, we introduce a number of encryption algorithms (based on symmetric key ciphers).

5.2.1 RC4

RC4 (Ron's Code 4) was designed by Ronald Rivest for RSA Data Security in 1984. It is a byte-oriented stream cipher. Each byte of a plaintext is XORed with a byte of a key to produce a byte of a ciphertext. Due to its simplicity and speed, RC4 is the most widely used stream cipher. It is used in WEP for both encryption and authentication. For the purpose of illustration, we download the following document[3] to use as a test file (while any document will suffice, if the reader uses the same document, the results will match those obtained here):

```
$ wget http://www.ietf.org/rfc/rfc2246.txt
```

We encrypt the *rfc2246.txt* file using RC4 with the key "secret":

```
$ openssl enc -rc4 -k secret -in rfc2246.txt \
> -out rfc2246.rc4
```

A file *rfc2246.rc4* is created which contains the ciphertext of the plaintext file, *rfc2246.txt*. While the file *rfc2246.txt* is readable, the contents of *rfc2246.rc4* is unintelligible. For this reason, we examine the two files using the command od. We display the first 32 bytes of the each file. It can be seen from these small extracts that the two files have completely different content:

```
$ od -N 32 -x rfc2246.txt
0000000 0a0a 0a0a 0a0a 654e 7774 726f 206b 6f57
0000020 6b72 6e69 2067 7247 756f 2070 2020 2020
0000040
$ od -N 32 -x rfc2246.rc4
0000000 6153 746c 6465 5f5f 64dd d70d bc80 67be
0000020 69b9 df66 9c00 30a5 adda 9e2c f85a ccb2
0000040
```

---

[3]This is the request for comment (RFC) document for the TLS protocol.

5.2.2 DES and Triple-DES

The data encryption standard (DES) is a symmetric key block cipher, published by
the National Institution of Standards and Technology (NIST). DES is vulnerable to
brute-force attacks due to the limited length of cipher key (64-bits). Also, its insecure internal structure allows the National Security Agency (NSA) to decrypt the
message without the cipher key. Triple-DES (the DES cipher repeated three times)
is designed to strengthen DES. It employs up to three 56-bit keys and makes three
encryption/decryption passes over the block. We encrypt *rfc2246.txt* using DES with
the command below:

```
$ openssl enc -des -k secret -in rfc2246.txt \
> -out rfc2246.des
```

To decrypt the ciphertext file (*rfc2246.des*), use the command below. As DES is
a symmetric key cipher (like RC4), the encryption and decryption passwords are the
same. When prompted, we issue the password: ("secret"):

```
$ openssl enc -des -d -in rfc2246.des
enter des-cbc decryption password:
```

5.2.3 AES

The advanced encryption standard (AES) was designed as a successor to DES and
published by the NIST in 2001. It is an encryption standard adapted by the US government. It has a fixed block size of 128-bits and employs keys lengths of either 128,
192, or 256 bits. While larger key sizes yield greater security, there is a performance
trade-off. This is illustrated by the command below which tests the performance of
AES in CBC mode for 128, 192 and 256 bit key sizes:

```
$ openssl speed aes
```

For brevity, the output of the command is omitted. Instead we summarise the
results in Table 5.1. We also compare the performance of RC4, DES (CBC mode)
and AES (CBC mode with 128-bit key). The results are presented in Table 5.2.
Again, we use OpenSSL:

```
$ openssl speed rc4 des-cbc aes-128-cbc
```

Table 5.1 Performance of AES

Block size (bits)	Performance (kbytes/s)				
	16 bytes	64 bytes	256 bytes	1024 bytes	8192 bytes
128	43631.54	69270.06	80642.73	84584.79	86576.97
192	40473.58	60079.55	68818.43	71977.98	73004.37
256	37277.10	53214.76	59966.29	61694.98	62859.95

Table 5.2 Performance comparison of RC4, DES and AES

Encryption method	Performance (kbytes/s)				
	16 bytes	64 bytes	256 bytes	1024 bytes	8192 bytes
rc4	165493.37	191814.14	189848.75	192289.45	185851.90
des-cbc	35471.77	36572.78	37149.53	37173.25	37372.56
aes-128-cbc	59936.06	77465.84	82522.97	85504.68	86649.51

5.3 Message Digests

A message digest is a transformation of a message of arbitrary length to a fixed length numerical value. Message digests are also known as hashes, digital fingerprints, or, simply, digests. Functions for computing message digests have three properties:

- Message digests are easy to compute
- It is very difficult to derive the message from the message digest
- It is unlikely that more than one message has the same message digest

Two simple forms of message integrity checks are *checksums* and *cyclic redundancy checks* (CRCs). Communication protocols employs checksums and CRCs in order to detect corruption in packets. Consider the checksum function for National Marine Electronics Association (NMEA) messages (called sentences) used in the global positioning system (GPS). NMEA sentences are a set of comma separated fields. The checksum is appended to the end of the sentence, delimited by a "*" character. An example of a NMEA sentence, including the checksum, is:

```
$GPVTG,,T,,M,0.00,N,0.0,K,N*1C
```

The checksum is computed over the message a character at a time. The commas are included, but the leading "$" and trailing "*" are removed. The Python script below computes the NMEA checksums.

```
#!/usr/bin/python

import sys

def checksum(nmealine):
    sentence, csum = nmealine.split('*')
    csum1 = "0x%s" % (csum.lower())
    csum2 = 0
    for s in sentence[1:]:
        csum2 = csum2 ^ ord(s)
    return csum1 ==  hex(csum2)

if __name__=='__main__':
```

```
for line in sys.stdin.readlines():
    print checksum(line.strip())
```

The script reads NMEA sentences from the standard input and returns True or False depending upon whether the computed checksum equals the checksum appended to the message. Run the script, then enter NMEA sentence:

```
$ ./checksum.py
$GPVTG,,T,,M,0.00,N,0.0,K,N*1C
True
```

In this case the computed checksum agrees with the checksum included with the sentence. We run the script again, but make slight change to the NMEA sentence:

```
$ ./checksum.py
$GPVTG,,T,,M,0.00,S,0.0,K,N*1C
False
```

Checksums and CRCs are predominantly used to detect errors introduced by unreliable communication channels. They are not based upon true cryptographic methods and are deemed unsuitable for security purposes. Nevertheless, CRC-32 was used as an integrity check in 802.11 before more rigorous methods were adopted. Two examples of message digests based upon cryptographic algorithms are: message digest 5 (MD5) and secure hash algorithm (SHA). Create a test file:

```
$ dd if=/dev/urandom of=testfile1 bs=1 count=64
```
Calculate a message digest using md5sum:

```
$ md5sum testfile1
2ca0b569cf50118c8a87cdda01a363ec  testfile1
```
Alternatively a message digest using MD5 can be generated using OpenSSL:

```
$ openssl dgst -md5 testfile1
MD5(testfile1)= 2ca0b569cf50118c8a87cdda01a363ec
```

Create a file *testfile2* with identical content to *testfile1*:

```
$ cp testfile1 testfile2
```

Examine the contents of *testfile2*:

```
$ od -x testfile2
0000000 eb39 7f93 eb5d f990 8bad 57be ef9b cdd1
0000020 6408 c2f5 9dac 424c 0047 0770 fac8 b806
0000040 cf2d f1ca 43af edbf 76a7 a480 7b8d 845d
0000060 b2ba e36f 65ce 5c48 1efd 34e5 a0bc 6967
0000100
```

Using a binary editor (like bvi), we make a slight change to the file. The value of the byte that appears on the last line in the far right column is altered from 67 to 66:

```
$ od -x testfile2
0000000 eb39 7f93 eb5d f990 8bad 57be ef9b cdd1
0000020 6408 c2f5 9dac 424c 0047 0770 fac8 b806
0000040 cf2d f1ca 43af edbf 76a7 a480 7b8d 845d
0000060 b2ba e36f 65ce 5c48 1efd 34e5 a0bc 6966
0000100
```

Whilst this represents a change of only one bit, the resultant message digest is completely different:

```
$ od -x testfile2
$ openssl dgst -md5 testfile2
MD5(testfile2)= 66b20cc640ef6b3f1eb9409b699ea387
```

MD5 is no longer recommended as a cryptographic message digest algorithm and its only real use is as a checksum for large files. It has been demonstrated that two (different) messages can be produced that have the same MD5 message digest. MD5, therefore, is subject to *collision* attacks. Furthermore, the speed of these attacks is increasing with the increase in computer processing power.

SHA is a set of cryptographic hash functions conceived by the National Security Agency (NSA) and is part of the US Federal Information Processing Standard (FIPS). Five algorithms are defined: SHA-1, SHA-224, SHA-256, SHA-384, and SHA-512. Vulnerabilities have been reported for SHA-1, but none have been reported to date for the remaining algorithms.

5.4 Digital Signatures

A digital signature consists of three algorithms. One algorithm is used to generate, at random, a public key and a (corresponding) private key. Another algorithm is used to *sign* messages using the private key. Finally, a signature verifying algorithm which, given a message, public key and signature, either accepts or rejects the message.

Messages can be authenticated by a digital signature. As messages can be large, the message itself is not signed. Instead, a message digest is generated (see Sect. 5.3 above), which is signed by encrypting it with the sender's private key. We present the following example using OpenSSL. Generate a SHA-1 message digest of the file *rfc2246.txt* and write it to a file (*rfc2246.dgst*):

```
$ openssl dgst -sha1 -out rfc2246.dgst rfc2246.txt
```

Check the digest:

```
$ cat rfc2246.dgst
SHA1(rfc2246.txt)=
13c9790c0ea8f61e0e080c2990b3d030695bbf43
```

We generate a 512-bit RSA key with the command below:

```
$ openssl genrsa -aes192 -out rsa_privkey.pem 512
Generating RSA private-key, 512 bit long modulus
......................++++++++++++
.........++++++++++++
e is 65537 (0x10001)
Enter pass phrase for rsa_privkey.pem:
Verifying - Enter pass phrase for rsa_privkey.pem:
```

Note that 512 bits is too short for any practical security purpose. The reader is advised to use a key of at least 1024-bits for real applications. The -aes192 option causes OpenSSL to prompt for a passphrase. At the prompt (and verification prompt), we entered "secret" (which is not echoed on the screen). Sign the digest of *rfc2246.txt*:

```
$ openssl dgst -sha1 -sign rsa_privkey.pem \
> -out rfc2246.sig rfc2246.txt
```

Create a corresponding public key for the private key in *rsa_privkey.pem*:

```
$ openssl rsa -in rsa_privkey.pem -out rsa_pubkey.pem \
> -pubout
```

Verify the signature (in *rfc2246.sig*) of *rfc2246.txt*:

```
$ openssl dgst -sha1 -verify rsa_pubkey.pem \
> -signature rfc2246.sig rfc2246.txt
Verified OK
```

5.5 Digital Certificates

A digital signature, created using a given private key, can be verified with the corresponding public key. This merely establishes that the owner of the public key is also the owner of private key, and did indeed create the signature. It does not, however, guarantee the validity of the key owner. In a large-scale network environment, it is difficult to distribute public keys securely in an ad-hoc fashion. Digital certificates were conceived to solve the public key distribution problem. A digital certificate is a mechanism for binding an identity to a public key (and its associated private key). The owner (with the given identity) of the public key can be an individual, an organisation, or a device.

Certificates are managed and maintained by trusted third party organisation called a certificate authority (CA). The CA establishes the binding by digitally signing the owner's identity data and the public key. The digital signature, identity data and public key form the digital certificate. A root certificate identifies the Root Certificate Authority (CA) and is either an unsigned or self-signed.

The International Telecommunication Union (ITU) X.509 recommendation is a digital certificate standard that is widely used. X.509 specifies the secure management, distribution and format of digitally signed certificates. An X.509 certificate

is a container for an X.500 Distinguished Name (DN). The structure of an X.509
certificate is shown below:

- Certificate
  - Version: The X.509 version of this certificate. Current certificates are typically
    version 3, which is required if the certificates has extensions.
  - Serial number: A unique serial number for the certificate.
  - Algorithm ID:
  - Issuer: The DN of the entity that signed the certificate.
  - Validity: The certificate is valid only for a limited period, specified by the Not
    Before and Not After fields below:
    · Not before: Certificate valid, not before this date.
    · Not after: Expires after this date.
  - Subject: The DN of the entity to be authenticated.
  - Subject public key info:
    · Public key algorithm:
    · Subject public key:
  - Issuer unique identifier (Optional)
  - Subject unique identifier (Optional)
  - Extensions (optional): The standard fields of X.509 were insufficient for many
    applications. The syntax of Version 3 was extended to include extensions that
    specified extra information about keys and procedures; and attributes of owners
    and issuers.
  - Certificate signature algorithm:
  - Certificate signature:

The specification for the X.509 certificate structure is in ASN.1 (abstract syntax
notation 1):

```
Certificate ::= SEQUENCE {
   tbsCertificate       TBSCertificate,
   signatureAlgorithm AlgorithmIdentifier,
   signatureValue       BIT STRING
}
TBSCertificate           ::= SEQUENCE {
   version              [0] EXPLICIT Version DEFAULT v1,
   -- If extensions are present, version MUST be v3
   serialNumber            CertificateSerialNumber,
   signature               AlgorithmIdentifier,
   issuer                  Name,
   validity                Validity,
   subject                 Name,
   subjectPublicKeyInfo SubjectPublicKeyInfo,
   extensions           [3] EXPLICIT Extensions OPTIONAL
}
Name ::= CHOICE {RDNSequence}
RDNSequence ::= SEQUENCE OF
```

```
  RelativeDistinguishedName
RelativeDistinguishedName ::= SET OF
  AttributeTypeAndValue
AttributeTypeAndValue ::= SEQUENCE {
  type AttributeType,
  value AttributeValue
}
AttributeType ::= OBJECT IDENTIFIER
AttributeValue ::= ANY DEFINED BY AttributeType
SubjectPublicKeyInfo ::= SEQUENCE {
  algorithm        AlgorithmIdentifier,
  subjectPublicKey BIT STRING
}
Extensions ::= SEQUENCE SIZE (1..MAX) OF Extension
Extension ::= SEQUENCE {
  extnId    OBJECT IDENTIFIER,
 critical BOOLEAN DEFAULT FALSE,
 extnValue OCTET STRING
}
```

In order to verify that a public key belongs to a valid user the following verification process is carried out:

- Verify the digital signature of the issuing CA upon the certificate contents.
- Check that the current time is within the validity period of the certificate.
- Check that the certificate is not on a certificate revocation list (CRL).

5.6 Generating Digital Certificates

In Chap. 8, we describe how to set up an RSN (robust security network). We use EAP-TLS for authentication, which requires digital certificates, for both the wireless client and the RADIUS server. We keep user accounting information for RADIUS in a MySQL database on a separate server. In order to strengthen security, we configure the RADIUS and MySQL servers to use SSL. Thus, we also need to generate a certificate for the MySQL server so that the RADIUS server can authenticate.

In order to test the certificates, we create two Xen virtual machines (VMs) called *radius* and *client*. In Chap. 8, we show how FreeRadius is configured on the radius VM. Thus, the radius VM will ultimately become the RADIUS server for the RSN. The client VM assumes the role of a "wireless" client, purely for the purpose of testing the certificates. It will communicate with the radius VM over the virtual bridge on the Xen host. It will not actually have any wireless connectivity.

It is important that the IP addresses of these hosts can be resolved. Either they must have records in DNS (domain name system) or the following entries must exist in the */etc/hosts* files:

```
172.16.20.70      radius
172.16.20.81      client, sta
```

Note that *client* is also known as *sta* because, when we generate the wireless client certificate, the CN component of the DN will be set to "sta".[4] Here, we verify the address resolution of radius and sta. From radius, ping sta (this also tests the communication path between the two hosts):

```
radius$ ping -q -c 3 sta
PING sta (172.16.20.81) 56(84) bytes of data.

--- sta ping statistics ---
3 packets transmitted, 3 received, 0% packet loss,
time 2001ms
rtt min/avg/max/mdev = 0.512/0.806/1.394/0.416 ms
```

Similarly, test radius from sta:

```
client$ ping -q -c 3 radius
PING radius (172.16.20.70) 56(84) bytes of data.

--- radius ping statistics ---
3 packets transmitted, 3 received, 0% packet loss,
time 2000ms
rtt min/avg/max/mdev = 0.494/1.740/4.164/1.714 ms
```

The certificates do not have to be generated on their respective hosts, but can be generated on any machine. We prepare a number of directories in which to work:

```
$ mkdir ca/{,crl,newcerts,private,demoCA}
$ cd ca
```

In the *ca* directory, create the following files:

```
$ echo "01" > serial
$ touch index.txt
```

5.6.1 Generating a Certificate Authority

Before we can generate the radius and sta certificates, we need a certificate authority (CA) to sign them. The command below generates a certificate authority:

```
srv$ openssl req \
> -new \
> -x509 \
```

---

[4]"STA" is the IEEE nomenclature for an 802.11 device.

```
> -out cacert.pem \
> -keyout private/cakey.pem \
> -passin pass:rootsecret \
> -passout pass:rootsecret \
> -days 3650
```

The OpenSSL command creates a private key (in *private/cakey.pem*) and displays the following message:

```
Generating a 1024 bit RSA private key
.................................................
.................................................
.....................++++++
.........++++++
writing new private key to 'private/cakey.pem'
-----
You are about to be asked to enter information that
will be incorporated into your certificate request.
What you are about to enter is what is called a
Distinguished Name or a DN.
There are quite a few fields but you can leave some
blank
For some fields there will be a default value,
If you enter '.', the field will be left blank.
-----
```

The user is prompted to enter a number of fields which make up the DN, as described in the output above.

```
Country Name (2 letter code) [AU]:UK
State or Province Name (full name) [Some-State]: Wilts
Locality Name (eg, city) []:.
Organization Name (eg, company) [Internet Widgits Pty
Ltd]:WLAN
Organizational Unit Name (eg, section) []:.
Common Name (eg, YOUR name) []:Root
Email Address []:.
```

Note that some fields are assigned and others left blank (when a . was input). If we check the policy_match section in the */etc/ssl/openssl.cnf* file, we see how the attributes are set:

```
# For the CA policy
[ policy_match ]
countryName                = match
stateOrProvinceName        = match
organizationName           = match
organizationalUnitName     = optional
```

```
commonName                    = supplied
emailAddress                  = optional
```

The attributes cannot be blank in the DN of the CA if the are set to "match". Furthermore, the corresponding attributes in the certificate request must match those in the CA. "Supplied" attributes must be set in the request. Attributes marked "optional" may be left blank. A file *cacert.pem* is created containing the CA. We can examine it with:

```
$ openssl x509 -in cacert.pem -noout -text
Certificate:
    Data:
        Version: 3 (0x2)
        Serial Number:
            ca:49:0b:69:d9:e3:70:15
        Signature Algorithm: sha1WithRSAEncryption
        Issuer: C=UK, ST=Wilts, O=WLAN, CN=Root
        Validity
            Not Before: Dec  3 13:44:59 2008 GMT
            Not After : Dec  1 13:44:59 2018 GMT
        Subject: C=UK, ST=Wilts, O=WLAN, CN=Root
        Subject Public Key Info:
            Public Key Algorithm: rsaEncryption
            RSA Public Key: (1024 bit)
                Modulus (1024 bit):
                                                                    :
                    00:ee:1e:15:bf:43:94:bb:c3:68:d0:
                    2d:46:fe:a1:c1:b1:36:2e:b4:3a:7c:
                    82:81:e3:f0:24:e8:61:45:80:cb:61:
                    5f:37:e7:46:ce:62:dd:ff:de:b5:c4:
                    86:2f:c9:99:f5:38:4b:c2:e6:80:bf:
                    25:6a:1b:eb:81:26:d4:03:40:7d:f6:
                    04:26:da:13:99:c0:ef:8c:e1:ce:a6:
                    78:79:d6:92:37:83:66:9c:8b:4d:59:
                    6b:0a:03:23:8c:27:55:a7:e0:de:fb:
                    30:85:64:e7:f9:c8:c7:6f:b8:ea:e4:
                    76:04:a5:cb:04:9f:59:02:8c:e7:d0:
                    16:c6:48:55:54:ec:9b:d9
                Exponent: 65537 (0x10001)
        X509v3 extensions:
            X509v3 Subject Key Identifier:
                E4:A0:36:B1:98:5F:3C:D4:6E:1B:3B:B3:52:
D9:9F:0E:76:C7:17:60
            X509v3 Authority Key Identifier:
                keyid:E4:A0:36:B1:98:5F:3C:D4:6E:1B:3B:
B3:52:D9:9F:0E:76:C7:17:60
```

```
DirName:/C=UK/ST=Wilts/O=WLAN/CN=Root
serial:CA:49:0B:69:D9:E3:70:15

X509v3 Basic Constraints:
    CA:TRUE
Signature Algorithm: sha1WithRSAEncryption
    7a:f3:38:34:0e:c0:96:e5:55:7c:e9:ea:a3:af:8f:
    12:9e:1b:4f:1f:1a:14:6b:1e:53:81:a1:ac:f0:47:
    fd:a9:96:fa:a4:5d:c5:bc:0b:af:16:a8:a7:5e:91:
    88:09:56:8c:6f:64:7b:98:d9:77:33:58:1a:1f:72:
    52:9c:d7:63:06:e3:f4:75:80:01:3e:ec:fa:26:42:
    40:2e:8f:49:3e:14:28:79:7b:79:69:ed:af:dd:2b:
    2a:53:13:ea:ad:93:98:87:ca:f8:a5:cb:34:9b:d7:
    17:da:81:a4:4b:53:fe:99:da:1e:70:35:ad:0d:50:
    ba:aa:d1:73:7b:36:ba:3a
```

The output from this command shows that the certificate is in human-readable form and conforms to the structure of an X.509 certificate, as described in Sect. 5.5. The CA:TRUE directive confirms that the certificate is a certificate authority. Also, the *Issuer* and *Subject* are the same because the certificate is self-signed. For signed certificates, the *Issuer* will be the *Subject* of the certificate that signed the request.

5.6.2 Generating Certificates

The generation of certificates involves a two step process:

- Generate a certificate request.
- Sign the certificate request using the CA.

OpenSSL commands require many options, and the resulting command-lines can be somewhat cumbersome. In order to overcome this, we assign the options to environment (array) variables and let the shell interpreter do the expansion for us. Set the options for the *radius* certificate request:

```
$ OPTS1[0]="-new"
$ OPTS1[1]="-nodes"
$ OPTS1[2]="-keyout rad_key.pem"
$ OPTS1[3]="-out rad_req.pem"
$ OPTS1[4]="-passin pass:certsecret"
$ OPTS1[5]="-passout pass:certsecret"
```

In order to avoid interaction with OpenSSL, we can use the -subj to specify the DN. We add this to the option array:

```
$ OPTS1[6]="-subj /C=UK/ST=Wilts/O=WLAN/CN=radius"
```

We can evaluate the shell variable (and view the option settings) with the command-line:

```
$ echo ${OPTS1[*]}
-new -nodes -keyout rad_key.pem -out rad_req.pem
-passin pass:certsecret -passout pass:certsecret
-subj /C=UK/ST=Wilts/O=WLAN/CN=radius
```

A certificate request (along with a private key) is generated with the command:

```
$ openssl req ${OPTS1[*]}
Generating a 1024 bit RSA private key
......++++++
.........++++++
writing new private key to 'rad_key.pem'
-----
```

Set the options for signing the certificate:

```
$ OPTS2[0]="-in rad_req.pem"
$ OPTS2[1]="-out rad_cert.pem"
$ OPTS2[2]="-key rootsecret"
```

The certificate request, in human-readable form, is shown below:

```
$ openssl req -in rad_req.pem -noout -text
Certificate Request:
    Data:
        Version: 0 (0x0)
        Subject: C=UK, ST=Wilts, O=WLAN, CN=radius
        Subject Public Key Info:
            Public Key Algorithm: rsaEncryption
            RSA Public Key: (1024 bit)
                Modulus (1024 bit):
                    00:b6:de:fa:1d:16:45:29:53:2c:04:3b:
                    48:2c:48:1a:a1:17:47:b7:52:72:43:8d:
                    43:31:90:06:11:95:2b:94:e1:7f:2a:2a:
                    96:7f:81:a2:1f:ec:c5:a4:65:4d:7a:16:
                    dd:9a:57:5d:60:36:ab:85:b4:46:4c:90:
                    a9:38:dd:04:11:2b:40:17:ea:77:d0:2e:
                    3c:cb:b4:10:29:91:08:23:93:ba:08:50:
                    b9:21:28:40:74:b1:12:04:ec:77:13:9e:
                    74:02:71:c4:f1:ea:78:78:05:08:74:d9:
                    ff:b8:46:18:a1:e1:f7:48:ff:9d:af:a8:
                    be:8a:0e:e0:9c:0a:6b:7e:c5
                Exponent: 65537 (0x10001)
        Attributes:
            a0:00
    Signature Algorithm: sha1WithRSAEncryption
```

```
61:ad:b6:b5:7f:c1:12:f0:6c:c9:80:1e:44:b9:62:6f:
fb:a7:6a:f6:2e:d1:82:11:d2:0d:6a:36:e6:7a:84:0d:
98:80:56:85:53:fc:cc:07:4b:15:76:1b:22:f5:4c:19:
58:98:4d:d8:f3:0a:29:33:7b:dc:98:aa:92:2d:3c:36:
75:58:02:e6:22:61:62:7c:20:7b:59:70:18:e6:98:68:
92:40:f7:cd:51:ff:3f:07:78:b5:60:7f:6f:71:85:61:
e6:81:ed:b1:dc:fd:06:8f:00:76:27:b8:29:61:a3:e8:
4f:a6:5b:14:64:2b:81:d8:97:43:64:73:5f:46:dd:c8
```

The command-line below signs the certificate (using the CA in *cacert.pem*). The OpenSSL ca command prompts the user (twice) to confirm the signing of the certificate (and the user should answer "y" on both occaisons). Interaction with the user is avoided by piping the output of the command yes to the openssl command:

```
$ yes | openssl ca ${OPTS2[*]}
Using configuration from /usr/lib/ssl/openssl.cnf
Check that the request matches the signature
Signature ok
Certificate Details:
        Serial Number: 1 (0x1)
        Validity
            Not Before: Nov 25 14:47:33 2008 GMT
            Not After : Nov 25 14:47:33 2009 GMT
        Subject:
            countryName             = UK
            stateOrProvinceName     = Wilts
            organizationName        = WLAN
            commonName              = radius
        X509v3 extensions:
            X509v3 Basic Constraints:
                CA:FALSE
            Netscape Comment:
                OpenSSL Generated Certificate
            X509v3 Subject Key Identifier:
                77:96:33:36:8A:03:5D:1A:77:05:49:1C:15:
17:4B:E7:C3:EB:E6:D5
            X509v3 Authority Key Identifier:
                keyid:80:A0:CE:6E:69:C1:F8:27:D3:0F:CC:
97:CF:8D:C6:E9:21:8A:98:E0

Certificate is to be certified until Nov 25 14:47:33
2009 GMT (365 days)
Sign the certificate? [y/n]:

1 out of 1 certificate requests certified, commit?
[y/n]Write out database with 1 new entries
Data Base Updated
```

View the certificate:

```
$ openssl x509 -in rad_cert.pem -noout -text
Certificate:
    Data:
        Version: 3 (0x2)
        Serial Number: 1 (0x1)
        Signature Algorithm: sha1WithRSAEncryption
        Issuer: C=UK, ST=Wilts, O=WLAN, CN=Root
        Validity
            Not Before: Dec  3 13:45:18 2008 GMT
            Not After : Dec  3 13:45:18 2009 GMT
        Subject: C=UK, ST=Wilts, O=WLAN, CN=radius
        Subject Public Key Info:
            Public Key Algorithm: rsaEncryption
            RSA Public Key: (1024 bit)
                Modulus (1024 bit):
                    00:b6:de:fa:1d:16:45:29:53:2c:04:3b:
                    48:2c:48:1a:a1:17:47:b7:52:72:43:8d:
                    43:31:90:06:11:95:2b:94:e1:7f:2a:2a:
                    96:7f:81:a2:1f:ec:c5:a4:65:4d:7a:16:
                    dd:9a:57:5d:60:36:ab:85:b4:46:4c:90:
                    a9:38:dd:04:11:2b:40:17:ea:77:d0:2e:
                    3c:cb:b4:10:29:91:08:23:93:ba:08:50:
                    b9:21:28:40:74:b1:12:04:ec:77:13:9e:
                    74:02:71:c4:f1:ea:78:78:05:08:74:d9:
                    ff:b8:46:18:a1:e1:f7:48:ff:9d:af:a8:
                    be:8a:0e:e0:9c:0a:6b:7e:c5
                Exponent: 65537 (0x10001)
        X509v3 extensions:
            X509v3 Basic Constraints:
                CA:FALSE
            Netscape Comment:
                OpenSSL Generated Certificate
            X509v3 Subject Key Identifier:
                9F:C7:F3:7D:0C:6D:2F:74:2C:74:36:65:55:
69:26:F7:D8:44:00:E4
            X509v3 Authority Key Identifier:
                keyid:E4:A0:36:B1:98:5F:3C:D4:6E:1B:3B:
B3:52:D9:9F:0E:76:C7:17:60

    Signature Algorithm: sha1WithRSAEncryption
        51:75:02:ee:f9:b9:f3:48:5f:da:02:b8:bc:46:df:7f:
        5c:b5:85:a0:a1:be:21:1c:10:5c:ba:1e:b4:5d:bc:cf:
        17:14:ee:68:bf:0c:24:53:d3:7d:8a:85:d8:01:81:e4:
        86:31:cd:cb:dd:78:7c:97:2a:78:59:ec:a3:53:f6:fd:
```

```
3c:f5:10:50:27:29:33:10:ec:d9:6c:50:b8:0c:79:36:
14:7a:01:a2:f7:47:46:e3:5b:95:2c:5c:d0:94:3a:40:
d5:84:21:22:dc:72:14:1b:1b:a5:d2:cd:34:11:08:a4:
0f:f6:13:1d:3c:c3:50:c9:9b:a6:e7:9d:99:16:48:00
```

Now we generate the certificate for the wireless device. Some of the options settings are common to both the radius server and the wireless client. We set the options which are different:

```
$ OPTS1[2]="-keyout sta_key.pem"
$ OPTS1[3]="-out sta_req.pem"
$ OPTS1[6]="-subj /C=UK/ST=Wilts/O=WLAN/CN=sta"
```

Set the options for signing:

```
$ OPTS2[0]="-in sta_req.pem"
$ OPTS2[1]="-out sta_cert.pem"
```

Generate a certificate request (along with a private key) and then sign it:

```
$ openssl req ${OPTS1[*]} && yes |
openssl ca ${OPTS2[*]}
Generating a 1024 bit RSA private key
.....................................................................
.................++++++
..........++++++
writing new private key to 'sta_key.pem'
-----
Using configuration from /usr/lib/ssl/openssl.cnf
Check that the request matches the signature
Signature ok
Certificate Details:
        Serial Number: 2 (0x2)
        Validity
            Not Before: Nov 25 14:55:33 2008 GMT
            Not After : Nov 25 14:55:33 2009 GMT
        Subject:
            countryName               = UK
            stateOrProvinceName       = Wilts
            organizationName          = WLAN
            commonName                = sta
        X509v3 extensions:
            X509v3 Basic Constraints:
                CA:FALSE
            Netscape Comment:
                OpenSSL Generated Certificate
            X509v3 Subject Key Identifier:
                25:29:FD:CA:7B:0C:D2:50:31:39:0D:CD:80:
```

```
A2:ED:50:31:F4:16:58
                X509v3 Authority Key Identifier:
                    keyid:80:A0:CE:6E:69:C1:F8:27:D3:0F:CC:
97:CF:8D:C6:E9:21:8A:98:E0

Certificate is to be certified until Nov 25 14:55:33
2009 GMT (365 days)
Sign the certificate? [y/n]:

1 out of 1 certificate requests certified, commit?
[y/n]Write out database with 1 new entries
Data Base Updated
```

Finally, we generate the certificate for the MySQL server:

```
$ OPTS1[2]="-keyout mysql_key.pem"
$ OPTS1[3]="-out mysql_req.pem"
$ OPTS1[6]="-subj /C=UK/ST=Wilts/O=WLAN/CN=mysql"
$ OPTS2[0]="-in mysql_req.pem"
$ OPTS2[1]="-out mysql_cert.pem"
$ openssl req ${OPTS1[*]} && yes |
  openssl ca ${OPTS2[*]}
```

We verify certificates for the radius, sta and mysql with the command:

```
$ openssl verify -CAfile cacert.pem rad_cert.pem \
> sta_cert.pem mysql_cert.pem
rad_cert.pem: OK
sta_cert.pem: OK
mysql_cert.pem: OK
```

5.6.3 Testing the Certificates

We will test the certificates by using the OpenSSL s_server and s_client commands to create an SSL tunnel. Data can be transmitted once the server and client have authenticated successfully. Copy the certificates, private keys and CA to the respective machines (radius and client):

```
$ scp rad*pem cacert.pem 172.16.20.79:
$ scp sta*pem cacert.pem 172.16.20.81:
```

This will also copy the certificate request (because of the use of the wild card). However, this is not required for the authentication process. Set the options for the s_server process:

```
radius$ OPTS[0]="-accept 8008"
radius$ OPTS[1]="-CAfile cacert.pem"
```

```
radius$ OPTS[2]="-cert rad_cert.pem"
radius$ OPTS[3]="-key rad_key.pem"
radius$ OPTS[4]="-Verify 1"
radius$ OPTS[5]="-state"
```

Some of these options require an explanation. The -accept option specifies the port on which to accept connections (in this case, 8008). Options -CAfile, -cert and -key specify the respective files containing the CA, the server's certificate and the private key. The -Verify option ensures that the radius server authenticates the wireless client. Without this option only, the radius server is authenticated (by the client) and the client will report:

```
No client certificate CA names sent
```

OpenSSL outputs useful information if the -state option is used. The (-debug option could also be used to give even more information). Start the OpenSSL server process on the server:

```
radius$ openssl s_server ${OPTS[*]}
verify depth is 1, must return a certificate
Using default temp DH parameters
Using default temp ECDH parameters
ACCEPT
```

The process waits to accept connections from a client. On the client, set the options:

```
client$ OPTS1[0]="-connect sta:8008"
client$ OPTS1[1]="-cert sta_cert.pem"
client$ OPTS1[2]="-key sta_key.pem"
client$ OPTS1[3]="-CAfile cacert.pem"
client$ OPTS1[4]="-state"
```

The -connect options tell the client on which port the server is waiting to accept connections. The other options are the same as for the server. The command line below opens up a tunnel to the OpenSSL server process and transmits the string "hello".

```
sta$ echo "hello" | openssl s_client ${OPTS1[*]}
```

The -www option causes the s_server to behave as a web server. Now we can test the certificates with a web client such as wget. On the client, set the options for wget:

```
sta$ OPTS2[0]="--certificate=sta_cert.pem"
sta$ OPTS2[1]="--private-key=sta_key.pem"
sta$ OPTS2[2]="--ca-certificate=cacert.pem"
```

Now download index.html of the secure tunnel:

```
client$ wget ${OPTS2[*]} https://radius:8008/
--15:03:08--  https://radius:8008/
           => 'index.html'
Resolving radius... 172.16.20.70
Connecting to radius|172.16.20.70|:8008... connected.
HTTP request sent, awaiting response... 200 ok
Length: unspecified [text/html]

    [ <=>                    ] 5,492          --.--K/s

15:03:08 (130.94 MB/s) - 'index.html' saved [5492]
```

5.7 Summary

In this chapter, we presented an overview of cryptography. We avoided a mathematical treatment of the subject and adopted a practical approach instead. We used the OpenSSL application and Python code extracts to demonstrate prinicples of cryptography.

There are two type of cipher: symmetric key and asymmetric key. Symmetric key is based upon a single shared key, whereas asymmetric key ciphers employs a pair of keys. Asymmetric key ciphers overcome the problem of secure key exchange.

We have discussed applications of cryptography; namely, encryption, message digests, digital signatures and digital certificates. We have shown how to create digital certificates which we will use in Chap. 8 for implementing a wireless LAN with enterprise security.

Chapter 6
Wireless Security

Security methods were not specified in the original 802.11 standard. Some vendors provided authentication based upon MAC addresses, whereby access-points maintained a list of MAC addresses of devices that were allowed to associate with them. This method suffers from scalability issues, as maintaining the access-list is problematic for networks with many devices. Furthermore, as MAC addresses can be spoofed, security can be circumvented with little effort. Wired equivalent privacy (WEP) was introduced with 802.11b, but suffered from a number of serious vulnerabilities. In order to overcome the shortcomings in the WEP, the IEEE introduced the 802.11i amendment. The aim of 802.11i was to produce a specification for a robust security network association (RSNA) designed to enchance:

- Authentication
- Key management
- Confidentiality and integrity

The Wi-Fi Alliance introduced an interim solution to WEP called Wi-Fi protected access (WPA). The aim of WPA was to address some of the vulnerabilities of WEP while 802.11i was being ratified (WPA was an implementation of a draft version of 802.11i). The 802.11i standard includes pre-RSNA algorithms. When 802.11i was ratified, the Wi-Fi alliance released WPA2.

Figure 6.1 summarises the authentication, key generation, confidentiality and integrity in 802.11i. We will discuss these methods in more detail in this chapter.

6.1 Pre-RSNA

Pre-RSNA algorithms originated from WEP which first appeared in the 802.11b amendment. WEP was introduced for the purpose of providing confidentiality, integrity and authentication. The RC4 stream cipher from RSA Security Inc. is used for confidentiality (encryption). A 32-bit cyclic redundancy check (CRC) is used for data integrity.

A. Holt, C.-Y. Huang, *802.11 Wireless Networks,*
Computer Communications and Networks,
DOI 10.1007/978-1-84996-275-9_6, © Springer-Verlag London Limited 2010

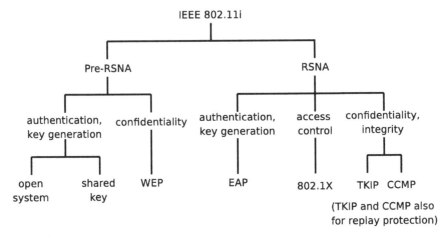

Fig. 6.1 Summary of 802.11i security

There are two pre-RSNA authentication methods; namely, open system and shared key authentication. With the exception of the open system authentication mechanism, all pre-RSNA algorithms have been deprecated. Despite this, WEP, and shared key authentication are still in wide-spread use.

6.1.1 Authentication

With open system, authentication is established by the transmission of two messages. Consider two wireless devices, A and B. Device A asserts its identity to device B by sending B an authentication request. B sends A the result of the request, which is either *success* or *failure*. The devices are mutually authenticated if the request is successful. As there is no criteria for authenticity, then the result is invariably "success". Authentication based on MAC address may be employed, thus, if the MAC address of a device does not appear in the access-point's access list, then a *failure* notification will result. MAC authentication, however, is not specified in the standard and is, therefore, vendor implemented at the discretion of the access-point manufacturer.

With shared key authentication, only devices that know the shared key can successfully authenticate. Shared-keys are distributed amongst participating devices by some secure mechanism outside the 802.11 framework (for example, by manual configuration by an administrator). Authentication is completed after a four-way handshake. Device A sends an authentication request to device B (first frame). B prepares a random 128-octet challenge text using a PRNG. The challenge is sent to A (second frame). A encrypts the challenge using RC4 (in the same way as it encrypts data frames) and sends the result to B (third frame). When B receives the third frame, it checks the ICV. If the ICV is correct, it verifies the challenge sent by A. If the challenge returned by A matches the original challenge text, B sends a "success" status code to A (fourth message). Otherwise, B responds by sending an "unsuccessful" status code.

The same shared key used for encryption is also used in the authentication process. The keystream K can be recovered by XORing the plaintext and ciphertext. Thus, the shared key is at its most vulnerable during the authentication stage because the plaintext challenge and the encrypted response are transmitted over the network. As the same key is used for both authentication and encryption, confidentiality is compromised due to flaws in the authentication method. While counter-intuitive, the open authentication method is actually more secure than the shared key method. This problem in compounded by the use of static keys which only change when the user manually changes them (which is, typically, infrequently).

The IV is 24-bits in length which is considered to be too small. On a busy network, the IV will frequently wrap around. IV collision (frames with the same IV), therefore, are relatively common. The likelihood of guessing the keystream increases with the IV collision rate. The problem is compounded by the lack of detail in the 802.11 specification regarding IV generation. Many wireless network cards do not make per-packet IV changes.

6.1.2 Encryption and Integrity

An integrity check value (ICV) is computed for each frame (M). The ICV is a 32-bit CRC and thus a plaintext frame M yields $\text{ICV} = \text{CRC}_{32}(M)$. The ICV is appended to a plaintext packet M to form $P = M|\text{ICV}$ (where $|$ denotes concatenation). A keystream is generated using a pseudo-random number generator (PRNG) from the WEP key K_{WEP} and a 24-bit initialisation vector (IV). A new IV is used for each frame (though IVs are reused every 24^2 frames). The IV is prepended to K_{WEP} to form a per-frame key, $K = \text{IV}|K_{\text{WEP}}$. P is then encrypted using the RC4 cipher. The ciphertext message C is derived by XORing the per-frame key K with P:

$$C = P \oplus K$$

The original WEP key was 40-bits in length (WEP-40). This was deemed to be too short for any serious security purpose. The length key was increased to 104 bits (WEP-104), though this did little to strengthen security.

A plaintext 802.11 MAC frame header is prepended to the ciphertext payload. One of the fields in the MAC frame header is the IV, thus the IV is transmitted as plaintext. The assembly of a WEP frame is shown in Fig. 6.2.

6.2 RSNA

802.11i introduced RSNA in response to the flaws in the original 802.11 security. RSNA algorithms provide enhancements to confidentiality, integrity authentication and key management.

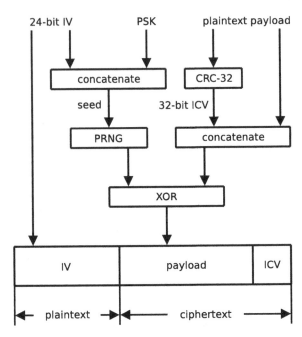

Fig. 6.2 Assembly of a WEP frame

6.2.1 Authentication

There are two RSNA authentication mechanisms specified in 802.11i:

- Pre-shared key (PSK)
- 802.1X

With PSK, a common secret key is installed on the wireless client and the access-point. Mutual authentication is established using a 4-way handshake. The distribution of the PSK is carried out outside the 802.11i framework. Typically, keys are installed on wireless devices manually. Clearly, the administrative overhead, in distributing keys to a large number of devices, can be considerable. For large networks IEEE 802.1X is recommended.

802.1X is a layer-2 protocol that supports the provisioning of port-based network access control. Communication over a 802.1X controlled port is blocked by the access-point until the wireless device has been successfully authenticated. 802.1X was originally designed for wired LANs but has been adapted for 802.11 networks. The extensible authentication protocol (EAP) is used to perform the authentication process. 802.1X defines how EAP packets are encapsulated in layer-2 frames. This is known as EAP over LAN (EAPOL). 802.1X defines three entities that are involved in the authentication process:

- Supplicant
- Authenticator
- Authentication server

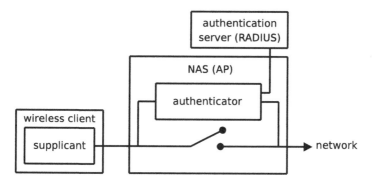

Fig. 6.3 802.1X

The diagram in Fig. 6.3 shows how the components of a 802.1X environment are interconnected. The supplicant is a piece of software that runs on the (wireless) client. The authenticator runs on the network authentication server (NAS). In an 802.11 network, the NAS is typically the access-point. The authentication server is typically a RADIUS server. The NAS is needed because the authentication server may not reside on the same layer-2 network as the client and the NAS blocks layer-3 packets from the client until it has authenticated. The NAS is configured with the IP address (or domain name) of the authentication server and forwards EAP packets from the client.

An access-point advertises its security capabilities in beacon frames or in responses to probe requests. A wireless client is, therefore, able to ascertain security capabilities either passively or actively. The wireless client then selects an access-point and "authenticates" using the open system authentication method. Authentication at this point is fairly weak and is simply to allow the device to associate with the access-point so that it can start sending EAP packets. All other communication is blocked.

The supplicant and the authentication server (RADIUS) perform the authentication (using one of a variety of methods) using the authenticator as an intermediate relay. Authentication can be client-only or mutual and depends upon the EAP method.

Upon successful authentication, the client and authentication server generate a common secret key called the master session key (MSK). The supplicant derives the pairwise master key (PMK) from the MSK. The authentication server transfers key material to the authenticator, enabling it to derive the PMK too. The supplicant and authenticator perform a 4-way handshake exchange which establishes the cipher suite and the pairwise transient key (PTK). Others keys are derived from the PTK, which are discussed in more detail below. At this point 802.1X unblocks the port and admits data packets to the network. At this point the supplicant and authenticator can now exchange frames securely.

EAP is an Internet standard for network client authentication. EAP was originally an extension to the point-to-point protocol (PPP). EAP was developed as a framework for end-points to negotiate which authentication mechanism to use. This

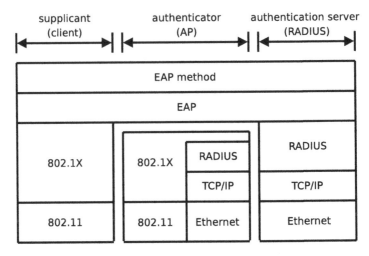

Fig. 6.4 EAP over LAN (EAPOL)

meant that new authentication mechanisms could be adopted without having to extend PPP.

When the supplicant associates, the authenticator sends an EAP-request/identity packet to the supplicant. The supplicant responds by sending the authenticator its identity with a EAP-Response/Identity. The authentication server sends the supplicant a challenge. The supplicant responds to the challenge and the authentication server sends back a success message if the client's credentials are valid.

The authenticator forwards EAP messages between the supplicant and authentication server. Messages traversing the wireless network are encapsulated in EAPOL packets (EAP over LAN). Messages traversing the wired network are encapsulated in RADIUS packets (over TCP/IP). The authenticator is responsible for the encapsulation (and de-encapsulation) of EAPOL and RADIUS packets. The relationship between EAP and 802.1X is summarised in Fig. 6.4.

A few of the current EAP methods are described below:

- EAP-PSK: Authentication based on pre-shared key.
- EAP-MD5: A minimal authentication method based upon a MD5 hash function. Authentication is not mutual; that is, only the authentication of the client is performed. It is vulnerable to dictionary and man-in-the-middle attacks. Furthermore, it is unsuitable for key generation.
- EAP-MSCHAPv2: Microsoft CHAP, version 2 is a challenge handshake authentication protocol. While version 1 was a client-only authentication mechanism, version 2 allows both client *and* server authentication.
- EAP-LEAP: Lightweight EAP is a proprietary EAP protocol from Cisco. EAP-LEAP provides mutual authentication based on password challenge-response.
- EAP-PEAP: Protected EAP protocol is a proprietary protocol co-developed by Microsoft, Cisco, and RSA Security. PEAP provides the secure mutual authentication of the client and server.

Fig. 6.5 802.11i key
hierarchy

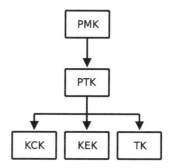

- EAP-TLS: Transport layer security (TLS) is based upon mutual certificate authentication. Certificates from both the client and the server are exchanged.
- EAP-TTLS: Tunneled transport layer security (TTLS) is an extension of TLS. Clients are authenticated by password, but server authentication is certificate based.

6.2.2 Key Management

The distribution of keys is closely linked to the authentication process. 802.11i uses different keys for different purposes. These keys form a key *hierarchy*, as shown in Fig. 6.5. At the top level is the PMK (pairwise master key) which is then used to derive other keys. If 802.1X is used for authentication, the PMK is established during the mutual authentication stage between the supplicant and authentication server. If the pre-shared key method is used for authentication, then the pre-shared key is used for the PMK. The PTK (pairwise transient key) is established on both the supplicant and the authenticator (access-point), Three more temporal keys are then derived from the PTK:

- EAPOL-key key confirmation key (KCK)
- EAPOL-key key encryption key (KEK)
- Temporal key (TK)

6.2.3 Encryption and Integrity

RSNA specifies two protocols for encryption (confidentiality) and integrity; namely, the temporal key integrity protocol (TKIP) and Counter mode with cipher block chaining message authentication code (CBC-MAC) protocol (CCMP). TKIP uses RC4 for encryption, but it is a much stronger implementation than that used by WEP. TKIP also feature a more sophisticated keying system which overcomes many of the shortcomings of WEP. The *Michael* algorithm is used for message integrity codes.

Fig. 6.6 TKIP frame

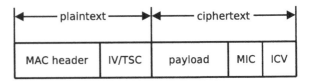

CCMP uses the advanced encryption standard (AES) in Counter mode for encryption and CBC-MAC for message integrity. CBC-MAC also supports confidentiality protection.

TKIP

Despite the improved security that 802.11i would bring, it was recognised that, the use of legacy 802.11 hardware would continue for some time to come. Firmware on legacy devices used WEP and, therefore, the RC4 cipher. In order to prevent the improper use of WEP (weak key scheduling, IV collisions and packet forgery), 802.11i specifies the TKIP sub-protocol. TKIP acts as wrapper around WEPs encryption, providing a more sophisticated key-mixing function. The 128-bit RC4 per-frame encryption key is derived from a temporal key (TK), the client's MAC address and an IV. The IV in TKIP also acts as a sequence counter to protect against simple replay attacks.

The TKIP mixing function operates in two phases. In the first phase, a TKIP-mixed transmit address and key (TTAK) is computed from the TK, MAC address (TA) and TKIP sequence counter (TSC). A per-frame key, called the WEP seed WEP_{seed} is generated in the second phase using the TTAK, TA and TSC.

The WEP_{seed} is passed to the WEP encapsulation process along with the plaintext frame M. From WEP_{seed}, WEP gets an RC4 key and an IV. Thus WEP_{seed} is used in place of the WEP key and WEP IV. WEP computes the ICV and encrypts M to produce the ciphertext frame. The TKIP frame format is shown in Fig. 6.6.

TKIP includes a 64 bit message integrity check (MIC) with every frame. The algorithm used to compute the MIC is called Michael. Its purpose is to prevent the sort of attacks that WEP was subjected to because of its weak CRC integrity check.

The MIC is computed over the source address (SA), destination address (DA), priority field (Pr), three reserved octets (Rsvd) and (plaintext) payload data (M) of the MAC frame:

$$MIC = Michael(SA|DA|Pr|Rsvd|M)$$

A per-frame TSC (TTKIP sequence counter) is used to protect against simple replay attacks. Frames that do not have increasing sequence numbers are dropped by the receiver. While Michael is an improvement of the CRC used in WEP, it is not infallible and it is possible to compromise message integrity. This is due to design constraints imposed on the implementation, requiring the support of legacy hardware. TKIP, therefore, implements countermeasures in order to reduce the likelihood of forgeries and limit information about the key. If an attack is suspected,

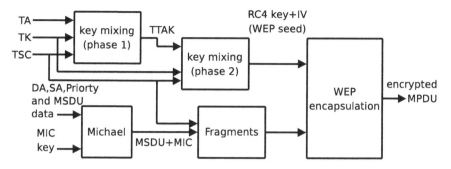

Fig. 6.7   TKIP encapsulation

TKIP operations are suspended for 60 seconds. Group and pairwise keys are then re-negotiated. Countermeasures are deployed if two frames arrive within a minute of each other with incorrect MICs.

The RC4 key and IV are used as the WEP seed, which is passed to the WEP encapsulation process. WEP uses this to generate an ICV and to encrypt the MPDU and the MIC (see Fig. 6.7). While an improvement on WEP, TKIP's MIC is still fairly weak in defending against message forgery. Nevertheless, it represents the best that can be achieved on legacy hardware.

CCMP

CCMP is a protocol is based upon AES's Counter mode with cipher-block chaining message authentication code (CBC-MAC). Counter mode is used for confidentiality and CBC-MAC for integrity. AES is much stronger than the RC4 cipher used in WEP and TKIP. However, it cannot run on legacy hardware.

802.11 MAC frames are passed to CCMP for processing. 802.11 frames consist of a MAC header, plaintext data and a frame check sequence (FCS). The MIC is encrypted along with the plaintext payload of the 802.11 frame. A CCMP header and the cipher text are appended to the original MAC header. An FCS is also appended. Figure 6.8 shows the expansion of a MAC frame into a CCMP frame.

Figure 6.9 shows the fields of the CCMP header. The CCMP header consists of a ExtIV, a KeyID and a packet number (PN). PN0 is the least significant byte of the PN. CCMP generates a new temporal key for each session and a nonce value for every frame. The nonce value is a 48-bit PN encrypted with the temporal key. The standard [17] warns that security can be compromised if the PN is reused with the same temporal key. The PN, therefore, is incremented for each frame.

Here we describe the CCMP encapsulation process. The additional authentication data (AAD) is constructed from fields in the MPDU header. The PN, the second address field (A2) and the priority field of the MAC header are used to construct the CCM nonce block:

$$nonce\ block = Prioriry|A2|PN$$

Fig. 6.8 Expanded CCMP
frame

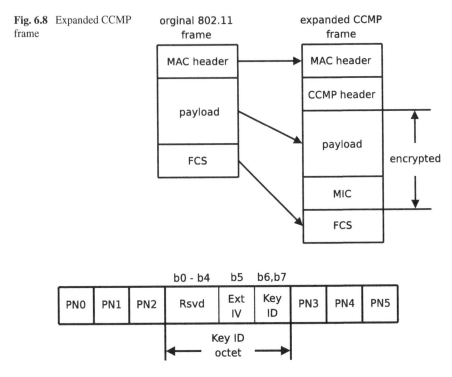

Fig. 6.9 CCMP header

The PN and key identifier are placed in the CCMP header. The concatenation of the payload data from the MAC frame and the MIC are encrypted with AES using the temporal key, AAD and nonce value. The encrypted frame is formed from the MAC header, the CCMP header and the ciphertext (see the diagram in Fig. 6.10).

The decryption process is as follows. Fields from the MAC and CCMP headers are extracted to construct the AAD and nonce value. The ciphertext is decrypted to produce the plaintext and the MIC. The original plaintext frame is reconstructed by appending the plaintext data to the MAC frame header. The diagram in Fig. 6.11 shows the CCMP decapsulation process.

6.3 Summary

The 802.11i amendment introduces RSNA (robust security network association). WEP (wired equivalent privacy) appears in the 802.11i standard under the pre-RSNA security methods. The flaws in WEP have been extensively studied and its use has been deprecated. TKIP (temporal key integrity protocol) is an enhancement of WEP that runs when using legacy 802.11 hardware. TKIP's security benefits from an extended IV (initialisation vector) space. Whereas WEP has a per-SSID encryp-

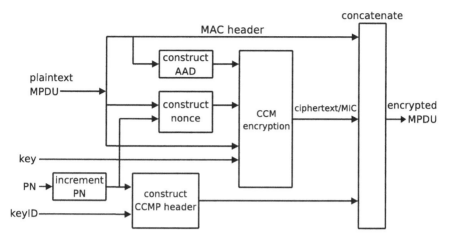

Fig. 6.10 CCMP encapsulation process

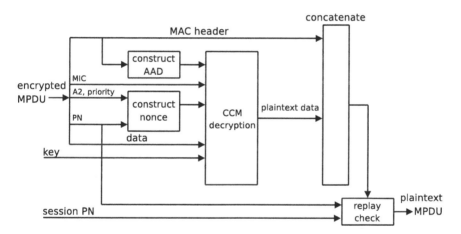

Fig. 6.11 CCMP decapsulation process

tion key, TKIP generates per user, per session keys. This prevents users on the same SSID from being able to decrypt each others' frames.

TKIP, like WEP, uses the RC4 cipher. TKIP implements a re-keying mechanism, a key mixing scheme and a MIC (message integrity check). Re-keying protects against recurrence-based PSK derivation attempts by generating per-packet encryption and integrity keys. The key mixing scheme introduces an IV sequence enforcement policy in order to protect against replay attacks. The Micheal MIC forms a counter measure against forgery attempts (but not packet replay forgeries).

TKIP is merely for backwards compatibility with legacy 802.11 hardware and for hardware that does not have the necessary capacity to run the CCMP encryption algorithm (we refer the reader to Table 5.2 which compares the performance of

RC4 and AES). CCMP offers stronger cryptographic methods and, for this reason, 802.11i recommends the use of CCMP over TKIP. The CCMP protocol is based on AES (advanced encryption standard) in Counter mode. CBC-MAC (cipher block chaining message authentication code) is used for data integrity.

Authentication in 802.11 is based upon either PSK (pre-shared key) of 802.1X. With 802.1X, clients are blocked until they have successfully authenticated. Within the 802.1X framework, the EAPOL (extensible authentication protocol over LAN) protocol is used to exchange authentication and key management information.

Chapter 7
Configuring Wireless Networks

In this chapter, we describe how to configure wireless equipment. A number of scenarios are presented using a variety of manufacturers, namely Cisco, Alcatel-Lucent and Meru Networks. We also describe how to build a router using open source software. Table 7.1 shows a summary of these three manufacturers. While they are three separate manufacturers, their command-line interfaces are similar, in that they resemble the Cisco IOS interface. All configuration commands must be entered when the controller is in configuration mode. To enter configuration mode, use the command from enable mode:

```
# configure terminal
```

Exit configuration mode by typing either, `exit` or `CTRL-Z`. Configuration commands take immediate effect but are not automatically saved to flash memory. Save the running configuration with:

```
# write memory
```

As we can see from Table 7.1, there are two different access-point architectures. Thick access-points operate stand alone and are managed directly. Each access-point maintains its own configuration data and performs its own security functions (such as authentication). Traffic is forwarded directly between network ports. Client roaming is performed in cooperation with the neighbouring access-points.

Conversely, thin access-points are lightweight and need to be managed from a separate controller. Configuration information is kept by the controller and pushed out to the access-points. Traffic also flows through the controller.

The initial deployment of thick access-points is relatively straightforward. Thick access-points, however, are more expensive than thin ones, but there are fewer infrastructure costs (no controllers required). Furthermore, they are more resilient; if an access-point fails, then coverage is only lost in a specific area. Thick access-points have scalability issues, as each access-point must be managed independently. Global changes to the network requires a configuration change on each access-point.

Thin access-points facilitate centralised administration. Troubleshooting is easier because data can be correlated in one place. Furthermore changes can be pushed to

A. Holt, C.-Y. Huang, *802.11 Wireless Networks,*
Computer Communications and Networks,
DOI 10.1007/978-1-84996-275-9_7, © Springer-Verlag London Limited 2010

Table 7.1 Summary of wireless equipment manufacturers

Manufacturer	Product	Architecture	Comment
Cisco	Aironet	Thick AP	Aironet is an Cisco aquisition
Alcatel-lucent	Omniaccess	Thin AP w/controller	OEM partnership w/aruba networks
Meru networks	n/a	Thin AP w/controller	

Table 7.2 Summary of laptops used to form an ad-hoc network

Manufacturer	Product	Distribution	Wireless card
Dell	Inspiron 510m	Ubuntu 9.04	Orinoco silver
Asus	Eee PC 4G	Xubuntu 7.04	Athereos AR5006EG

all access-points at once. Roaming can be coordinated by the controller, resulting in the seamless transition of a device from one access-point to another. In contrast, hand-overs between thick access-point can take hundreds of milliseconds.

Thin access-points cannot operate autonomously and are tightly coupled to a controller. Any problems experienced by the controller will affect the operation of all the access-points under its management.

7.1 Ad-hoc Network

Wireless devices can connect to each other without an access-point. This is referred to as *ad-hoc* mode. In this section, we show how to configure two GNU/Linux laptops to form an ad-hoc network. The two laptops are a Dell Insprion and an Asus Eee PC running Ubuntu 7.04 and Xubuntu 7.04 respectively (see Table 7.2).

On the Dell laptop, enter the command-line below (note that commands issued on the Dell are preceded by the dell$ prompt and commands issued on the Asus have the prompt asus$). This configures the mode as ad-hoc (as opposed to managed):

```
dell$ sudo iwconfig eth1 mode ad-hoc
```

Configure the ESSID with the command-line:

```
dell$ sudo iwconfig eth1 essid wnet
```

An attempt to configure the Eee PC in a similar way yields an error message.

```
asus$ sudo iwconfig ath0 essid wnet mode ad-hoc
Error for wireless request "Set Mode" (8B06) :
    SET failed on device ath0 ; Invalid argument.
```

The following command shows that the device has a get_mode function, but not a set_mode:

```
asus$ iwpriv ath0 | grep "[s|g]et_mode"
    get_mode         (8BE3) : set    0       & get    6 char
```

Whereas the wireless device on the Dell has both:

```
dell$ iwpriv eth1 | grep "[s|g]et_mode"
    set_mode         (8BE2) : set    1 int  & get    0
    get_mode         (8BE3) : set    0       & get   80 char
```

Remove the ath0 interface:

```
asus$ sudo wlanconfig ath0 destroy
```

Create a new interface, setting it to ad-hoc mode:

```
asus$ sudo wlanconfig ath0 create wlandev wifi0 \
> wlanmode adhoc
```

This creates a wireless interface ath1 (note that it is in the state of Not-Associated):

```
ath1  IEEE 802.11g  ESSID:""  Nickname:""
      Mode:Ad-Hoc  Frequency:2.452 GHz  Cell: Not-Assoc
iated
      Bit Rate:0 kb/s  Tx-Power=17 dBm  Sensitivity=1/1
      Retry:off  RTS thr:off  Fragment thr:off
      Power Management:off
      Link Quality:56/70  Signal level:-42  Noise level
=-98 dBm
      Rx invalid nwid:0  Rx invalid crypt:0  Rx invalid
frag:0
      Tx excessive retries:0  Invalid misc:0  Missed
beacon:0
```

Set the ESSID:

```
asus$ sudo iwconfig ath0 essid ahnet
```

The Asus is now associated with the Dell, forming an ad-hoc network (issuing this command on the Dell for interface eth1 will result in a similar output):

```
ath1  IEEE 802.11b  ESSID:"wnet"  Nickname:""
      Mode:Ad-Hoc  Frequency:2.452 GHz  Cell:
06:15:AF:8C:CE:D5
      Bit Rate:2 kb/s  Tx-Power=17 dBm  Sensitivity=1/1
      Retry:off  RTS thr:off  Fragment thr:off
      Power Management:off
      Link Quality:56/70  Signal level:-42  Noise level
=-98 dBm
```

```
        Rx invalid nwid:0   Rx invalid crypt:0   Rx invalid
frag:0
        Tx excessive retries:0   Invalid misc:0     Missed
beacon:0
```

Give the wireless interface on the Dell an IP address:

```
dell$ sudo ifconfig eth1 10.0.0.1 netmask 255.0.0.0
```

Configure the wireless interface on the Asus with an IP address in the same range:

```
asus$ sudo ifconfig ath1 10.0.0.2 netmask 255.0.0.0
```

Confirm communication between the two laptops:

```
asus$ ping -c 5 10.0.0.1
PING 10.0.0.1 (10.0.0.1) 56(84) bytes of data.
64 bytes from 10.0.0.1: icmp_seq=1 ttl=255 time=1.83 ms
64 bytes from 10.0.0.1: icmp_seq=2 ttl=255 time=1.92 ms
64 bytes from 10.0.0.1: icmp_seq=3 ttl=255 time=1.96 ms
64 bytes from 10.0.0.1: icmp_seq=4 ttl=255 time=1.88 ms
64 bytes from 10.0.0.1: icmp_seq=5 ttl=255 time=1.90 ms

--- 10.0.0.1 ping statistics ---
5 packets transmitted, 5 received, 0% packet loss, time
3999ms
rtt min/avg/max/mdev = 1.833/1.902/1.965/0.051 ms
```

7.2 WEP

As mentioned above, WEP (wired equivalent privacy) has suffered from many security issues and has since been deprecated in the 802.11 standard. Its usage, however, is still fairly common. In this section, we show how to configure a wireless infrastructure network on an Cisco Aironet access-point. Enter configuration mode and configure a dot11 ssid profile, thus:

```
dot11 ssid network-wep
  authentication open mac-address mac_methods
```

Now configure the radio interface:

```
interface Dot11Radio0
  encryption key 1 size 128bit 0 012345678901234567890112345 transmit-key
 encryption mode wep mandatory
 ssid network-wep
 station-role root access-point
```

We authenticate and associate with this ESSID using the GNU/Linux command-line:

```
asus$ sudo iwconfig ath0 mode managed
asus$ sudo iwconfig ath0 essid key \
> 012345678901234567890123456789012345
```

7.3 WPA with Pre-shared Key

WPA was an interim solution to 802.11i, introduced by the Wi-Fi Alliance. In this section, we show how to set up WPA pre-shared key security on an Alcatel-Lucent Omniaccess platform. Omniaccess APs are thin access-points and, therefore, download their configuration from a centralised controller.

When a new controller is powered on, it runs an initial configuration sequence, prompting the user for some basic details. This initial configuration sequence can be accessed through the console. Connect to the controller's console using a terminal emulator (such as minicom) with the serial settings of 9600 baud, 8 bits, 1 stop bit and no parity. The initial configuration procedure is described in Appendix B.

In configuration mode, define a virtual LAN (VLAN):

```
vlan 1001
interface vlan 1001
  ip address 172.16.11.2 255.255.255.0
```

Configure the Ethernet interface:

```
interface fastethernet 1/0
  switchport mode trunk
  switchport trunk native vlan 1001
  switchport trunk allowed vlan 1001
  no shutdown
```

The next task is to provision an access-point. When a OAW-AP boots it attempts to locate the master controller and download its configuration. If the access-point is connected to the same layer-2 network as the controller then it can use the Alcatel-Lucent discovery protocol (ADP) to find the controller. If the access-point and controller are separated by a layer-3 router, then the access-point relies on a combination of DHCP and DNS. The OAW-APs are factory-configured to connect to a controller with a domain name of "aruba-master". An entry for aruba-master must, therefore, exist in the DNS server. The IP details for the access-point have to be provided by a local DHCP server.

In order to avoid configuring auxiliary systems (such as DHCP or DNS), the access-point can be configured statically. Connect to the access-point (using a terminal emulator set to 9600 baud, 8N1) and power it up. The dialogue below will appear on the screen

```
APBoot 0.0.8.7 (build 16693)
Built: 2007-11-03 at 16:59:28
AP-12x: OCTEON CN30XX-SCP revision: 2
```

```
     Core clock: 500 MHz, DDR clock: 267 MHz (534 Mhz
data rate)
Power: POE
DRAM:   64 MB
Flash: 16 MB
Clearing DRAM...... done
BIST check passed.
Starting PCI
PCI Status: PCI 32-bit
PCI BAR 0: 0x00000000, PCI BAR 1: Memory 0x00000000 PCI
0xf8000000
Net:    en0, en1
Radio: ar9160#0, ar9160#1
```

The autoboot sequence can be interrupted by hitting the enter key when this line appears:

```
Hit <Enter> to stop autoboot:   0
```

This will drop out to the apboot prompt. Set the IP address, subnet mask and default gateway:

```
apboot> setenv ipaddr 172.16.11.10
apboot> setenv netmask 255.255.255.0
apboot> setenv gatewayip 172.16.11.1
```

Set the IP address of the master controller:

```
apboot> setenv master 172.16.11.2
```

Configure the DNS server:

```
apboot> setenv serverip 192.168.1.2
```

Resume the access-point's boot process with the command:

```
apboot> boot
```

Check the access-point is active on the controller:

```
(controller)#show ap active

Active AP Table
---------------
Name                    Group     IP Address   11g Clients
----                    -----     ----------   -----------
11g Ch/Pwr  11a Clients 11a Ch/Pwr    AP Type
----------  ----------- ----------    -------
Flags  Uptime
-----  ------
```

```
00:1a:1e:c9:59:dc   default   172.31.2.17   0
AP:HT:1/15   0                 AP:HT:104-/15   OAW-AP125
A        3m:27s

Flags: R = Remote AP; P = PPPOE; E = Wired AP
enabled;
A = Enet1 in active/standby mode;
       L = Active Load Balancing Enabled; D =
Disconn.
Extra Calls On; B = Battery Boost On
       X = Maintenance Mode; d = Drop Mcast/Bcast On

Num APs:1
```

Change the name of the access-point:

```
(controller)#ap-rename ap-name 00:1a:1e:c9:59:dc ap1
```

Show the AP database:

```
#show ap active

Active AP Table
---------------
Name            Group              IP Address
----            -----              ----------
11g Clients  11g Ch/Pwr   11a Clients   11a Ch/Pwr
-----------  ----------   -----------   ----------
AP Type     Flags  Uptime
-------     -----  ------

ap1              wtest-group          172.31.2.17
0                AP:HT:11/30   0          AP:HT:56-/30
OAW-AP125   A        13m:51s

Flags: R = Remote AP; P = PPPOE; E = Wired AP enabled;
A = Enet1 in active/standby mode;
       L = Active Load Balancing Enabled; D = Disconn.
xtra Calls On; B = Battery Boost On
       X = Maintenance Mode; d = Drop Mcast/Bcast On

Num APs:1
```

Enter configuration mode and configure dot1x authentication:

```
aaa authentication dot1x "wtest-wpa-dot1x"
```

Set up an AAA profile:

```
aaa profile "wtest-wpa-aaa-profile"
  authentication-dot1x "wtest-wpa-dot1x"
```

Set up an SSID profile, specifying the WPA passphrase, operation mode and the ESSID:

```
wlan ssid-profile wtest-wpa-ssid-profile
  wpa-passphrase letallin
  opmode wpa-psk-tkip
  essid "wtest-wpa"
```

Configure a virtual access-point:

```
wlan virtual-ap wtest-wpa-vap
  vap-enable
  vlan 1001
  ssid-profile wtest-wpa-ssid-profile
  aaa-profile wtest-wpa-aaa-profile
```

Assign the virtual-ap configured above to the ap-group *wtest-group*:

```
ap-group "wtest-group"
  virtual-ap wtest-wpa-vap
```

Exit configuration mode and assign ap1 to the group, wtest-group:

```
(controller)#ap-regroup ap-name ap1 wtest-group
```

Now we show how to configure a wireless device to connect using WPA. Here we use the Asus Eee PC (if the Asus still has the configuration from the ad-hoc network example, it might be a good idea to reboot).

From the GNU/Linux shell, we generate a passphrase and redirect the output to a file *wtest.conf*

```
asus$ wpa_passphrase wtest letallin | tee wtest.conf
network={
ssid="wtest"
#psk="letallin"
        psk=8b2daf45eca90b5d33080a75b3dfaf6bf9172e2e90
d9c58cf9643a7f55f74212
}
```

Edit *wtest.conf* such that the content is as follows:

```
ctrl_interface=/var/run/wpa_supplicant

network={
        ssid="wtest"
        scan_ssid=1
        proto=WPA RSN
        key_mgmt=WPA-PSK
```

```
      pairwise=CCMP TKIP
      group=CCMP TKIP
#psk="letallin"
      psk=8b2daf45eca90b5d33080a75b3dfaf6bf9172e2e90
d9c58cf9643a7f55f74212
}
```

Run the supplicant with the command-line:

```
$ sudo wpa_supplicant -Dwext -iath0 -c wtest.conf
```

7.4 Multiple SSIDs

It is possible to operate multiple SSIDs on one access-point. Each SSID can offer different security methods. In this section, we show how to set up a Cisco Aironet for dual SSIDs. One SSID will be configured for WEP security and the other SSID for WPA. Furthermore, traffic is mapped to different VLANs according to which SSID the device is associated with (Fig. 7.1 shows how the SSIDs are mapped to VLANs).

Enter configuration mode and configure the SSID for WEP devices:

```
dot11 ssid wtest-wep
  vlan 1
  authentication open
```

Then, configure the SSID for WPA:

```
dot11 ssid wtest-wpa
  vlan 2
  authentication open
  wpa-psk ascii 0 letallin
  authentication key-management wpa
```

Configure the radio interface:

```
interface Dot11Radio0
  encryption vlan 1 key 1 size 128bit 0 012345678901234
56789012345 transmit-key
  encryption vlan 1 mode wep mandatory
  encryption vlan 2 mode ciphers tkip
```

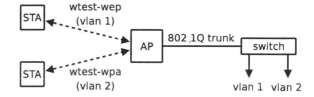

Fig. 7.1 An Aironet AP running dual SSIDs

```
  ssid wtest-wep
  ssid wtest-wpa
  mbssid
  station-role root
  no keepalive
```

Configure the radio sub-interface for VLAN 1:

```
interface Dot11Radio0.1
  encapsulation dot1Q 1 native
  no ip route-cache
  bridge-group 1
  bridge-group 1 subscriber-loop-control
  bridge-group 1 block-unknown-source
  no bridge-group 1 source-learning
  no bridge-group 1 unicast-flooding
  bridge-group 1 spanning-disabled
```

Configure the radio sub-interface for VLAN 2:

```
interface Dot11Radio0.2
  encapsulation dot1Q 2
  no ip route-cache
  bridge-group 2
  bridge-group 2 subscriber-loop-control
  bridge-group 2 block-unknown-source
  no bridge-group 2 source-learning
  no bridge-group 2 unicast-flooding
  bridge-group 2 spanning-disabled
```

Now configure the Ethernet sub-interfaces for VLAN 1 and 2:

```
interface FastEthernet0.1
  encapsulation dot1Q 1 native
  no ip route-cache
  no keepalive
  bridge-group 1
  no bridge-group 1 source-learning
  bridge-group 1 spanning-disabled

interface FastEthernet0.2
  encapsulation dot1Q 2
  no ip route-cache
  no keepalive
  bridge-group 2
  no bridge-group 2 source-learning
  bridge-group 2 spanning-disabled
```

Configure the bridge interface:

```
interface BVI1
  ip address 172.16.1.2 255.255.0.0
  no ip route-cache
```

Note that both SSIDs will operate on the same radio frequency. On the Omniaccess and Meru platform, multiple "virtual" access-points can be defined on a physcial access-point. In this way, multiple SSIDs can be operated on different frequencies.

7.5 Wireless Distribution System

The distribution system (DS) for 802.11 is (typically) a wired network technology, such as 802.3 or Ethernet. Some manufacturers, however, support a wireless distribution system (WDS). WDS is not part of the 802.11 standard, though a number of manufacturers use 802.11s mesh nomenclature to describe their WDS offering. In this section, we show how to configure a WDS on a Meru Networks platform (see Appendix B for instructions on how to perform the initial controller configuration). Meru calls this feature *Mesh Enterprise*. The network, however, does not form a full mesh, but rather a hub-spoke configuration [26]. The network diagram in Fig. 7.2 shows a "mesh" conprising two access-points. One access-point is a *gateway* and is connected to the controller by a wired LAN (in this case, Ethernet). The other access-point is a *leaf* node and uses the 5 GHz wireless interface for the DS. In this examples, we use AP150s which are dual radio access-points (some of the Meru access-points do not support WDS, check the manual for more information). One radio is for the 2.4 GHz band (802.11b/g) and the other is for the 5 GHz band (802.11a).

Power up the two AP150s and connect them to the controller using an Ethernet switch or hub. Once the access-points have completed their boot procedure, they should come up Enabled and Online on the controller:

```
controller# show ap
AP ID AP Name  Serial Number      Op State Availability
Runtime          Connectivity AP Role   AP Model

7     AP-7     00:0c:e6:05:55:88 Enabled  Online
3.5-53           L2           access     AP150
8     AP-8     00:0c:e6:05:70:3d Enabled  Online
3.5-53           L2           access     AP150
```

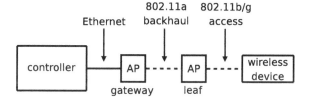

Fig. 7.2 Wireless distribution system

In our example, the access-points came up as AP-7 and AP-8. We will use AP-7 as the gateway and AP-8 as the leaf node. As the access-points are dual radio, they have two Dot11Radio interfaces. The first interface if for the 2.4 GHz band and the second for the 5GHz band. We will use the 5 GHz band as the back-haul for the mesh network. Configure the radio interface of AP-7 so that the back-haul channel is 44:

```
interface Dot11Radio 7 2
  channel 44
```

Configure the gateway access-point (AP-7):

```
ap 7
  connectivity l2-only
  description gw1
  role gateway
  dataplane-encryption on
  end
```

Configure the leaf access-point, specifying AP-7 as the parent access-point:

```
ap 8
  connectivity l2-only
  description n1
  role wireless
  parent-ap 7
  dataplane-encryption on
```

Reload the access-points:

```
# reload
```

Eventually, both access-points will come up on-line and enabled. Notice that the access-points have assumed new names according to their description fields. That is, AP-7 is called gw1 and AP-8 is called n1:

```
controller# show ap
AP ID AP Name  Serial Number       Op State Availability
Runtime          Connectivity AP Role   AP Model

7     gw1      00:0c:e6:05:55:88  Enabled  Online
3.5-53           L2               gateway   AP150
8     n1       00:0c:e6:05:70:3d  Enabled  Online
3.5-53           L2               wireless  AP150
```

The leaf access-point n1 should be using the wireless back-haul (through gw1) to access the controller. That being the case, disconnect the Ethernet cable of n1. Configure a BSS for wireless devices to connect using WPA security (with pre-shared key):

```
security-profile wds-profile
  allowed-l2-modes wpa-psk
  encryption-modes tkip
  psk key letallin
```

Configure an SSID:

```
essid wtest
  security-profile wds-profile
  no ess-ap 7 1
```

Note that we have disabled gw1 from providing a BSS on its 2.4 GHz interface. This is merely to ensure that, when a wireless device connects to the BSS, it does so on n1 and is, therefore, forced to use the WDS. Under normal circumstances, it would be desirable for both gw1 and n1 to provide the BSS (for greater coverage), in which case, the no ess-ap 7 1 command is omitted.

Using our Asus Eee PC, we associate with the BSS:

```
asus$ sudo wpa_supplicant -Dwext -iath0 -c wtest.conf
```

Verify that the wireless device is associated with n1:

```
controller# show station
```

```
MAC Address          IP Type      AP Name           L2 Mode
L3 Mode Authenticated User Name   Tag   Client IP

00:15:af:8c:ce:d5 DHCP         n1                    wpa-psk
clear                               0   172.16.50.83
```

7.6 Wireless Bridge

A bridge is a device that connects two networks (typically) at Layer 2 (Data Link Layer). Packets are received by the bridge on one port and re-transmitted on another port. Bridges have been used in wired LANs for many years. For example, the IEEE 802.1D [22] is a bridging standard for IEEE MAC layer LANS. The distinction between a bridge and a router is that, with a bridge, packets do not have to traverse a protocol stack and network devices are interconnected as though they were on the same network.

An access-point performs a similar function to a bridge except that it connects a set of clients (wireless devices) to a network as opposed to connecting two networks. There are wireless devices that can connect to an access-point, as a client, and act as a bridge for a wired network. The diagram in Fig. 7.3 shows an access-point connected to the a DS (distribution system). A wireless bridge is associated with the access-point and, in turn, connected to a wired LAN. Devices on the wired LANs are interconnected via the wireless channel between the access-point and wireless

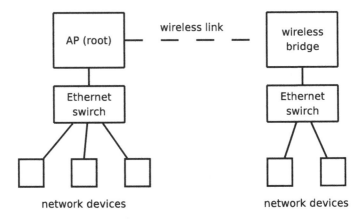

Fig. 7.3 A wireless bridge topology

bridge. This feature is useful if two wired LANs need to be connected but running a cable between them is problematic.

In this section, we describe how to set up a wireless LAN bridge using two Cisco Aironet APs. We one Aironet access-point the role of *access-point*. It is configured as a root access-point (as shown in Fig. 7.3). The other Aironet access-point is configured for the role of wireless bridge. We use WPA with a pre-shared key for security. We describe the configuration of the root access-point first. Configure the hostname of the access-point:

```
hostname br1
```

Next, assign an IP address and set the interface to administratively up (no shutdown):

```
int BVI 1
   ip address 10.0.0.1 255.255.255.0
   no shutdown
```

Configure the ssid "wbridge":

```
dot11 ssid bridge-test
   authentication open
   authentication key-management wpa
   authentication client username br2 password 0 letmein
   max-associations 1
   wpa-psk ascii 0 letmein2
```

The configuration lines above, specify the name of the client (in this case br2) and the password it must authenticate with ("letmein"). A pre-shared key is also required ("letmein2"). For further security, we set the maximum associations to 1, so that once the (legitimate) client has associated, no other devices may associate, even if they supply the correct authentication password and pre-shared key.

Finally, configure the wireless interface setting the station-role as the root:

```
interface Dot11Radio0
  encryption mode ciphers tkip
  ssid wbridge
  station-role root
  no shut
```

Configure the name of the Aironet access-point designated as the wireless bridge:

```
hostname br2
```

Configure the IP address:

```
int BVI 1
  ip address 10.0.0.2 255.255.255.0
  no shutdown
```

Configure the SSID ("wbridge"):

```
dot11 ssid wbridge
  authentication open
  authentication key-management wpa
  authentication client username br1 password 0 letmein
  wpa-psk ascii 0 letmein2
```

We specify the hostname of the root access-point (br1) with the corresponding password and pre-shared key.

Configure interface setting the station role as non-root:

```
interface Dot11Radio0
  encryption mode ciphers tkip
  ssid wbridge
  station-role non-root
  no shutdown
```

One the configuration is complete, br2 should associate with br1. This can be confirmed by the command:

```
(br2)#show dot11 associations

802.11 Client Stations on Dot11Radio0:

SSID [wbridge] :

MAC Address     IP address      Device        Name
0022.9099.bf30  10.0.0.1        11g-bridge    br1

Parent          State
–               Assoc
```

7.7 Build an Open Source Access-Point

This chapter describes how to build an AP using open source software. Any PC with an appropriate wireless card can be used; however, there are a number of embedded systems available which would be more suitable.

PCs and laptops tend to have extraneous hardware, such as hard disks, sound cards, graphic adapters and DVD drives. Furthermore, the processing power (and memory) within these devices is excessive for this sort of application. Embedded devices consume less power and generate less heat (as well as noise) than a regular PC or laptop. There are many examples of embedded systems designed specifically for building network devices. In this chapter, we use a Soekris net4521 [39] which has a 133 MHz AMD ElanSC520 processor, two Ethernet interfaces and two PCM-CIA slots. A compact flash card is used instead of a hard disk. The installation procedure is as follows:

- Build the root filesystem along AP application software.
- Compile and install the Linux kernel.
- Install the bootloader and root file system on to the compact flash.
- Configure the system to operate as an AP.

7.7.1 Root Filesystem

The root filesystem is a hierarchy of directories containing the operating system applications, configuration files and the kernel. A typical modern GNU/Linux distribution is huge, comprising many gigabytes of data. A few years ago, the limited size of compact flash cards (in the order of 64 to 128 megabytes) meant that it was a challenge to build a complete operating system small enough to fit onto a card. The directory hierarchy, along with the configuration files, had to be created manually and individual packages had to be compiled from source. It was a painstaking task to even build a minimal system. Adding new packages was complex because it often required compiling a number of dependencies.

Nowadays, 1 gigabyte compact flash cards are relatively inexpensive. While still too small for a full modern distribution, this does mean we do not have to be as parsimonious with regard to size of the operating system. A great deal of time can be saved by using the debootstrap application to create a small (if not minimal) operating system.

For convenience we use environment variables, in this case, to define the directories under which we build the new system:

```
$ export BASE=${HOME}/ap
$ export SRC=${BASE}/src
$ export ROOT=${BASE}/root
```

The instructions below reference environment variables, so it is important that they are assigned in the current shell. We must remember to re-assign them if we close the current shell and start a new one. Create the directory structure in which to work:

```
$ mkdir $BASE/{,src,root}
```

The ${ROOT} directory will be the *root* for the new system. We use the $SRC directory in which to build the Linux kernel. We can specify which packages to include along with the packages in the base system:

```
$ OPTS[0]="--include=grub,locales,pciutils,pcmciautils,
> udev,dnsutils,openssh-client,openssh-server,
> linux-wlan-ng,wireless-tools,wpasupplicant"
```

We can also specify packages to exclude:

```
$ OPTS[1]="--exclude=manpages,gcc-4.1-base,nano"
```

Create the system by running debootstrap thus:

```
$ sudo debootstrap ${OPTS[*]} etch ${ROOT}
```

7.7.2 Administration

We need to download firmware for the card we are using, in this case an ASUS WL-100 (which is a Prism 2.5 card). Download the firmware with:

```
$ cd $BASE
$ wget http://www.red-bean.com/~proski/firmware/\
> 1.1.0.tar.bz2
$ wget http://www.red-bean.com/~proski/firmware/\
> 1.4.2.tar.bz2
```

Extract the firmware files:

```
$ tar jxvf 1.1.0.tar.bz2
$ tar jxvf 1.4.2.tar.bz2
```

Install them within the AP's directory structure:

```
$ sudo cp sf010100.hex $ROOT/lib/firmware/
$ sudo cp sf010402.hex $ROOT/lib/firmware/
```

For convenience, we carry out the remaining instructions from within a chroot "jail":

```
$ cd $ROOT
$ sudo chroot.
```

Configure the filesystem information by entering the following lines into the */etc/fstab* file:

```
proc /proc proc rw,nodev,nosuid,noexec 0 0
tmpfs /dev/shm tmpfs defaults 0 0
tmpfs /tmp tmpfs defaults 0 0
```

Enable a `getty` process on the serial port by adding the line below in
/etc/inittab:

```
T0:23:respawn:/sbin/getty -L ttyS0 19200 vt100
```

In order to extend the life of the compact flash, it is necessary to reduce the
number of write operations to the filesystem. System logfiles are located in */log/var*.
Mounting a temporary filesystem on */log/var* avoids writes to the filesystem on the
compact flash, redirecting Create a file */etc/init.d/mountvar.sh*, with the following
content:

```sh
#!/bin/sh

PATH=/lib/init:/sbin:/bin

TMPFS_SIZE=
[ -f /etc/default/tmpfs ] && . /etc/default/tmpfs

KERNEL="$(uname -s)"

. /lib/lsb/init-functions
. /lib/init/mount-functions.sh

do_start () {
    domount tmpfs "" /var/log tmpfs \
            -onoexec,nosuid,mode=0620
        cd /var
        /bin/tar xvf log.tar
}

case "$1" in
  "")
echo "Warning: mountvar should be called with
    the 'start' argument." >&2 do_start
;;
  start)
do_start
;;
  restart|reload|force-reload)
echo "Error: argument '$1' not supported" >&2
exit 3
;;
  stop)
# No-op
;;
  *)
echo "Usage: mountvar [start|stop]" >&2
```

```
exit 3
;;
esac
```

Make the script executable:

```
# chmod +x /etc/init.d/mountvar.sh
```

Create a symbolic link to the script in the */etc/rcS.d* directory:

```
# cd /etc/rcS.d
# ln -s ../init.d/mountvar.sh S05mountvar
```

7.7.3 Configuring the Access-Point

In this subsection we describe how configure the access-point. Edit the */etc/hostapd/ hostapd.conf* file and enter the following content:

```
bridge=br0
interface=wlan0
driver=hostap
logger_syslog=-1
logger_syslog_level=2
logger_stdout=-1
logger_stdout_level=2
debug=0
dump_file=/tmp/hostapd.dump
ssid=wtest
ctrl_interface=/var/run/hostapd
```

Now configure the Ethernet, wireless and bridge interfaces. Edit */etc/network/ interfaces*:

```
auto eth0

auto wlan0
iface wlan0 inet static
  wireless-mode master
  wireless-essid wtest
  fw_primary /lib/firmware/sf010100.hex
  fw_secondary /lib/firmware/sf010402.hex

auto br0
iface br0 inet static
  address 10.10.1.10
  netmask 255.255.255.0
  broadcast 10.10.1.255
  bridge_ports wlan0 eth0
```

7.7.4 *Installing Grub*

We use Grub (GRand Unified Bootloader) to bootstrap the kernel. For my details on Grub see [14]. Still in the *chroot* jail, create the directory */boot/grub*:

```
# mkdir /boot/grub
```

Copy files to the `grub` directory:

```
# cp /usr/lib/grub/i386-pc/* /boo/grub
```

Create the Grub menu file */boot/grub/menu.lst* and add the following content:

```
default 0
timeout 3

title 2.6.28.10
        root (hd0,0)
        kernel /boot/bzImage-2.6.28.10 ro \
               root=/dev/hda1 console=ttyS0,19200n8
```

Exit the chroot jail:

```
# exit
```

7.7.5 *Compile the Kernel*

In this subsection, we describe how to compile the Linux kernel. In this example, we will use version 2.6.28.10. Download the source code with:

```
$ cd $SRC
$ wget http://www.kernel.org/pub/linux/kernel/v2.6/\
> linux-2.6.28.10.tar.gz
```

Unpack the source file and prepare to compile:

```
$ tar zxvf linux-2.6.28.10.tar.gz
$ cd linux-2.6.28.10/
```

Set the CFLAGS environment variable:

```
$ export CFLAGS="-march=i486 -O3"
```

Configure kernel options with the command below. Kernel options are selected using the menu based application shown in Fig. 7.4.

```
$ make menuconfig
```

A full explanation of all of the kernel variables is beyond the scope of this book. For more information, refer to [24]. You need to ensure that the Ext3 journalling filesystem is built into the kernel (as opposed to being a loadable module). The options below can be found under *File systems*:

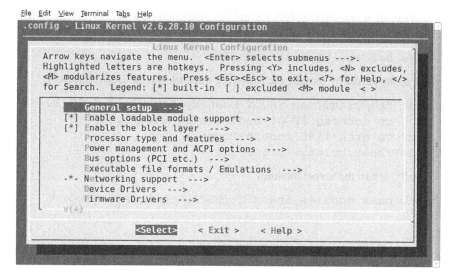

File Edit View Terminal Tabs Help

.config - Linux Kernel v2.6.28.10 Configuration

Linux Kernel Configuration
Arrow keys navigate the menu. <Enter> selects submenus --->.
Highlighted letters are hotkeys. Pressing <Y> includes, <N> excludes,
<M> modularizes features. Press <Esc><Esc> to exit, <?> for Help, </>
for Search. Legend: [*] built-in [ ] excluded <M> module < >

       General setup --->
   [*] Enable loadable module support --->
   [*] Enable the block layer --->
       Processor type and features --->
       Power management and ACPI options --->
       Bus options (PCI etc.) --->
       Executable file formats / Emulations --->
  -*- Networking support --->
       Device Drivers --->
       Firmware Drivers --->
   v(+)

              <Select>   < Exit >   < Help >

Fig. 7.4   Output of make menuconfig command

```
<*> Ext3 journalling file system support
[ ]     Default to 'data=ordered' in ext3 (legacy option)
[*]     Ext3 extended attributes
[*]        Ext3 POSIX Access Control Lists
[*]        Ext3 Security Labels
```

Ensure PCI is configured as built-in to the kernel. Under *Bus options*, set the following options:

```
[*] PCI support
<*> PCCard (PCMCIA/CardBus) support   --->
```

Also, under *PCCard (PCMCIA/CardBus) support*, select:

```
<*>    CardBus yenta-compatible bridge support
```

The Ethernet card is a National Semiconductor DP83815. The kernel option for this driver can be found under *Device Driver/Network device support/Ethernet (10 or 100 Mbit)*:

```
<M>    National Semiconductor DP8381x series PCI
       Ethernet support
```

Ensure the Host AP drivers are enabled. We are using an ASUS WL-100, which is a Prism 2.5 cardbus device. The options below can be found under sections, *Device Driver/Network device support/Wireless LAN*:

```
<M> IEEE 802.11 for Host AP (Prism2/2.5/3 and WEP/TKIP
    /CCMP)
<M>    Host AP driver for Prism2.5 PCI adaptors
```

Exit out of `make menuconfig` and save the configuration. Now compile the kernel and modules:

```
$ make bzImage && make modules
```

Install the kernel by moving the following three files to the `boot` directory:

```
$ sudo cp System.map $ROOT/boot/System.map-2.6.28.10
$ sudo cp .config $ROOT/boot/config-2.6.28.10
$ sudo cp arch/i386/boot/bzImage \
> $ROOT/boot/bzImage-2.6.28.10
```

Finally, install the kernel modules:

```
$ sudo make modules_install INSTALL_MOD_PATH=$ROOT
```

7.7.6 Install Root Directory Structure onto Compact Flash

Use the tar command to "archive" the root directory structure:

```
$ cd $BASE
$ sudo tar zcvf root.tar.gz root/
```

Connect a compact flash (CF) card to the host machine. Unless the host machine you are using has a built-in CF card reader, an external (typically USB) card reader is required. After connecting the CF card, check the name of the device:

```
$ dmesg | tail
[ 4396.244886] sd 2:0:0:0: [sdb] 3928176 512-byte
hardware sectors (2011 MB)
[ 4396.247856] sd 2:0:0:0: [sdb] Write Protect is off
[ 4396.247867] sd 2:0:0:0: [sdb] Mode Sense:
0b 00 00 08
[ 4396.247872] sd 2:0:0:0: [sdb] Assuming drive cache:
write through
[ 4396.253841] sd 2:0:0:0: [sdb] 3928176 512-byte
hardware sectors (2011 MB)
[ 4396.256870] sd 2:0:0:0: [sdb] Write Protect is off
[ 4396.256881] sd 2:0:0:0: [sdb] Mode Sense:
0b 00 00 08
[ 4396.256886] sd 2:0:0:0: [sdb] Assuming drive cache:
write through
[ 4396.256898]  sdb: sdb1
```

In our case, the CF card is called */dev/sdb* and the first partition is */dev/sdb1* (most probably, this will be a Windows FAT filesystem). If it has mounted automatically, unmount it:

```
$ sudo umount /dev/sdb1
```

Now run `fidsk` to create a partition table entry:

```
$ sudo fdisk /dev/sdb1
```

If there is a current partition table entry, delete it (if there is more than one, delete them all):

```
Command (m for help): d
Partition number (1-4): 1
```

Create a primary partition:

```
Command (m for help): n
Command action
   e    extended
   p    primary partition (1-4)
p
Selected partition 1
First cylinder (1-992, default 1): 1
Last cylinder or +size or +sizeM or
+sizeK (1-992, default 992):
Using default value 992
```

Make the partition bootable:

```
Command (m for help): a
Partition number (1-4): 1
```

Write the partition table to the disk:

```
Command (m for help): w
```

Make an Ext3 filesystem:
```
$ sudo mkfs.ext3 /dev/sdb1
```

Tune the filesystem with the command:

```
$ sudo tune2fs -c0 -i0 /dev/sdb1
```

Mount the filesystem:

```
$ sudo mount /dev/sdb1 root
```

Untar the root directory structure onto the compact flash filesystem:

```
$ sudo tar zxvf root.tar.gz
```

We use Grub as the bootloader. Install the bootloader by running the command:

```
$ sudo grub
```

This takes us into an interactive session. Specify the device:

```
grub> device (hd0) /dev/sdb
```

Specify the root filesystem:

```
grub> root (hd0,0)
```

Install the bootloader in the MBR:

```
grub> setup (hd0)
 Checking if "/boot/grub/stage1" exists... yes
 Checking if "/boot/grub/stage2" exists... yes
 Checking if "/boot/grub/e2fs_stage1_5" exists... yes
 Running "embed /boot/grub/e2fs_stage1_5 (hd0)"...  15
sectors are embedded.
succeeded
 Running "install /boot/grub/stage1 (hd0) (hd0)1+15 p
(hd0,0)/boot/grub/stage2 /boot/grub/menu.lst"...
succeeded
Done.
```

Quit Grub:

```
grub> quit
```

Unmount the compact flash card:

```
$ umount /dev/sdb1
```

Place the compact flash into the CF slot of the Soekris. Once it has booted it will advertise the SSID for *wtest*.

7.8 Summary

In this chapter, we have shown how to configure a number of wireless networks. We have used a number of manufacturers' equipment; namely, Cisco, Alactel-Lucent and Meru. Alactel-Lucent and Meru equipment is controller based (thin access-point). While Cisco has controller based systems, we used thick access-points in our examples. We also showed how to build an access-point from open source software on a Soekris PC.

In all of our examples, we only demonstrated Open, WEP and WPA (PSK) security. Full 802.11i (WPA2) security methods involve greater complexity. We dedicate the next chapter to building an wireless network based upon enterprise security.

Chapter 8
Robust Security Network

This chapter describes how to set up a robust security network (RSN) association. The diagram in Fig. 8.1 shows the network infrastructure for the RSN. We use an Alcatel-Lucent Omniaccess controller as the NAS (network authentication server). The Omniaccess switch (OAW-4504) is also the controller for a OAW-AP125 thin access-points.

We use EAP-TLS for authentication. We need a number of supporting services; that is, a RADIUS server and a database server. FreeRadius and MySQL are used for the RADIUS database server servers, respectively. A DHCP server is also required for serving IP details to (thin) APs and wireless clients. Table 8.1 gives the details of the host machines and their respective IP addresses.

For convenience, we use Xen (running on a Debian distribution) to create multiple virtual machines in order to emulate a multi-server environment. Clearly, the physical host on which Xen, and all the virtual machines runs, represents a single point of failure. In reality, these services would run on separate physical machines. Furthermore, it would be prudent to operate these servers in a high-availability (HA) configuration. Detailed instructions of how to set up a HA environment is beyond the scope of this book. Nevertheless, it would be fairly straightforward to build a HA environment based upon the implementation presented in this chapter. HA for the RADIUS server can be achieved by having multiple hosts running RADIUS. The AP controller can be configured to use a list of RADIUS servers.

With FreeRadius, user account information can be configured in flat files or in a database.[1] Using a database (instead of flat files, which is the default) involves greater complexity. However, if multiple RADIUS servers are used (for HA), then, ideally we need to centralise the user account information (which we cannot do with flat files). For this reason, we show how to setup a MySQL database server to hold the RADIUS user account details.

The MySQL server, however, represents another single point of failure. This problem can be overcome by implementing a MySQL cluster for HA and load bal-

---

[1] Alternatively, LDAP could be used.

A. Holt, C.-Y. Huang, *802.11 Wireless Networks*,
Computer Communications and Networks,
DOI 10.1007/978-1-84996-275-9_8, © Springer-Verlag London Limited 2010

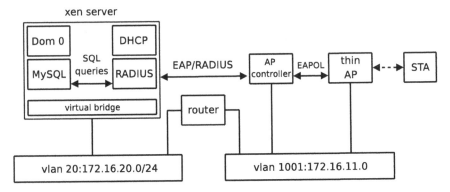

Fig. 8.1 RSN architecture

Table 8.1 IP addresses

Hostname	Address/mask	Comment
Xen	172.16.20.2/24	Dom 0
Radius	172.16.20.70/24	RADIUS server
Mysql	172.16.20.79/24	MySQL server
Dhcp	172.16.20.57/24	DHCP server
Al-ctl	172.16.11.51/24	WLAN controller

ancing. Again, this is outside the scope of this book. The reader is referred to [33] for details on MySQL clustering.

We tested the infrastructure using two laptops as wireless clients. We used a DELL inspiron and an Eee PC running Ubuntu 7.04 and 8.04 respectively. For the supplicant, we used the `wpa_supplicant`, which was installed using the distribution's package management system.

An RSN environment involves a number of separate (disparate) hardware and software systems. Setting up an enterprise level wireless infrastructure is, therefore, a complex process. At each stage of the process, we show how to test the various components.

8.1 Installing FreeRadius

FreeRadius can be installed using a Debian distribution package management utility. On the VM designated as the RADIUS server, issue the following command:

```
radius$ sudo apt-get install freeradius
```

The TLS module is not compiled by default. For this reason, we have to recompile FreeRadius from source. Install the GCC compiler:

```
$ sudo apt-get install -y gcc g++
```

Also install these packages:

```
radius$ sudo apt-get install -y apt-src dpkg-dev
fakeroot
```

Install MySQL client:

```
radius$ sudo apt-get install -y mysql-client
```

Create a directory in which to work:

```
radius$ mkdir ~/src
radius$ cd ~/src
```

Download the FreeRadius source package:

```
radius$ apt-src install freeradius
```

In the file */src/debian/rules*, edit the line that begins with the string "buildssl=" so that the option "–without-rlm_eap_tls" reads, "–with-rlm_eap_tls". In the file *~/src/debian/control*, add "libssl-dev" and "libpq-dev" to the end of the line that begins *Build-Depends*.

Comment out the current `Build-Conflicts` line:

```
#Build-Conflicts: libssl-dev
```

And add this line:

```
Build-Conflicts:
```

Now install libssl-dev and libpq-dev packages:

```
radius$ sudo apt-get install -y libssl-dev libpq-dev
```

Append this line to ~/src/debian/changelog:

```
* Add tls support for compilation

  -- Alan Holt <aholt@ip-performance.co.uk>  30.10.2008
```

Build:

```
radius$ cd ~/src
$ sudo apt-src build freeradius
```

Create user, freerad:

```
radius$ sudo addgroup --gid=103 freerad
radius$ sudo adduser --uid=101 --gid=103 \
> --shell=/bin/false freerad
```

Install the freeradius and freeradius-mysql packages:

```
radius$ sudo dpkg -i freeradius_1.1.3-3_i386.deb
radius$ sudo dpkg -i \
> freeradius-mysql_1.1.3-3_i386.deb
```

Change the group and set the permission on the */var/run/freeradius/* directory:

```
radius$ sudo chgrp freerad /var/run/freeradius/
radius$ sudo chmod g+w /var/run/freeradius/
```

8.2 Configuring FreeRadius

The configuration files for FreeRadius are located in the */etc/freeradius* directory. Configure FreeRadius so that is allows the localhost (127.0.0.1) to be a client of RADIUS server. An entry should already exist in the file */etc/freeradius/clients.conf*. Edit this entry so that it resembles:

```
client 127.0.0.1 {
        secret          = letmein
        shortname       = localhost
        nastype         = other
}
```

This will enable us to do preliminary testing of the FreeRadius installation. Configure a test user by creating the file */etc/freeradius/users.test* with the following content:

```
test1  Auth-Type := Local, User-Password == "secret"
        Reply-Message = "Hello, %u"
```

In the file, */etc/freeradius/users*, add the line:

```
$INCLUDE users.test
```

Hangup signal forces FreeRadius to reload its configuration files:

```
$ sudo killall --signal=HUP freeradius
```

Now we can test FreeRadius usng the `radtest` application (which is a wrapper for `radclient`):

```
radius$ radtest test1 secret localhost 1812 letmein
Sending Access-Request of id 161 to 127.0.0.1 port 1812
        User-Name = "test1"
        User-Password = "secret"
        NAS-IP-Address = 255.255.255.255
        NAS-Port = 1812
```

Now we run a test from a remote machine. We use the client host we created earlier. We need to install the FreeRadius package for the `radclient` and `radtest` applications. As we do not need TLS functionality in FreeRadius, we can simply install the package using the package management utility:

```
client$ sudo apt-get install freeradius
```

We do not want to run the RADIUS server on the client, so we shut it down:

```
client$ sudo /etc/init.d/freeradius stop
```

To prevent FreeRadius from starting up again when the host reboots, use the Debian runlevel configuration tool, `rcconf` (which can be installed in the usual way with the package management utility). The client machine (IP address 172.16.20.81) needs to be configured on the FreeRadius server as a RADIUS client. Add the following entry to the */etc/freeradius/clients.conf* file on the radius machine:

```
client 172.16.20.81 {
        secret          = letmein
        shortname       = sta
}
```

For this, test we show how to view the FreeRadius debugging information. First, we stop the current freeradius daemon:

```
radius$ sudo /etc/init.d/freeradius stop
```

Then, we run freeradius as a foreground process:

```
radius$ sudo /usr/sbin/freeradius -X
Starting - reading configuration files ...
reread_config:   reading radiusd.conf
Config:    including file: /etc/freeradius/proxy.conf
Config:    including file: /etc/freeradius/clients.conf
Config:    including file: /etc/freeradius/snmp.conf
Config:    including file: /etc/freeradius/eap.conf
Config:    including file: /etc/freeradius/sql.conf
   :
   :
Listening on authentication *:1812
Listening on accounting *:1813
Ready to process requests.
```

The `-X` option causes FreeRadius to output many lines of debugging messages. Run radclient on the client:

```
client$ radclient -f rad.conf 172.16.20.70 auth letmein
Received response ID 81, code 2, length = 38
        Reply-Message = "Hello, test1"
```

Note: we use radclient instead of radtest merely to demonstrate an alternative way of testing the FreeRadius account. On *radius* the FreeRadius server outputs the following debug messages:

```
rad_recv: Access-Request packet from host 172.16.20.81:
1024, id=156, length=49
        User-Name = "test1"
        User-Password = "secret"
```

```
  Processing the authorize section of radiusd.conf
modcall: entering group authorize for request 0
  modcall[authorize]: module "preprocess" returns ok
for request 0
  modcall[authorize]: module "chap" returns noop for
request 0
  modcall[authorize]: module "mschap" returns noop for
request 0
    rlm_realm: No '@' in User-Name = "test1", looking
up realm NULL
    rlm_realm: No such realm "NULL"
  modcall[authorize]: module "suffix" returns noop
for request 0
  rlm_eap: No EAP-Message, not doing EAP
  modcall[authorize]: module "eap" returns noop for
request 0
    users: Matched entry DEFAULT at line 152
    users: Matched entry test1 at line 1
  modcall[authorize]: module "files" returns ok for
request 0
modcall: leaving group authorize (returns ok) for
request 0
  rad_check_password:  Found Auth-Type Local
auth: type Local
auth: user supplied User-Password matches local
User-Password
radius_xlat:  'Hello, test1'
Sending Access-Accept of id 156 to 172.16.20.81 port
1024
        Reply-Message = "Hello, test1"
Finished request 0
```

8.3 Configure FreeRadius to use MySQL

Create a new virtual machine, *mysql*. Install mysql-server and mysql-client packages:

```
mysql$ sudo apt-get install mysql-server mysql-client
```

The password for the MySQL root account is not set at this point. For obvious security reasons, we assign one:

```
mysql$ mysqladmin --user=root password letmein
```

In */etc/mysql/my.cnf*, add the following lines to the [mysqld] section:

```
ssl-ca=/etc/mysql/cacert.pem
ssl-cert=/etc/mysql/mysql_cert.pem
ssl-key=/etc/mysql/mysql_key.pem
```

Also, in */etc/mysql/my.cnf*, make the following edit to the file:

```
bind-address                 = 172.16.20.79
```

Using the MySQL shell, we create the radius database. Run the `mysql` client:

```
mysql$ mysql --user=root --password=letmein
```

Create the database:

```
mysql> CREATE DATABASE radius;
```

Create a radius account and configure for SSL authentication:

```
mysql> GRANT ALL ON radius.* TO "radius"@"radius"
    -> IDENTIFIED BY "letmein"
    -> REQUIRE subject "/C=UK/ST=Wilts/O=WLAN/CN=radius"
    -> AND issuer "/C=UK/ST=Wilts/O=WLAN/CN=Root";
```

Flush the privileges and terminate the `mysql` session:

```
mysql> FLUSH PRIVILEGES;
mysql> exit
```

Restart the MySQL server:

```
mysql$ sudo /etc/init.d/mysql restart
```

Now, we need to configure *radius* to use the MySQL server. Install the *rad_cert.pem, rad_key.pem cacert.pem* files to the directory */etc/freeradius/certs*:

```
radius$ cd /etc/freeradius
radius$ sudo cp ~/rad_*.pem ~/cacert.pem certs
```

Add the lines below to the [client] section of the file */etc/mysql/my.cnf* (on radius):

```
ssl-ca=/etc/freeradius/certs/cacert.pem
ssl-cert=/etc/freeradius/certs/rad_cert.pem
ssl-key=/etc/freeradius/certs/rad_key.pem
```

Create the file, *random*:

```
radius$ sudo openssl rand -out random 128
```

Create the file, *dh*:

```
radius$ sudo openssl dhparam -check -text -5 -out dh
512 Generating DH parameters, 512 bit long safe prime,
generator 5
This is going to take a long time
```

```
. . . . . . . . . . . . . . . . . . . . . . . . . . . . . . . . . . . . . . . . . . . +. . . . . . .
. . . . . . . . . . . . . . . . .+. . . . . . . . . . . . . . . . . . . . . . . . . . . . . . . . .
     :
     :
. . . . . . . . . . . . . . . . . .+. . . . . . . . . . . .+. . . . . . . . . . . . . . . . . . . .
. . . . . .++*++*++*++*++*++*
DH parameters appear to be ok.
```

Change the owner and group (do this as superuser rather than using sudo):

```
$ sudo su
# cd /etc/freeradius
# chown root:freerad certs/rad_*.pem
# chown root:freerad certs/cacert.pem
# chown root:freerad {dh,random}
```

Change the permissions:

```
radius# chmod 0640 certs/rad_*.pem
radius# chmod 0640 certs/cacert.pem
radius# chmod 0640 {dh,random}
```

Exit from the superuser account:

```
radius# exit
```

Set the following parameters in the file */etc/freeradius/sql.conf*:

```
sql {
    :
        server = "172.16.20.70"
        login = "radius"
        password = "letmein"
        radius_db = "radius"
    :
}
```

Also in */etc/freeradius/sql.conf*, uncomment the line:

```
sql_user_name = "%{Stripped-User-Name:
-%{User-Name:-DEFAULT}}"
```

And comment out this one:

```
# sql_user_name = "%{User-Name}"
```

In the file */etc/freeradius/radiusd.conf*, uncomment the line in the authorize{} section:

```
sql
```

Also enable the sql setting in the accounting{} (and, optionally, in the session{} and apost-auth{} sections). In the authorize{} sectionm comment out the line:

```
# files
```

Under the [client] section in the file */etc/mysql/my.cnf*, enter the following lines:

```
ssl-ca=/etc/freeradius/certs/cacert.pem
ssl-cert=/etc/freeradius/certs/rad_cert.pem
ssl-key=/etc/freeradius/certs/rad_key.pem
```

We can run the following test to verify that the RADIUS server can connect to the radius database on the MySQL server. If the command returns the current data, then access to the MySQL server has been successful:

```
radius$ mysql --host=172.16.20.79 --user=radius \
> --password=letmein --execute="SELECT CURRENT_DATE();"
+----------------+
| CURRENT_DATE() |
+----------------+
| 2009-01-07     |
+----------------+
```

Create the tables for the radius database. There is a script in the FreeRadius source directory for this:

```
radius$ cd ~/src/freeradius-1.1.3/doc/examples
radius$ mysql --host=mysql --user=radius \
> --password=letmein < mysql.sql
```

To examine the tables created by the script *mysql.sql* (and confirm that it has run successfully), issue the following SQL statement:

```
$  mysql --host=172.16.20.79 --user=radius \
> --password=letmein radius --execute="SHOW TABLES;"
+------------------+
| Tables_in_radius |
+------------------+
| nas              |
| radacct          |
| radcheck         |
| radgroupcheck    |
| radgroupreply    |
| radpostauth      |
| radreply         |
| usergroup        |
+------------------+
```

Start FreeRadius in the foreground with debugging enabled:

```
radius$ sudo /usr/sbin/freeradius -X
```

8.4 Testing

Configure a test user in the tables of the radius database:

```
$  mysql --host=172.16.20.79 --user=radius \
> --password=letmein radius
```

Use the following SQL statement to enter the user, test2:

```
mysql> INSERT INTO radcheck
    -> (UserName, Attribute, op, Value)  VALUES
    -> ('test2','Password',':=', 'secret');
```

Specify the Repy-Message:

```
mysql> INSERT INTO radreply
    -> (UserName, Attribute, op, Value) VALUES
    -> ('test2','Reply-Message',':=', 'Hello, %u');
```

Run a test from the host machine *client*:

```
client$ radtest test2 secret 172.16.20.70 1812 letmein
Sending Access-Request of id 208 to 172.16.20.70 port
1812
        User-Name = "test2"
        User-Password = "secret"
        NAS-IP-Address = 255.255.255.255
        NAS-Port = 1812
rad_recv: Access-Accept packet from host 172.16.20.70:
1812, id=208, length=38
        Reply-Message = "Hello, test2"
```

The debug output from FreeRadius looks like this:

```
rad_recv: Access-Request packet from host 172.16.20.81:
1024, id=208, length=61
        User-Name = "test2"
        User-Password = "secret"
        NAS-IP-Address = 255.255.255.255
        NAS-Port = 1812
  Processing the authorize section of radiusd.conf
modcall: entering group authorize for request 0
  modcall[authorize]: module "preprocess" returns ok
for request 0
  modcall[authorize]: module "chap" returns noop for
request 0
  modcall[authorize]: module "mschap" returns noop for
request 0
    rlm_realm: No '@' in User-Name = "test2",
looking up realm NULL
```

```
    rlm_realm: No such realm "NULL"
  modcall[authorize]: module "suffix" returns noop for
request 0
    rlm_eap: No EAP-Message, not doing EAP
  modcall[authorize]: module "eap" returns noop for
request 0
radius_xlat:  'test2'
rlm_sql (sql): sql_set_user escaped user --> 'test2'
radius_xlat:  'SELECT id, UserName, Attribute, Value,
op            FROM radcheck          WHERE Username =
'test2'          ORDER BY id'
rlm_sql (sql): Reserving sql socket id: 4
radius_xlat:  'SELECT radgroupcheck.id,radgroupcheck.
GroupName,radgroupcheck.Attribute,radgroupcheck.Value,
radgroupcheck.op  FROM radgroupcheck,usergroup WHERE
usergroup.Username = 'test2' AND usergroup.
GroupName = radgroupcheck.GroupName ORDER BY
radgroupcheck.id'
radius_xlat:  'SELECT id, UserName, Attribute, Value,
op            FROM radreply          WHERE Username =
'test2'          ORDER BY id'
radius_xlat:  'SELECT radgroupreply.id,radgroupreply.
GroupName,radgroupreply.Attribute,radgroupreply.Value,
radgroupreply.op  FROM radgroupreply,usergroup WHERE
usergroup.Username = 'test2' AND usergroup.
GroupName = radgroupreply.GroupName ORDER BY
radgroupreply.id'
rlm_sql (sql): Released sql socket id: 4
  modcall[authorize]: module "sql" returns ok for
request 0
modcall: leaving group authorize (returns ok) for
request 0
auth: type Local
auth: user supplied User-Password matches local
User-Password
radius_xlat:  'Hello, test2'
Sending Access-Accept of id 208 to 172.16.20.81 port
1024
        Reply-Message := "Hello, test2"
Finished request 0
```

If this is unsuccessful, try running radtest locally on *radius*.

8.5 Configure EAP

Configure /etc/freeradius/radiusd.conf. In the `authorize{}` section, making sure the `eap` line is uncommented:

```
authorize {
    :
    eap
    :
}
```

Check that `eap` is also set in the `authenticate{}` section:

```
authenticate {
    :
    eap
    :
}
```

Check */etc/freeradius/eap.conf*:

```
eap {
    default_eap_type = md5
    md5 {
    }
}
```

In MySQL, insert table entries for wireless users. Configure test user `test3` with an authentication type of EAP:

```
mysql> INSERT INTO radcheck
    -> (UserName, Attribute, op, Value)
    -> VALUES ('test3','Auth-Type', ':=', 'EAP');
```

Configure the password for `test3`:

```
mysql> INSERT INTO radcheck
    -> (id, UserName, Attribute, op, Value) VALUES
    -> (6, 'test3','User-Password',':=', 'secret');
```

Send FreeRadius a hangup signal to force it to reload the radius database:

```
$ sudo killall --signal=HUP freeradius
```

Now we can test EAP with MD5 authentication using the `radeapclient`. Create a file (on the client machine), *md5.conf* with the content:

```
User-Name = "test3"                            ì
EAP-MD5-Password = "secret"
EAP-Type-Identity = "test3"
EAP-Code = Response
EAP-Id = 210
```

Run radeapclient:

```
client$ radeapclient -x 172.16.20.70 auth
letmein <md5.conf

+++> About to send encoded packet:
        User-Name = "test3"
        EAP-MD5-Password = "secret"
        EAP-Type-Identity = "test3"
        EAP-Code = Response
        EAP-Id = 210
        Message-Authenticator = 0x00
Sending Access-Request of id 68 to 172.16.20.70
port 1812
        User-Name = "test3"
        Message-Authenticator = 0x00000000000000000000000
00000000000
        EAP-Message = 0x02d2000a017465737433
rad_recv: Access-Challenge packet from host
172.16.20.70:1812, id=68, length=80
        EAP-Message = 0x01d30016041054e878544ca74d5ea3c
6a9309534b2d2
        Message-Authenticator = 0x43c1911b9da95d9665ae5
9e9958ec1cf
        State = 0x76385576c0744e98d52fd4552f83c217
<+++ EAP decoded packet:
        EAP-Message = 0x01d30016041054e878544ca74d5ea3c
6a9309534b2d2
        Message-Authenticator = 0x43c1911b9da95d9665ae5
9e9958ec1cf
        State = 0x76385576c0744e98d52fd4552f83c217
        EAP-Id = 211
        EAP-Code = Request
        EAP-Type-MD5 = 0x1054e878544ca74d5ea3c6a9309534
b2d2

+++> About to send encoded packet:
        User-Name = "test3"
        EAP-MD5-Password = "secret"
        EAP-Code = Response
        EAP-Id = 211
        Message-Authenticator = 0x00000000000000000000000
00000000000
        EAP-Type-MD5 = 0x1034f472cd292173a3ba32c068d783
c7d0
        State = 0x76385576c0744e98d52fd4552f83c217
```

```
Sending Access-Request of id 69 to 172.16.20.70 port
1812
        User-Name = "test3"
        Message-Authenticator = 0x00000000000000000000000
00000000000
        State = 0x76385576c0744e98d52fd4552f83c217
        EAP-Message = 0x02d30016041034f472cd292173a3ba3
2c068d783c7d0
rad_recv: Access-Accept packet from host 172.16.20.70:
1812, id=69, length=51
        EAP-Message = 0x03d30004
        Message-Authenticator = 0x04e2f53c1e293e957ecb6
81e95eca0ee
        User-Name = "test3"
<+++ EAP decoded packet:
        EAP-Message = 0x03d30004
        Message-Authenticator = 0x04e2f53c1e293e957ecb6
81e95eca0ee
        User-Name = "test3"
        EAP-Id = 211
        EAP-Code = Success
```

We can see from the last line of the debug output that the authentication was successful.

8.6 Configure TLS

Edit */etc/freeradius/eap.conf* and configure the default EAP type to tls:

```
default_eap_type = tls
```

Also (in */etc/freeradius/eap.conf*), configure the tls{} section:

```
tls {
    private_key_password = letmein
    private_key_file = ${raddbdir}/certs/rad_key.pem
    certificate_file = ${raddbdir}/certs/rad_cert.pem
    CA_file = ${raddbdir}/certs/demoCA/cacert.pem
    dh_file = ${raddbdir}/dh
    random_file = ${raddbdir}/random
    fragment_size = 1024
    include_length = yes
}
```

On the MySQL server (*mysql* run the mysql client command:

```
mysql$ mysql --user=radius --password=letmein radius
```

Create an account in the database for *sta*:

```
mysql> INSERT INTO radcheck
    -> (UserName, Attribute, op, Value) VALUES
    -> ('sta','Auth-Type', ':=', 'EAP');
```

Add an entry to the database so that the default action is to reject the request:

```
mysql> INSERT INTO radcheck
    -> (id, UserName, Attribute, op, Value)
    -> VALUES (100000, 'DEFAULT','Auth-Type',':=',
    -> 'Reject');
mysql> INSERT INTO radreply
    -> (id, UserName, Attribute, op, Value)
    -> VALUES (100000, 'DEFAULT','Reply-Message', '=',
    -> '%u not authorised');
```

Force FreeRadius to reload the configuration files and the radius database:

```
$ sudo killall --signal=HUP freeradius
```

8.7 NAS Configuration

In this section we demonstrate hoe to configure the access-point controller to act as a NAS. In this example, we use the Alcatel-Lucent Omniaccess controller. In configuration mode, specify the RADIUS server:

```
aaa authentication-server radius radius
   host 172.16.20.70
   key letmein
   enable
```

Configure the server group:

```
aaa server-group rsn-server-group
   auth-server radius
```

Set AAA authentication:

```
aaa authentication dot1x rsn-dot1x
```

Configure the AAA profile:

```
aaa profile rsn-aaa-profile
   authentication-dot1x rsn-dot1x
   dot1x-server-group rsn-server-group
```

Specify the SSID profile. Here, we define the ESSID to be "wlan":

```
wlan ssid-profile rsn-ssid-profile
   essid wlan
   opmode wpa2-aes
```

Set up the virtual AP:

```
wlan virtual-ap rsn-ap
   ssid-profile "rsn-ssid-profile"
   vlan 1001
   aaa-profile "rsn-aaa-profile"
```

Specify the `rsn-ap` virtual access-point as part of the `wlan` ap-group:

```
ap-group wlan
   virtual-ap "rsn-ap"
```

View the RADIUS server details:

```
# show aaa authentication-server radius radius

RADIUS Server "radius"
--------------------------
Parameter      Value
---------      -----
Host           172.16.20.70
Key            ********
Auth Port      1812
Acct Port      1813
Retransmits    3
Timeout        5 sec
NAS ID         N/A
NAS IP         N/A
Use MD5        Disabled
Mode           Enabled
```

From the NAS (Omniaccess controller), test the radius server:

```
(al-ctl) #aaa test-server pap radius test2 secret

Authentication successful
```

8.8 Wireless Client

The result of the scan below shows that the `wlan` SSID is active. Note, however, that the scan reveals two instances of `wlan` (one for 802.11bg and one for 802.11a). This is because we are using a dual radio access-point:

```
sta$ iwlist eth1 scan
eth1      Scan completed :
          Cell 01 - Address: 00:1A:1E:86:13:A0
                    ESSID:"wlan" Protocol:IEEE
                    802.11bg Mode:Master Channel:11
```

```
                              Encryption key:on Bit Rates:1
                              Mb/s; 2 Mb/s; 5.5 Mb/s; 11 Mb/s;
                              6 Mb/s
                                        9 Mb/s; 12 Mb/s;
                                        18 Mb/s; 24 Mb/s; 36
                                        Mb/s 48 Mb/s; 54 Mb/s
                              Quality=95/100  Signal level=-33
                              dBm  Noise level=-33 dBm IE:
                              IEEE 802.11i/WPA2 Version 1
                                   Group Cipher : CCMP
                                   Pairwise Ciphers (1) : CCMP
                                   Authentication Suites (1)
                                   : 802.1X
                              Extra: Last beacon: 1660ms ago
                    Cell 02 - Address: 00:1A:1E:86:13:B0
                              ESSID:"wlan" Protocol:IEEE
                              802.11a Mode:Master Channel:40
                              Encryption key:on Bit Rates:6
                              Mb/s; 9 Mb/s; 12 Mb/s; 18 Mb/s;
                              24 Mb/s
                                        36 Mb/s; 48 Mb/s;
                                        54 Mb/s
                              Quality=83/100  Signal level=-51
                              dBm  Noise level=-75 dBm IE:
                              IEEE 802.11i/WPA2 Version 1
                                   Group Cipher : CCMP
                                   Pairwise Ciphers (1) : CCMP
                                   Authentication Suites (1)
                                   : 802.1X
```

Create a directory to work in:

```
sta$ mkdir rsn
sta$ cd rsn
```

Copy the *sta_cert.pem*, *sta_req.pem* and *cacert.pem* files over to the wireless client (place in the *rsn* directory). Create a configuration file *wlan.conf* for the wireless supplicant:

```
# WPA2-EAP/CCMP using EAP-TLS

ctrl_interface=/var/run/wpa_supplicant

network={
        ssid="wlan"
        identity="sta"
        key_mgmt=WPA-EAP
```

```
        proto=WPA2
        pairwise=CCMP
        group=CCMP
        eap=TLS
        ca_cert="cacert.pem"
        client_cert="sta_cert.pem"
        private_key="sta_key.pem"
        private_key_passwd="certsecret"
}
```

Run the supplicant with the command-line:

```
$ sudo wpa_supplicant -Dwext -ieth1 -cwlan.conf
```

The `wpa_supplicant` command above generates many lines of output. If authentication has been successful the last few lines of the output should resemble:

```
CTRL-EVENT-EAP-SUCCESS EAP authentication completed
successfully
WPA: Key negotiation completed with 00:1a:1e:86:13:a0
[PTK=CCMP GTK=CCMP]
CTRL-EVENT-CONNECTED - Connection to 00:1a:1e:86:13:a0
completed (auth) [id=0 id_str=]
```

The results of the `iwconfig` command on the device below indicates that the authentication (and association) has been successful:

```
sta$ wconfig eth1
eth1      IEEE 802.11g  ESSID:"wlan"
          Mode:Managed  Frequency:2.462 GHz  Access
          Point: 00:1A:1E:86:13:A0 Bit Rate:54
          Mb/s   Tx-Power:15 dBm Retry limit:15
          RTS thr:off  Fragment thr:off Power
          Management:off Link Quality=92/100  Signal
          level=-37 dBm  Noise level=-38 dBm Rx
          invalid nwid:0  Rx invalid crypt:0  Rx
          invalid frag:0 Tx excessive retries:0
          Invalid misc:3073   Missed beacon:0
```

This merely indicates that the initial open system authentication has been successful. Confirmation of open system authentication can be gathered from the AP controller:

```
(al-ctl) #show ap association

Flags: W: WMM client, A: Active, R: RRM client

PHY Details: HT: High throughput; 20: 20MHz; 40: 40MHz
```

```
            <n>ss: <n> spatial streams

Association Table
----------------
Name                  bssid                 mac
----                  -----                 ---
00:1a:1e:c0:61:3a  00:1a:1e:86:13:a0  00:18:de:a5:ca:c2


auth  assoc  aid  l-int  essid  vlan-id  tunnel-id
----  -----  ---  -----  -----  -------  ---------
y     y      1    10     wlan   1001     0x108a


phy  assoc. time  num assoc  Flags
---  -----------  ---------  -----
g    22m:28s      2          A
```

Num Clients:1

A successful open system authentication allows the device to associate. This does not necessarily mean that the 802.1X authentication has succeeded. If 802.1X has failed, user data will not be forwarded (regardless of a successful open system authentication). We can gather further information from the controller. The command below displays the supplicant information for 802.1X. The results show that the 802.1X authentication has succeeded:

```
(al-ctl) #show dot1x supplicant-info list-all

802.1x User Information
-----------------------
      MAC              Name     Auth   AP-MAC
-----------          --------   ----   ------
      Enc-Key/Type
------------------
00:18:de:a5:ca:c2   sta


 Auth-Mode      EAP-Type   Remote
-----------    ---------   ------
   Yes     00:1a:1e:86:13:a0


* * * * * * * */WPA2-AES  Explict Mode  EAP-TLS    No
```

Station Entries: 1

Now that 802.1X authentication has been successful, we can obtain an IP address (default route and DNS server) using DHCP:

```
$ sudo dhclient eth1
```

8.9 Summary

In this chapter, we described how to set up a robust security network. We used FreeRadius as the authentication server. User accounting information was stored in a MySQL database running on a separate server. In order to protect the exchange of messages between RADIUS and database servers and prevent eavedropping, we configured MySQL to use SSL. The other benefit of SSL is that authentication between the two servers require shared password and digital certificate verification.

EAP-TLS was implemented as it requires mutual authentication between the wireless client and the authentication (RADIUS) server. WPA2 was specified to ensure the strongest encryption (AES).

Chapter 9
MAC Layer Performance Analysis

In this chapter, we present a number of mathematical models of the 802.11 MAC sub-layer and show how to build them using Maple. Using these models, we carry out an analysis of the effects of the 802.11 MAC on performance.

9.1 Fragmentation

In a "hostile" RF environment, fragmentation can mitigate the harmful effects of frame loss. Conversely, excessive fragmentation introduces high levels of overhead. The maximum size of a MSDU is 2304 octets. The fragmentation threshold determines the maximum size of the MPDU (but is limited to 2312 octets). Setting the fragmentation threshold (and, thus, the maximum size of the MPDU) effectively disables fragmentation. The degree of fragmentation increases as the fragmentation threshold decreases below the maximum size of the MSDU. Fragmentation with the MAC sub-layer was described in Sect. 3.3.5 below.

The following analysis examines the trade-off introduced in setting the fragmentation threshold. Consider the transmission of an MSDU over a wireless network. The probability of an MSDU transmission failure P_{msdu}, is given by the expression:

$$F_{msdu} = 1 - (1 - (F_{mpdu})^{M-1})^N \qquad (9.1)$$

Equation (9.1) is implemented in Maple with the function:

```
> Fmsdu := (M,N, Fmpdu) -> 1 - (1 - Fmpdu^(M-1))^N:
```

The expression below produces the graph shown in Fig. 9.1. It shows the probability of MSDU transmission failure (F_{msdu}) for values of N (number of fragments per MSDU) between 2 and 12 and M (maximum retransmission attempts) fixed at 7.

```
> plot3d(Fmsdu(7,n,p), n=2..12, p=0..1,
    labels=["N", "Fmpdu", "Fmsdu"], labeldirections=
```

A. Holt, C.-Y. Huang, *802.11 Wireless Networks,*
Computer Communications and Networks,
DOI 10.1007/978-1-84996-275-9_9, © Springer-Verlag London Limited 2010

Fig. 9.1 Probability of
MSDU transmission failure.
The maximum number of
fragments, N, varies between
2 and 12. The maximum
retransmission attempts is set
to $M = 7$

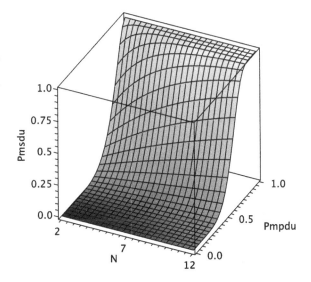

```
["horizontal", "horizontal", "vertical"],
axes=BOXED);
```

It can be seen that the probability of MSDU transmission failure is small (less than 0.0082) as long as the MPDU loss rate P_{mpdu} does not exceed 0.4. The probability of MSDU transmission failure, however, rises steeply as P_{mpdu} increases above 0.4.

Figure 9.2 shows the P_{msdu} for values of M between 3 and 10 and N set to 5. The Maple expression below produces the graph in Fig. 9.2.

```
> plot3d(Fmsdu(m,5,p), m=3..10, p=0..1,
    labels=["M", "Fmpdu", "Fmsdu"], labeldirections=
    ["horizontal", "horizontal", "vertical"], axes=BOXED);
```

9.2 Analysis of Multiple Hops

In a mesh environment, the path between a user device and the wired network infrastructure may consist of multiple wireless links. Here, we present an analysis of the successful frame transmission rates over a multi-hop wireless mesh network. The probability of a frame successfully traversing multiple wireless links l (based on the BER theoretical perspective in [35]) is given by:

$$P_{links} = (1 - F_{msdu})^l \qquad (9.2)$$

Where F_{msdu} is defined in (9.1) above. The P_{links} function is implemented in Maple thus:

```
> Plinks := (M,N,Fmpdu,l) -> (1-Fmsdu(M,N,Fmpdu)) ^ l:
```

Fig. 9.2 Probability of
MSDU transmission failure.
The maximum retransmission
attempts M varies between 3
and 10. The maximum
number of fragments is set to
$N = 5$

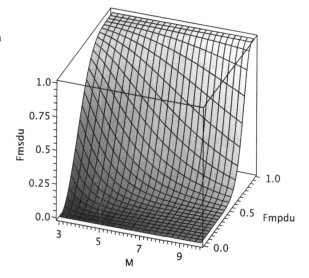

Fig. 9.3 Probability of
successful frame transmission
over multiple wireless links

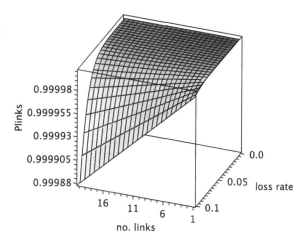

The graph in Fig. 9.3 shows the frame transmission success probability as a function of the number of links and F_{msdu}. The retransmission limit is set to $M = 7$ and the (average) number of fragments is $N = 6$. The graph is rendered with the command:

```
> plot3d(Plinks(7,6,p,l), l=1..20, p=0..0.1,
  axes=BOXED, labels=["no. links", "loss rate",
  "Plinks"],
  labeldirections=["horizontal", "horizontal",
  "vertical"]);
```

The results show that, the fragmentation/retransmission mechanism is quite reliable. Even for 20 links and a frame fragmentation loss rate of 10%, the probability of frame success is quite high ($P_{\text{links}} \approx 0.99$). This is due to the high retransmission limit of $M = 7$. For $M = 4$, the probability of a successful frame transmission is much lower: $P_{\text{links}} \approx 0.89$. There is a cost associated with reliability, in that a high number of retransmissions, will add to the transmission delay of the frame.

9.3 Throughput

When a device sends data, it is transmitted as one or more MSDUs, depending upon the size of the data message. The MSDUs, in turn, are encapsulated in MPDUs. If the size of an MSDU exceeds the maximum MPDU size, the MSDU is fragmented and sent as multiple MPDUs. Here, we define a set of generic functions for fragmenting messages. Consider a message of size s and a fragmentation threshold f. When the message undergoes fragmentation, it is divided into zero or more fragments of size f plus a runt fragment of size $0 \leq s_{\text{runt}} < f$. The number of fragments n_{frag} (of size f) is given by:

$$n_{\text{frag}} = \lfloor s/f \rfloor \tag{9.3}$$

The size of the runt fragment is:

$$s_{\text{runt}} = s \mod f \tag{9.4}$$

n_{frags} and s_{runt} are implemented by the Maples functions below: Number of (additional) fragments:

```
> nfrags := (s,f) -> trunc(s/f);
```

$$\text{nfrags} := (s, f) \rightarrow \text{trunc}\left(\frac{s}{f}\right)$$

```
> runt := (s,f) -> s mod f;
```

$$\text{runt} := (s, f) \rightarrow s \mod f$$

To transmit a message of size s, the number of MSDUs of maximum size (MSDUsize) is given by the function:

```
> nmsdu := (s) -> nfrags(s, MSDUsize);
```

$$\text{nmsdu} := s \rightarrow \text{nfrags}(s, \text{MSDUsize})$$

The size of the MSDU runt is given by:

```
> msdurunt := s -> runt(s, MSDUsize);
```

$$\text{msdurunt} := s \rightarrow \text{runt}(s, \text{MSDUsize})$$

The function below generates a sequence of MSDU sizes for a given message of size s:

```
> msduseq := (s) -> piecewise((s mod MSDUsize) = 0,
      [seq(MSDUsize, i=1..nmsdu(s))],
      [seq(MSDUsize, i=1..nmsdu(s)), msdurunt(s)]);
```

$$\text{msduseq} := s \to \text{piecewise}(s \bmod \text{MSDUsize} = 0,$$
$$[\text{seq}(\text{MSDUsize}, i = 1 \ldots \text{nmsdu}(s))],$$
$$[\text{seq}(\text{MSDUsize}, i = 1 \ldots \text{nmsdu}(s)), \text{msdurunt}(s)])$$

Define the maximum size of an MSDU (in bits):

```
> MSDUsize := 8 * 2304:
```

$$\text{MSDUsize} := 18432$$

The transmission of a 4 kilobyte message (32768 bits) results in two MSDUs, one 18432 bits in size (equal to MSDUsize) and one of 14336 bits (the runt MSDU because it is less than the MSDUsize):

```
> msduseq(32768);
```

$$[18432, 14336]$$

An MSDU may be fragmented further into multiple MPDUs, resulting in zero or more fragments The number of MPDUs is given by:

```
> nmpdu := (s) -> nfrags(s, MPDUsize);
```

$$\text{nmpdu} := s \to \text{nfrags}(s, \text{MPDUsize})$$

Where MPDUsize is the maximum size of an MPDU. The function for the runt MPDU :

```
> mpdurunt := (s) -> runt(s, MPDUsize);
```

$$\text{mpdurunt} := s \to \text{runt}(s, \text{MPDUsize})$$

The function below generates a sequence of MPDUs

```
> mpduseq := (s) -> piecewise((s mod MPDUsize) = 0,
      [seq(MPDUsize, i=1..nmpdu(s))],
      [seq(MPDUsize, i=1..nmpdu(s)), mpdurunt(s)]);
```

$$\text{mpduseq} := s \to \text{piecewise}(s \bmod \text{MPDUsize} = 0,$$
$$[\text{seq}(\text{MPDUsize}, i = 1..\text{nmpdu}(s))],$$
$$[\text{seq}(\text{MPDUsize}, i = 1..\text{nmpdu}(s)), \text{mpdurunt}(s)])$$

If we set the maximum MPDU size (MPDUsize) higher than the MSDUsize, then the MSDUs will not be fragmented. Set the MPDUsize to 18496 bits:

```
> MPDUsize := 8 * 2312;
```

$$\text{MPDUsize} := 18496$$

Comparing the results above with the sequence of MPDUs, we can see that the number and size of the MPDUs is the same as the sequence of MSDUs:

```
> mpduseq(32768);
```

$$[[18432], [14336]]$$

If, however, we set the MPDUsize to a value less than the MSDUsize, the fragmentation of MSDUs will occur:

```
> MPDUsize := 8 * 1500;
```

$$\text{MPDUsize} := 12000$$

The sequence of MPDUs is given by:

```
> F1 := mpsduseq(FILESIZE);
```

$$F1 := [[12000, 6432], [12000, 2336]]$$

Each MPDU needs to be acknowledged. The function below appends an acknowledgment frame to a sequence of MPDUs:

```
> addack := (q) -> [seq(op([q[i],ACKsize]), i in q)];
```

$$> \text{addack} := q \rightarrow [\text{seq}(\text{op}([q_i, \text{ACKsize}]), i \ \epsilon \ q)]$$

Define the size of the acknowledgment frame in bits:

```
> ACKsize := 112:
```

Show the sequence of MPDUs with acknowledgments:

```
> F2 := map(addack, F1);
```

$$F2 := [[12000, 112, 6432, 112], [12000, 112, 2336, 112]]$$

In RTS/CTS mode, and MSDU (and its corresponding sequence of MPDUs) is proceeded by an RTS and CTS frame. Define RTS and CTS frame sizes (in bits):

```
> RTSsize := 160:
> CTSsize := 112:
```

The function below prepends an RTS/CTS sequence to each MSDU sequence of MPDUs:

```
> rtscts := (q) -> map(op, [[RTSsize, CTSsize],q]);
```

$$\text{rtscts} := q \rightarrow \text{map}(\text{op}, [[\text{RTSsize}, \text{CTSsize}], q])$$

The sequence of frames in RTS/CTS mode is given by:

```
> F3 := map(rtscts,F2);
```

$$F3 := [[160, 112, 12000, 112, 6432, 112], [160, 112, 12000, 112, 2336, 112]]$$

Now, we calculate the transmission time of each frame in the sequence. The frame transmission time will depend upon the transmission rate over the wireless channel. The function below returns transmission rate for a given mode of 802.11b:

```
txrate := (mode) -> piecewise(mode=1,   1000000,
                              mode=2,   2000000,
                              mode=3,   5500000,
                              mode=4, 11000000,
                                        1000000);
```

$$\text{txrate} := \text{mode} \to \text{piecewise}(\text{mode} = 1, 1000000, \text{mode} = 2, 2000000,$$
$$\text{mode} = 3, 5500000, \text{mode} = 4, 11000000, 1000000)$$

Each MAC frame is appended to a PLCP preamble and a PLCP header. The size of those headers (in bits) is defined below:

```
> PREAMBLEsize := 144;
```

$$\text{PREAMBLEsize} := 144$$

```
> PLCPsize := 48;
```

$$\text{PLCPsize} := 48$$

In order to interoperate with legacy forms of 802.11, the PLCP preamble and header are transmitted at either 1 or 2 Mb/s, regardless of the transmission rate of the MPDU body. The max(2,mode) term ensure that the preamble transmission speed is capped at 2 Mb/s. The PLCP preamble transmission time is defined as:

```
> tPLCPpreamble := (mode) -> PREAMBLEsize /
                             txrate(max(2,mode));
```

$$\text{tPLCPpreamble} := \text{mode} \to \frac{\text{PREAMBLEsize}}{\text{txrate}(\max(2, \text{mode}))}$$

Similarly, the function of the PLCP header transmission time is given by:

```
> tPLCPheader := PLCPheader / txrate(max(2,PLCPmode));
```

$$\text{tPLCPheader} := \text{mode} \to \frac{\text{PLCPsize}}{\text{txrate}(\max(2, \text{mode}))}$$

The function below gives the transmission delay of a MAC frame:

```
> txdelay := (data, mode) -> tPLCPpreamble
             + tPLCPheader
             + (data+FRAMEheader+FCS)/txrate(mode);
```

$$\text{txdelay} := (\text{data}, \text{mode}) \to \text{tPLCPpreamble}(\text{PLCPmode})$$
$$+ \text{tPLCPheader}(\text{PMCPmode})$$
$$+ \frac{\text{data} + \text{FRAMEheader} + \text{FCS}}{\text{txrate}(\text{mode})}$$

The *FRAMEheader* term is the size (in bits) of a MAC frame header, it defined as:

```
> FRAMEheader := 224;
```

$$\text{FRAMEheader} := 224$$

We also need a 32-bit frame check sequence:

```
> FCS := 32;
```

$$\text{FCS} := 32$$

The function *framedelay* applies the *txdelay* function to a sequence MAC frames:

```
> framedelay := (q, mode) -> [seq(map(txdelay, i, mode),
  i in q)];
```

$$\text{framedelay} := (q, \text{mode}) \rightarrow [\text{seq}(\text{map}(\text{txdelay}, q_i, \text{mode}), i \in q))]$$

We compute the sequence of delays involved in transmitting a frame (*framedelay*) with the statement:

```
> D1 := framedelay(F3,3);
```

$$D1 := \left[\left[\frac{59}{343750}, \frac{28}{171875}, \frac{799}{343750}, \frac{28}{171875}, \frac{41}{31250}, \frac{21}{171875} \right], \right.$$
$$\left. \left[\frac{59}{343750}, \frac{28}{171875}, \frac{799}{343750}, \frac{28}{171875}, \frac{41}{31250}, \frac{21}{171875} \right] \right]$$

We are fortunate to have, from an unrelated research project, an empirical value for WLAN frame latency (ϕ). We derive frame latency as a function of the distance between wireless devices. In [2], time-of-flight (TOF) measurements were presented for frames over a wireless channel. The TOF of a frame between two wireless devices with negligible separation was 410 clock ticks, where, for a 44 MHz clock, one clock tick is approximately 0.023 μs. We define the CLOCKtick term:

```
> CLOCKtick := 1/44000000
```

$$\text{CLOCKtick} := \frac{1}{44000000}$$

Each time the distance between two nodes was increased by 3.4 meters; the round trip TOF increased by one clock tick. The distance that the signal travels in one (44 MHz) clock tick is 6.8 meters, therefore the signal travels 3.4 meters per half a clock tick. Define a function for latency:

```
> latency := (d) -> CLOCKtick * (410 + (d)/3.4)/2;
```

$$\text{latency} := d \rightarrow \text{CLOCKtick}\left(410 + \frac{d}{3.4}\right)$$

```
L20 := latency(20);
```

$$L20 := 0.000009451871657$$

Define the DIFS and SIFS times:

```
> aDIFSTime := 50/milliseconds;
```

$$\text{aDIFSTime} := \frac{1}{20000}$$

```
> aSIFSTime := 10/milliseconds;
```

$$\text{aSIFSTime} := \frac{1}{100000}$$

After waiting for a DIFS, the transmitting device initiates a back-off period. We use the analysis in [16] to derive a value for the average backoff interval t_{backoff}:

$$t_{\text{backoff}} = \sum_{i=1}^{k} \phi(i) \frac{\text{CW}_i}{2} \cdot \text{aSlotTime} \tag{9.5}$$

where, k is the maximum number of retries, aSlottime is the slot time and $\phi(i)$ is the probability of a successful frame transmission after the ith attempt:

$$\phi(i) = (1 - P_s)^{i-1} P_s \tag{9.6}$$

P_s is the probability that a frame is successfully transmitted and is given by:

$$P_s = p_s^{\text{rts}} p_s^{\text{data}} \tag{9.7}$$

p_s is the probability of a successful RTS/CTS exchange:

$$p_s^{\text{rts}} = (1 - p_e^{\text{rts}})(1 - p_e^{\text{cts}})(1 - p_c^{\text{rts}}) \tag{9.8}$$

p_s is the probability of a successful data/acknowledgment frame exchange:

$$p_s^{\text{data}} = (1 - p_e^{\text{data}})(1 - p_e^{\text{ack}}) \tag{9.9}$$

where:

- p_e^{rts} is the RTS frame error rate (FER)
- p_e^{cts} is the CTS frame FER
- p_c^{rts} is the RTS collision rate
- p_e^{data} is the data frame error rate
- p_e^{ack} is the acknowledgment frame error rate

For the purpose of illustration, we give values to the FERs. The FER for the data frame is set higher because data frames are typically higher than management frame. Otherwise, the settings are somewhat arbitrary, and chosen for convenience:

```
> perts  := 0.00001:
> pects  := 0.00001:
> peack  := 0.00001:
> pedata := 0.0001:
```

We also set the RTS frame collision rate:

```
> pcrts := 0.000001:
```

Calculate p_s^{rts}:

```
> psrts := (1 - perts) * (1 - pects) * (1 - pcrts);
```

$$p_s^{rts} := 0.9999790001$$

Calculate p_s^{data}:

```
> psdata := (1 - pedata) * (1 - peack);
```

$$p_s^{data} := 0.999890001$$

Calculate P_s:

```
> Ps := psrts * psdata;
```

$$P_s := 0.9998690034$$

The function for $\phi(i)$ (9.6) is given by:

```
> phi := (i) -> P_s * (1 - P_s)^(i-1); phi(4);
```

$$\phi(i) := i \to (1 - P_s)^{i-1} P_s$$

Set CWmin and CWmax:

```
> CWmin := 31;
```

$$CWmin := 31$$

```
> CWmax := 1023
```

$$CWmax := 1023$$

$CW(i)$ is defined as:

```
> CW := (i) -> min(2^{(i-1)} * (CWmin+1) - 1, CWmax);
```

$$CW := i \to \min(2^{(i} - 1)(CWmin + 1) - 1, CWmax);$$

Define a function for the average back-off interval:

```
> tBackoff := (k) -> sum(aSlotTime * phi(i) * CW(i)/2,
                          i=1..k);
```

$$tBackoff := k \to \sum_{i=1}^{i=k} \frac{1}{2} aSlotTime\phi(i)CW(i)$$

These delays are incorporated into the function below:

```
> adddelays := (q) -> map(op, [[aDIFSTime,tBackoff(7),
                          q[1]], seq([aSIFSTime,i, L20],
                          i in q[2..-1])]);
```

$$addelays := q \to map(op, [\,[aDIFSTime, tBackoff(7), q_1], \\ seq([aSIFSTime, q_i, L20], i \in q_{2\,..\,-1})]);$$

Calculate the delays:

```
> D2 := map(adddelays,D1):
```

Calculate the total delay in sending the file:

```
> DT := add(i, i in map(op, D2));
```

$$DT := 0.009225427811$$

Procedure returns delays for all four modes:

```
> Delay := proc(msgsize)
    local mode,delays,F1,F2,D1;
    delays := [];
    for mode in [1,2,3,4]
    do
      F1 := map(addack, frameseq(msgsize));
      F2 := map(rtscts,F1);
      D1 := map(adddelays,framedelay(F2, mode));
      delays := [op(delays), [txrate(mode)/megabits,
                add(d, d in map(op, D1))]];
    end do;
    return delays;
  end proc:
```

Calculate the delay to send a 10 megabyte file for each mode in 802.11b; that is, at 1, 2, 5.5 and 11 Mb/s:

```
> delays := Delay(8*10*2^10);
```

$$delays := \left[[1, 0.09097819910], [2, 0.04649819910], \left[\frac{11}{2}, 0.01819274451\right], \right.$$
$$\left. [11, 0.01010547177] \right]$$

The MPDUSize is set to 2312 bytes, so there is no fragmentation. Create a graph plot of delay against mode:

```
> G1 := pointplot(delays, connect=true,
  labeldirections=["horizontal", "vertical"],
  labels=["rate (Mb/s)", "delay (s)"], legend=[2312],
  linestyle=SOLID, color=black,font=[times,roman,12]):
```

Change the MPDUsize to 1024 so that the MSDUs are fragmented. Create a graph plot:

```
> MPDUsize := 8 * 1024:
> G2 := pointplot(Delay(8*10*2^10), connect=true,
  labeldirections=["horizontal", "vertical"],
  labels=["rate (Mb/s)", "delay (s)"], legend=[1024],
  linestyle=DASH, color=black,font=[times,roman,12]):
```

Change the MPDUsize to 512, and create a graph plot:

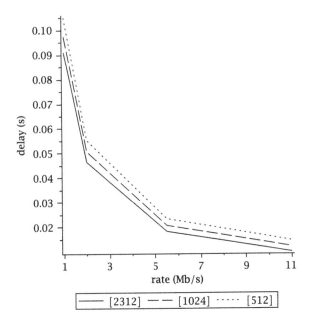

Fig. 9.4 File transfer times for varying degrees of fragmentation

```
> MPDUsize := 8 * 512:
> G3 := pointplot(Delay(8*10*2^10), connect=true,
  labeldirections=["horizontal", "vertical"],
  labels=["rate (Mb/s)", "delay (s)"], legend=[512],
  linestyle=DOT, color=black,font=[times,roman,12]):
```

The statement below produces the graph shown in Fig. 9.4:

```
> display(G1,G2,G3);
```

9.4 Summary

We have presented a number of models of the 802.11 MAC sub-layer in this chapter. Using Maple, we have used them to investigate the effects of the MAC on performance. First, we investigated the reliability of frame delivery with respect to the retransmission and fragmentation thresholds.

Finally, we developed a model of the DCF using collision avoidance (RTS/CTS) and analysed the effects of different fragmentation thresholds on performance.

Chapter 10
Link Rate Adaptation

Many factors affect the performance of a wireless communication channel; namely, protocol overhead, congestion and link speed. In this chapter, we focus on the speed of the wireless link. Wireless link speeds are governed by the effects of the environment on the transmitted signal.

802.11b is capable of transmitting at 11 Mb/s. Transmitters can drop the link speed to 5.5, 2 or 1 Mb/s depending upon the quality of the channel. Similarly, 802.11a/g are capable of 54 Mb/s, but can drop the speed to 48, 36, 24, 18, 12, 11, 9 or 6 Mb/s. This function is called link rate adaptation. There is no link rate adaptation scheme specified in the 802.11 standard. Link rate adaptation is, therefore, vendor dependent. Nevertheless, link rates will be selected based upon the received signal strength and noise.

In this chapter, we present a number of models for radio signal loss. We incorporate these loss models into link rate adaptation models in order to analyse the affect of RF conditions on the link speeds.

10.1 Walffish-Ikegami Model

In this section, we present the Walfish-Ikegami Model loss model, which applies to urban environments, where the path loss is given by:

$$L_{wi} = FSPL + 10\log_{10}(W) + 10\log_{10}(f) + 20\log_{10}(\Delta h_m) + L(\phi) \qquad (10.1)$$

The parameters and values used are described below:

W: street width (10 m)
f: carrier frequency (2.412 GHz)
Δh_m: average roof top height above mobile antenna (2 m)

A. Holt, C.-Y. Huang, *802.11 Wireless Networks,*
Computer Communications and Networks,
DOI 10.1007/978-1-84996-275-9_10, © Springer-Verlag London Limited 2010

$L(\phi)$ is the loss due to the angle of incident to the road ϕ and is given by:

$$L(\phi) = \begin{cases} -10 + 0.354 * \phi & 0° \le \phi < 35° \\ 2.5 + 0.075(\phi - 35) & 35° \le \phi < 55° \\ 4 - 0.114(\phi - 55) & 35° \le \phi < 55° \end{cases} \qquad (10.2)$$

The WI function is the Maple representation of L_{wi}:

```
> WI := (f,d,W,phi,dh) -> FSPL(f,d,K) - 16.9 +
  10*log10(W) + 10*log10(f) + 20*log10(dh) + L(phi);
```

$$WI := (f, d, \phi, K) \rightarrow FSPL(f, d, \phi, K) - 16.9 + 10\log_{10}(W)$$
$$+ 10\log_{10}(f) + 20\log_{10}(hd) + L(\phi)$$

The free-space loss term FSPL, is defined in Sect. 2.2.1. The constant K determines the units for frequency and distance. In this example, frequency and distance are in MHz and meters, respectively, thus:

```
> K := 20*log10(4*Pi*MHz/c): evalf(K);
```

$$-27.55221678$$

We define the $L(\phi)$:

```
L := (phi) -> piecewise(0 <= phi and phi < 35, -10
    + 0.354*phi, 35<= phi and phi < 55, 2.5 + 0.075
    * (phi - 35), 55 <= phi and phi <= 90, 4 -
    (0.114 * (phi - 55)));
```

$$L := \phi \rightarrow piecewise(0 \le \phi \text{ and } \phi < 35, -10 + 0.354\phi, 35 \le \phi \text{ and } \phi < 55,$$
$$2.5 + 0.075(\phi - 35), 55 \le \phi \text{ and } \phi \le 90,$$
$$4 - (0.114(\phi - 55)))$$

We compute the loss for a distance d, where $1 \le d \le 100$ and angle of incident $0° \le \phi \le 90°$:

```
> wl := [seq(seq([d,phi,WI(2437,d,10,phi,2)], d=1..100),
  phi=0..90)]:
```

The statement below produces the 3D graph shown in Fig. 10.1. The path loss increases with an angle of incident up to 55°, then diminishes as the angle approaches 90°.

```
> pointplot3d(wl, axes=BOXED, font=[TIMES,ROMAN,12],
  labels=["distance (m)", "angle (deg)", "loss (dB)"],
  labeldirections=[HORIZONTAL, HORIZONTAL, VERTICAL]):
```

10.2 Berg Model

Another model for outdoor path loss in urban street environments is the Berg model [38]. Consider the street plan example shown in Fig. 10.2. The filled circle denotes

Fig. 10.1 Walfish-Ikegami
model path loss

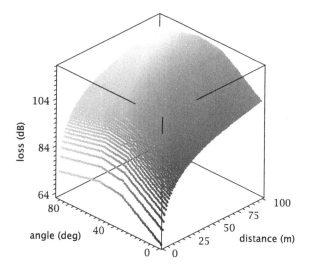

Fig. 10.2 Street plan

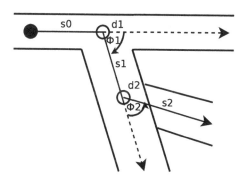

the access-point location in street s_0. Signals propagate along adjoining streets as if
from "virtual" access-points located at the junctions. Here, we use the Berg model
to analyze the path loss of the back-haul links forming a WDS (wireless distribution
system). The path loss L_{berg} is given by:

$$L_{\text{berg}} = 20 \log_{10} \frac{4\pi d_l}{\lambda} \tag{10.3}$$

where l is the street number. The distance d_l is given by the recursive function:

$$\begin{aligned}
d_0 &= 0, & d_m &= k_m \cdot s_{m-1} + d_{m-1} & l \geq m > 0 \\
k_0 &= 1, & k_m &= k_{m+1} + d_{m-1} \cdot q_{m-1} & l \geq m > 0
\end{aligned} \tag{10.4}$$

The angle of dependency to the adjoining street s_m (to s_{m-1}) is q_m:

$$q_0 = 0, \qquad q_m(t_m) = \left(q_{90°} \frac{\phi_m}{90} \right)^v \quad l \geq m > 0 \tag{10.5}$$

We follow the conventions in [38] and use, $q_{90°} = 0.5$ and $v = 1.5$. We define these constants in Maple:

```
> v := 1.5;
```

$$v := 1.5$$

```
> q90 := 0.5;
```

$$q90 := 0.5$$

The recursive terms q, d and k are defined as piecewise functions:

```
> q := (m) -> piecewise(m = 0, 0, q90 * angle[m]/90);
```

$$q := m \rightarrow \text{piecewise}\left(m = 0, 0, \frac{1}{90}q90 \ \text{angle}_m\right)$$

```
> d := (m) -> piecewise(m = 0, 0, k(m)*s[m] + d(m-1));
```

$$d := m \rightarrow \text{piecewise}(m = 0, 0, k(m)s_m + d(m-1))$$

```
> k := (m) -> piecewise(m = 0, 1,
                         k(m-1) + d(m-1)*q(m-1));
```

$$k := m \rightarrow \text{piecewise}(m = 0, 1, k(m-1) + d(m-1)q(m-1))$$

Finally, the Berg loss model in Equation (10.3) is defined as:

```
> berg := (f,l) -> 20 * log10(4*Pi*f*d(l)/c);
```

$$\text{berg} := (f, l) \rightarrow 20\log_{10}\left(\frac{4\pi f d(l)}{c}\right);$$

Using the street plan from Fig. 10.2, we analyze the path loss in an urban street area for a network operating on a channel with a centre frequency of 5.32 GHz (802.11a). The junction leading to street s_1 is 40 m (along s_0) from the access-points and branches at an angle of 30°. The junction leading to s_2 is 25 m down from the s_0/s_1 junction and branches off at an angle of 45°. The path loss along street s_0 is modeled as a sequence of short "streets", 10 m in length, at an angle 0°:

```
> s := [seq(10,i=1..12)];
```

$$s := [10, 10, 10, 10, 10, 10, 10, 10, 10, 10, 10, 10]$$

```
> angle := [seq(0,i in s)];
```

$$\text{angle} := [0, 0, 0, 0, 0, 0, 0, 0, 0, 0, 0, 0]$$

Calculate the path loss along street s_0 (at 10 m intervals) and create a graph object:

```
> loss1 := [seq([add(s[j],j=1..i), berg(5.32*10^9,i)],
  i=1..nops(s))]:
> G3 := pointplot(loss1, connect=true, color=black,
  legend=["street 0"]);
```

Now calculate the path loss along street s_1. The junction for s_1 is 40 m from the access-point. After the junction, we model s_1 as a sequence of short streets at 0° angles:

```
> s := [0,40,seq(10, i=1..8)];
```
$$s := [0, 40, 10, 10, 10, 10, 10, 10, 10, 10]$$

```
angle := [0,30,seq(0, i in s[3..-1])];
```
$$\text{angle} := [0, 30, 0, 0, 0, 0, 0, 0, 0, 0, 0, 0]$$

Calculate the path loss and create a graph object:

```
> loss2 := [seq([add(s[j],j=1..i),berg(5.32*10^9,i)],
  i=2..nops(s))]:
> G4 := pointplot(loss2, connect=true, color=black,
  linestyle=DASH, legend=["street 1"]);
```

Now calculate the path loss along street s_2, where the junction for s_2 is 25 m from the junction of s_1x at as angle of 45°:

```
> s := [0,40,25, seq(10, i=1..6)];
```
$$s := [0, 40, 25, 10, 10, 10, 10, 10, 10]$$

```
angle := [0,30,45, seq(0, i in s[4..-1])];
```
$$\text{angle} := [0, 30, 45, 0, 0, 0, 0, 0, 0]$$

Calculate the path loss and create a graph object:

```
> loss3 := [seq([add(s[j],j=1..i) , berg(5.32*10^9,i)],
  i=3..nops(s))]:
> G5 := pointplot(loss3, connect=true, color=black,
  linestyle=DASH, legend=["street 1"]);
```

The graph shown in Fig. 10.3 shows the path loss curves for each street and was produced by the command:

```
> display(G3, G4, G5);
```

10.3 802.11b Link Rate Adaptation

For regulation purposes, we must consider the equivalent isotropically radiated power (EIRP). EIRP is the (theoretical) power that would be emitted by an isotropic antenna in the direction of maximum antenna gain. EIRP is given by the equation:

$$\text{EIRP} = P_{tx} - L_c + G_{tx} \qquad (10.6)$$

In Europe, the maximum legal EIRP is 20 dBm (100 mW). For the purpose of this analysis, we assume that the transmitter is operating at the maximum legal limit (e.g. 20 dBm).

Fig. 10.3 Signal loss in an
urban area (Berg model)

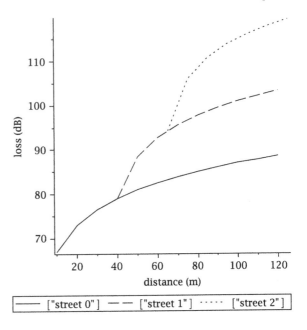

["street 0"] — — ["street 1"] ····· ["street 2"]

Table 10.1 Modulation
techniques supported by
802.11b for signal-to-noise
ratios and bit-error-rate

SNR/dB	BPSK	QPSK	CCK5.5	CCK11
1	1.2e−5	5e−3	8e−2	1e−1
2	1e−6	1.2e−3	4e−2	1e−1
3	6e−8	2.1e−4	1.8e−2	1e−1
4	7e−9	3e−5	7e−3	5e−2
5	2.3e−10	2.1e−6	1.2e−3	1.3e−2
6	2.3e−10	1.5e−7	3e−4	5.2e−3
7	2.3e−10	1e−8	6e−5	2e−3
8	2.3e−10	1.2e−9	1.3e−5	7e−4
9	2.3e−10	1.2e−9	2.7e−6	2.1e−4
10	2.3e−10	1.2e−9	5e−7	6e−5
11	2.3e−10	1.2e−9	7e−8	2.1e−5
12	2.3e−10	1.2e−9	1.2e−8	7e−6
13	2.3e−10	1.2e−9	1.7e−9,1	7e−6
14	2.3e−10	1.2e−9	1.7e−9	5e−7

First, we consider 802.11b (operating in the 2.4 GHz band). The data provided
in Table 10.1 shows the relationship between SNR (signal-to-noise ratio) and bit-
error-rate (BER) reported in [18] for modulation techniques supported by 802.11b.
The data rates for CCK5.5 and CCK11 are 5.5 and 11 Mb/s respectively. BPSK and
QPSK are from the original 802.11 standard and operate at 1 and 2 Mb/s respec-

tively. We calculate the signal strength (in dBm) at the receiver:

$$P_r = \text{EIRP} - \text{FSPL} + G_{rx} - L_c \qquad (10.7)$$

We use the free-space loss model (2.8) at $f = 2.437$ GHz. It is assumed that the end-user device has an internal antenna and that $G_{rx} = L_c = 0$. The signal-to-noise ratio (SNR/dB) is, therefore, the difference between the receive power P_r and the signal noise S_{noise} (in dB):

$$\text{SNR} = P_r - S_{\text{noise}} \qquad (10.8)$$

We define the bit error rates for BPSK in a list:

```
> BPSK := [1.2e-05, 1.0e-06, 6.0e-08, 7.0e-09,
  2.3e-10, 2.3e-10, 2.3e-10, 2.3e-10, 2.3e-10,
  2.3e-10,2.3e-10, 2.3e-10, 2.3e-10, 2.3e-10]:
```

The index to each BER value represents its corresponding SNR value. For example, if we want the BER for an SNR of 4 dB:

```
> BPSK[4];
```

$$7.0 \times 10^{-9}$$

Similarly, we define the BER/SNR relationship for QPSK, CCK5.5 and CCK11 in their respective lists:

```
> QPSK := [5.0e-03, 1.2e-03, 2.1e-04, 3.0e-05,
  2.1e-06, 1.5e-07, 1.0e-08, 1.2e-09, 1.2e-09,
  1.2e-09, 1.2e-09, 1.2e-09, 1.2e-09, 1.2e-09]:
> CCK5 := [8.0e-02, 4.0e-02, 1.8e-02, 7.0e-03,
  1.2e-03, 3.0e-04, 6.0e-05, 1.3e-05, 2.7e-06,
  5.0e-07, 7.0e-08, 1.2e-08, 1.7e-09, 1.7e-09]:
> CCK11 := [1.0e-01, 1.0e-01, 1.0e-01, 5.0e-02,
  1.3e-02, 5.2e-03, 2.0e-03, 7.0e-04, 2.1e-04,
  6.0e-05, 2.1e-05, 7.0e-06, 1.7e-06, 5.0e-07]:
```

The link rate adaptation R_b for 802.11b is given by:

$$R_b = \begin{cases} 11 & \text{BER} \geq \text{CCK11(SNR)} \\ 5.5 & \text{CCK11(SNR)} > \text{BER} \geq \text{CCK5(SNR)} \\ 2 & \text{CCK5(SNR)} > \text{BER} \geq \text{QPSK(SNR)} \\ 1 & \text{BER} \geq \text{BPSK(SNR)} \end{cases} \qquad (10.9)$$

The Maple function that implements (10.9) is:

```
> Rb := (s,b) -> piecewise(round(s) < 1, 0,
                 round(s) > 14,          11,
                 b > CCK11[round(s)],    11,
                 b > CCK5[round(s)],     5.5,
                 b > QPSK[round(s)],     2,
                 b > BPSK[round(s)],     1, 0):
```

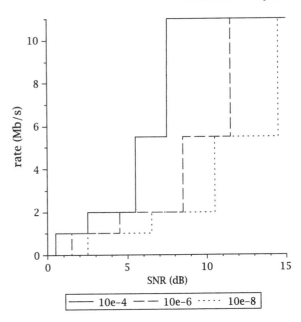

Fig. 10.4 802.11b Link rate adaptation versus SNR (dB)

We create graphs plots of the link rate against SNR for loss rates of 10^{-4}, 10^{-6} and 10^{-8}:

```
> G1 := plot(Rb(s,10e-4), s=0..15,
    labeldirections=["horizontal", "vertical"],
    labels=["SNR (dB)", "rate (Mb/s)"], legend=["10e-4"],
    linestyle=SOLID, color=black), font=[times,roman,12]:
> G2 := plot(Rb(s,10e-6), s=0..15,
    labeldirections=["horizontal", "vertical"],
    labels=["SNR (dB)", "rate (Mb/s)"], legend=["10e-6"],
    linestyle=DASH, color=black,font=[times,roman,12]):
> G3 := plot(Rb(s,10e-8), s=0..15,
    labeldirections=["horizontal", "vertical"],
    labels=["SNR (dB)", "rate (Mb/s)"], legend=["10e-8"],
    linestyle=DOT, color=black,font=[times,roman,12]):
```

The statement below produces the graph shown in Fig. 10.4:

```
> display(G1,G2,G3);
```

We calculate the signal-to-noise ratio as a function of the received signal P_r and the noise level. We derive P_r from the EIRP and the free-space loss model.

```
> SNR := (f,d) -> (EIRP - FSPL(f,d,K1)) - NOISE:
```

Set the EIRP and the noise level:

```
> EIRP := 20:
> NOISE := -90:
```

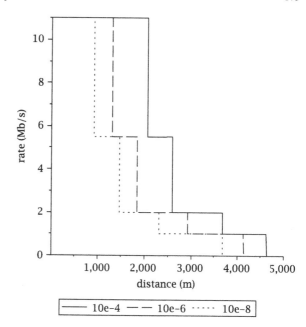

Fig. 10.5 802.11b Link
adaptation for strong LOS
with noise at −90 dB

We create graph plots of link rate adaptation against distance (for a frequency $f =$ 2.437 GHz):

```
> G4 := plot(Rb(SNR(2.437*10^9, d), 10e-4), d=10..5000,
  labeldirections=["horizontal", "vertical"],
  labels=["distance (m)", "rate (Mb/s)"],
  legend=["10e-4"],
  linestyle=SOLID, color=black,font=[times,roman,12]):
> G5 := plot(Rb(SNR(2.437*10^9, d), 10e-6), d=10..5000,
  labeldirections=["horizontal", "vertical"],
  labels=["distance (m)", "rate (Mb/s)"],
  legend=["10e-6"],
  linestyle=DASH, color=black,font=[times,roman,12]):
> G6 := plot(Rb(SNR(2.437*10^9, d), 10e-8), d=10..5000,
  labeldirections=["horizontal", "vertical"],
  labels=["distance (m)", "rate (Mb/s)"],
  legend=["10e-8"],
  linestyle=DOT, color=black,font=[times,roman,12]):
```

The graph in Fig. 10.5 shows the 802.11b link rate adaptation over distance for various error rates. The graph is rendered using the Maple display command.

The results shows that, assuming a free-space loss model, long distances can be achieved (even when European regulations are adhered to). We double the signal noise and repeat the analysis. The graph in Fig. 10.6 shows the link rate adaptation for NOISE = −87 dB.

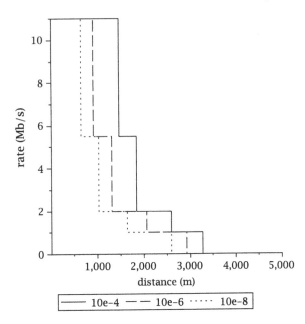

Fig. 10.6 802.11b Link adaptation for strong LOS with noise at −87 dB

10.4 Link Rate Adaptation in an Urban Area

We can examine link rate adaptation in urban environments by using the Walfish-Ikegami model in (10.1). We consider receivers in households located perpendicular and nearly perpendicular to the access-point (in the street). We define a signal-to-noise ratio function which uses the Walfish-Ikegami loss model instead of the free-space loss model:

```
> SNR2 := (f,d) -> EIRP - WI(2437,d,10,phi,2) - NOISE;
```

Now we set the angle from the access-point between the street and the wireless device. Here, the device is perpendicular to the access-point in the street:

```
> phi := 90:
```

Create graph plots for various BER (frequency is expressed in MHz):

```
> H1 := plot(Rb(SNR2(2437, d), 10e-4), d=10..50,
    labeldirections=["horizontal", "vertical"],
    labels=["distance (m)", "rate (Mb/s)"],
    linestyle=SOLID, color=black,font=[times,roman,12],
    legend=["10e-4"]):
> H2 := plot(Rb(SNR2(2437, d), 10e-6), d=10..50,
    labeldirections=["horizontal", "vertical"],
    labels=["distance (m)", "rate (Mb/s)"],
    linestyle=DASH, color=black,font=[times,roman,12],
    legend=["10e-6"]):
> H3 := plot(Rb(SNR2(2437,d), 10e-8), d=10..50,
```

Fig. 10.7 Link adaptation of
802.11b in an urban area
(Walfish-Ikegami model).
The wireless device is located
perpendicular to access-point
($\phi = 90°$) in the street

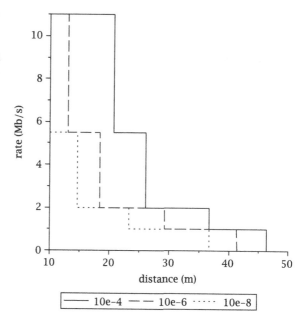

```
labeldirections=["horizontal", "vertical"],
labels=["distance (m)", "rate (Mb/s)"],
linestyle=DOT, color=black,font=[times,roman,12],
legend=["10e-8"]):
```

Render the graph in Fig. 10.7 with the statement:

```
> display(H1,H2,H3);
```

We repeat the analysis above for $\phi = 55$:

```
> phi := 55:
```

The graphs shown in Figs. 10.7 and 10.8 show link rate adaptation for the Walfish-Ikegami loss model (at 90° and 55° respectively). It can be seen that the results are more conservative than when using the free-space loss model. Perpendicular to the road ($\phi = 90°$), the maximum operating distance is approximately 60–80 m. At $\phi = 55°$ the operating distance of the channel is little more than 40–50 m. At more acute angles ($\phi < 55°$) the operating distance increases. For example, at $\phi = 20°$, the operating distance is around 50–65 m. This is due, mainly, to the signals travelling *along* (almost) the path of the street. We leave the reader to verify this analysis. The graph in Fig. 10.9 shows how the link rate adaptation varies with angle of incidence (for BER of 10^{-4}).

Fig. 10.8 Link adaptation of
802.11b in an urban area
(Walfish-Ikegami model) The
wireless device is located at
$\phi = 55°$ to the access-point in
the street

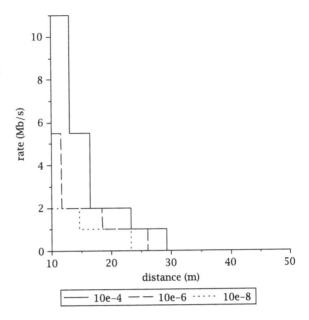

Fig. 10.9 Walfish-Ikegami
model link rate adaptation for
BER 10^{-4}

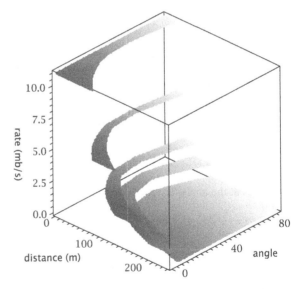

10.5 802.11a Link Rate Adaptation

In this section we consider a 802.11a backhaul network. Two wireless routers form a
link in the 5 GHz band. Both devices have external antennas connected by low-loss
cable. For 802.11a, [6]. provides empirical data for link rate adaptation. Furthermore, it includes measurements for environments with multipath and packet errors.
Table 10.2 shows the relationship between SNR and the link rate.

| **Table 10.2** 802.11a Link | Fading | Packet | Link rate | | | | | | |
| rate adaptation (empirical | | error | 6 | 12 | 18 | 24 | 36 | 48 | 54 |
data)									
	None	None	−2–3	3–6	6–9	9–12	12–16	16–18	18
	Multipath	None	0–5	5–12	n/a	12–19	19–22	22–27	27
	Multipath	5%	7–10	10–15	15–16	16–21	21–24	24–26	26

We implement the link rate adaptation model in Table 10.2 as a Maple function below. For no fading and no packet errors, the function is:

```
Ra1 := (s) -> piecewise(-2 < s and s <= 3, 6,
                         3 < s and s <= 6, 12,
                         6 < s and s <= 9, 18,
                         9 < s and s <= 12, 24,
                        12 < s and s <= 16, 36,
                        16 < s and s <= 18, 48,
                        18 < s, 54, 0):
```

Multipath fading and no packet errors:

```
Ra2 := (s) -> piecewise(0 < s and s <= 5, 6,
                         5 < s and s <= 12, 12,
                        12 < s and s <= 19, 24,
                        19 < s and s <= 22, 36,
                        22 < s and s <= 27, 48,
                        27 < s, 54, 0):
```

Multipath fading and 5% packet errors:

```
Ra3 := (s) -> piecewise(7 < s and s <= 10, 6,
                        10 < s and s <= 15, 12,
                        15 < s and s <= 16, 18,
                        16 < s and s <= 21, 24,
                        21 < s and s <= 24, 36,
                        24 < s and s <= 26, 48,
                        26 < s, 54, 0);
```

Create a graph of link rate adaptation against signal-noise-signal:

```
> I1 := plot(Ra1(s), s=-3..30,
  legend=["no fade/no error"],
  labels=["SNR (dB)", "rate (Mb/s)"],
  labeldirections=["horizontal", "vertical"],
  color=black, linestyle=SOLID):
> I2 := plot(Ra2(s), s=-3..30,
  legend=["mpath fade/no packet error"],
  labels=["SNR (dB)", "rate (Mb/s)"],
  labeldirections=["horizontal", "vertical"],
```

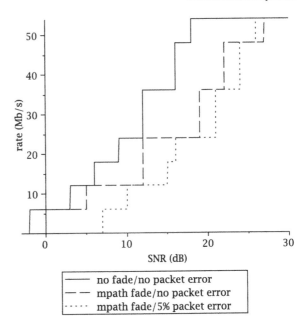

Fig. 10.10 802.11a link rate adaptation versus SNR

— no fade/no packet error
– – mpath fade/no packet error
· · · · · mpath fade/5% packet error

```
  color=black, linestyle=DASH):
> I3 := plot(Ra3(s), s=-3..30,
  legend=["mpath fade/5% packet error"],
  labels=["SNR (dB)", "rate (Mb/s)"],
  labeldirections=["horizontal", "vertical"],
  color=black, linestyle=DOT):
```

The graph shown in Fig. 10.10, rendered using the `display` command, shows the link rate adaptation for various environments.

In this scenario, the power of the receive signal is given by:

$$P_{rx} = \text{EIRP} - \text{FSPL} + G_{rx} - L_c \tag{10.10}$$

Note that antenna gain (G_{tx}) and cable loss at the transmit end are intrinsic to EIRP and, therefore, do not feature in (10.10). Gains and losses due to the antenna and cable are mitigated by an adjustment of the transmission power that is necessary in order to comply with a region's regulations. For the purpose of this example we assume European regulations and set the maximum EIRP to 20 dB:

```
> EIRP := 20:
```

We define a signal-to-noise ratio function:

```
> SNR3 := (f,d) -> EIRP - FSPL(f,d,K1) + Grx - Lc
                   - NOISE:
```

We assume an antenna with a gain $G_{rx} = 6$ dB and that the cable loss is $L_c = 2$ dB:

Fig. 10.11 Link rate versus distance for 802.11a

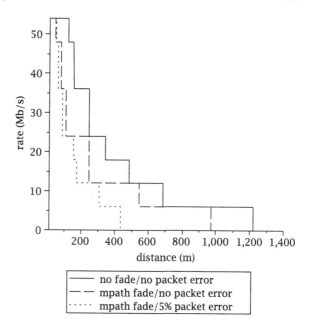

— no fade/no packet error
– – mpath fade/no packet error
····· mpath fade/5% packet error

```
> Grx := 6:
> Lc := 2:
```

Set the noise level:

```
> NOISE := -87;
```

Create graphs of the effects of link rate adaptation over distance:

```
> I4 := plot(Ra1(SNR3(5.5*10^9,d,K1)), d=10..2000,
  legend=["no fade/no packet error"],
  labels=["distance (m)", "rate (Mb/s)"],
  labeldirections=["horizontal", "vertical"],
  color=black, linestyle=SOLID):
> I5 := plot(Ra2(SNR3(5.5*10^9,d,K1)), d=10..2000,
  legend=["mpath fade/no packet error"],
  labels=["distance (m)", "rate (Mb/s)"],
  labeldirections=["horizontal", "vertical"],
  color=black, linestyle=DASH):
> I6 := plot(Ra3(SNR3(5.5*10^9,d,K1)), d=10..2000,
  legend=["mpath fade/5% packet error"],
  labels=["distance (m)", "rate (Mb/s)"],
  labeldirections=["horizontal", "vertical"],
  color=black, linestyle=DOT):
```

The graph in Fig. 10.11 (rendered with the display command) shows how the link rate drops as the distance between the devices increases.

10.6 Link Rate Experiments

In this section, we present an experimental analysis of link rate adaptation. We investigate a point-to-point outdoor link between two buildings in an urban-city environment. The test environment comprises two Cisco Aironet 1300 series access-points 16 dBi Yagi-Udo antennas. We use the Cisco *linktest* feature to investigate the performance of an outdoor point-to-point wireless link. The modulation scheme, and consequently the transmission speed, is determined by the link rate adaptation function. The `linktest` command, however, allows the operator to override the link rate adaptation and set the link rate at which the test is performed.

For example, the command below send 5000 packets of size 1024 at a rate of 2 Mb/s[1]:

```
#dot11 dot11Radio 0 linktest count 5000 packet-size
1024 rate 2.0
```

The results of the test above are automatically displayed on the console. If logged in over the network, the results can be recovered with the command:

```
#show dot11 linktest

GOOD (0 % retries) Time Strength(dBm) SNR SNR     Retries
                   msec    In     Out   In  Out    In Out
    Sent :5000, Avg 10  - 63    - 63   14   31 Tot: 2    5
Lost to Tgt: 0, Max 18  - 61    - 62   20   38 Max: 1    1
Lost to Src: 0, Min  9  - 65    - 65   10   11

Rates (Src/Tgt)     2Mb 5000/5000
Linktest Done in 51.956 msec
```

The results show the distribution (mean, maximum and minimum) of the response times, signal strength and signal-to-noise ratio. In addition, they also show the retransmission (retries) statistics. The `Tot` field shows all the retransmissions for the entire test. It can be seen that there were only 5 retransmissions (for both the in and out directions). The `Max` fields shows the maximum number of transmission attempts incurred by a single packet (for both in and out directions). The test is repeated for a rate of 24 Mb/s. As we are only interested in the retransmission results, we just show the `Retries` fields:

```
        Retries
      In    Out
Tot:  30    10
Max:   2     2
```

---

[1] The command-line below should appear on a single line. The width of the page means that it appears split over two lines.

It can be seen that the retransmissions are an order of magnitude higher than those for 2 Mb/s. Retransmissions are even higher for 36 Mb/s

```
          Retries
       In    Out
Tot:  469     2
Max:   40     2
```

However, when we attempt to run the test at 48 Mb/s, the console displays the following error:

```
*Mar   1 00:58:02.754: %DOT11-4-MAXRETRIES: Packet to
client 0022.9099.bf80 react
*Mar   1 00:58:02.755: %DOT11-6-DISASSOC: Interface
Dot11Radio0, Deauthenticatin
```

The test at this speed has resulted in a packet's retransmission attempt reaching the MAXRETRIES threshold, causing the link to disassociate. This means that the channel conditions cannot support rates of 48 Mb/s or above. Even at 36 Mb/s, retransmission rates are high and could, at times, reach the MAXRETRIES threshold. It would be advisable to limit the rate of the link to 24 Mb/s. In addition to the link

Table 10.3 Retransmissions

Direction	Link rate (Mb/s)				
	2	5.5	11	24	36
In	2	5	20	30	469
Out	5	7	10	20	67

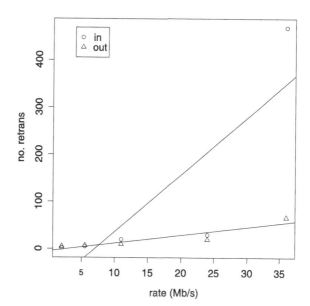

Fig. 10.12 Retransmissions versus link rate

rate test for 2, 24 and 36 Mb/s, we also ran the test for 5.5 and 11 Mb/s. The retransmission frequency results are summarised in Table 10.3. The graph in Fig. 10.12 shows the effect of the link rate on frame retransmissions.

10.7 Summary

In this chapter, we developed a number of link rate adaptation models for 802.11 devices. We have shown how to implement two signal loss models; namely, the Walffish-Ikegami and the Berg model. Along with published research data on link rate adaptation, we have used these models to analyse wireless coverage under a range of conditions.

Appendix A
Build a Xen Server

In this appendix, we describe how to set up Xen (Dom0) and how to configure the virtual machines (DomUs) that we use in this book.

A.1 Install Xen

Download and install packages:

```
$ sudo apt-get install
xen-linux-system-2.6.18-4-xen-686 \
> libc6-xen
```

Download bridge utilities package:

```
$ sudo apt-get install bridge-utils
```

Reboot:

```
$ sudo reboot
```

```
$ uname -a
Linux xen 2.6.18-4-xen-686 #1 SMP Thu May 10 03:24:35
UTC 2007 i686 GNU/Linux
```

In */etc/xen/xend-config.sxp*, uncomment the line:

```
(network-script network-bridge)
```

Install xen-tools:

```
$ sudo apt-get install xen-tools
```

In the file */etc/xen-tools/xen-tools.conf*, change the *kernel* and *initrd* parameters to reflect the system:

```
kernel = /boot/vmlinuz-2.6.18-4-xen-686
initrd = /boot/initrd.img-2.6.18-4-xen-686
```

A. Holt, C.-Y. Huang, *802.11 Wireless Networks*,
Computer Communications and Networks,
DOI 10.1007/978-1-84996-275-9, © Springer-Verlag London Limited 2010

Also, adjust the settings below:

```
dir = /home/xen
debootstrap = 1
size = 4Gb # Disk image size.
memory = 128Mb
swap = 128Mb
fs = ext3 # use the EXT3 filesystem
dist = etch # Default distribution
image = sparse # Sparse vs. full disk images.
```

Create a directory for xen guests:

```
$ sudo mkdir /home/xen/{,domains}
```

Here, we describe how to configure Xen to support multiple network (Ethernet) interfaces. Add a logical bridge:

```
$ sudo brctl addbr xenbr1
```

Turn off spanning tree:

```
$ sudo brctl stp xenbr1 off
```

Set the learning state time to zero:

```
$ sudo brctl setfd xenbr1 0
```

Activate the bridge:

```
$ sudo ip link set xenbr1 up
```

Check the bridge interfaces:

```
$ /usr/sbin/brctl show
bridge name bridge id               STP enabled interfaces
xenbr0      8000.feffffffffff no            vif0.0
                                            peth0
                                            vif26.0
                                            vif26.1

xenbr1      8000.000000000000 no
```

Add eth1 to xenbr1:

```
$ sudo brctl addif xenbr1 eth1
```

Configure */etc/xen/ipp-radius.cfg*:

```
vif = [ 'bridge=xenbr0', 'bridge=xenbr1' ]
```

Create the script file */etc/xen/scripts/int2-script*:

```
#!/bin/bash

dir=${dirname "$0")
```

```
$dir/network-bridge" start vifnum=0 \
                     netdev=eth0 bridge=xenbr0
$dir/network-bridge" start vifnum=1 \
                     netdev=eth1 bridge=xenbr1
```

In the file */etc/xen/xend-config.sxp*, enter the line:

```
(network-script int2-script)
```

A.2 DomU Configuration

In this section, we provide details of the configuration of the DomU virtual machines used in this book.

A.2.1 RADIUS Server

/etc/fstab:
```
/dev/hda1 /      ext3 errors=remount-ro      0 1
/dev/hda2 none   swap sw                      0 0
proc      /proc proc rw,nodev,nosuid,noexec 0 0
```

/etc/hostname:

```
radius
```

/etc/hosts:
```
172.16.20.70     radius
172.16.20.79     mysql
172.16.20.80     server
172.16.20.81     client sta
```

```
# The following lines are desirable for IPv6 capable
hosts
::1      ip6-localhost ip6-loopback
fe00::0 ip6-localnet
ff00::0 ip6-mcastprefix
ff02::1 ip6-allnodes
ff02::2 ip6-allrouters
ff02::3 ip6-allhosts
```

/etc/network/interfaces:

```
iface lo inet loopback

# The primary network interface
auto eth0
iface eth0 inet static
  address 172.16.20.70
  network 172.16.20.0
  gateway 172.16.20.1
  netmask 255.255.255.0
  dns-nameservers 192.168.1.201 192.168.1.203
```

/etc/xen/raduis.cfg:

```
kernel = '/boot/vmlinuz-2.6.18-4-xen-686'
ramdisk = '/boot/initrd.img-2.6.18-4-xen-686'

memory = '128'
root    = '/dev/hda1 ro'

disk
    = ['file:/home/xen/domains/radius/disk.img,hda1,w',\
       'file:/home/xen/domains/radius/swap.img,hda2,w']

name = 'radius'

vif = [ 'bridge=xenbr0' ]

on_poweroff = 'destroy'
on_reboot   = 'restart'
on_crash    = 'restart'
```

A.2.2 MySQL Server

The files, */etc/hosts* and */etc/fstab* are the same as for the RADIUS server, described in Sect. A.2.1 above.
/etc/hostname:

```
mysql
```

/etc/network/interfaces:

```
iface lo inet loopback

# The primary network interface
auto eth0
iface eth0 inet static
```

```
  address 172.16.20.79
  network 172.16.20.0
  gateway 172.16.20.1
  netmask 255.255.255.0
```

/etc/xen/mysql.cfg:

```
kernel = '/boot/vmlinuz-2.6.18-4-xen-686'
ramdisk = '/boot/initrd.img-2.6.18-4-xen-686'

memory = '128'
root    = '/dev/hda1 ro'

disk
   = ['file:/home/xen/domains/mysql/disk.img,hda1,w',\
       'file:/home/xen/domains/mysql/swap.img,hda2,w']

name = 'mysql'

vif = [ 'bridge=xenbr0' ]

on_poweroff = 'destroy'
on_reboot   = 'restart'
on_crash    = 'restart'
```

A.2.3 DHCP Server

The files, */etc/hosts* and */etc/fstab* are the same as for the RADIUS server described in Sect. A.2.1 above.
/etc/hostname:

```
dhcp
```

/etc/network/interfaces:

```
iface lo inet loopback

# The primary network interface
auto eth0
iface eth0 inet static
  address 172.16.20.57
  network 172.16.20.0
  gateway 172.16.20.1
  netmask 255.255.255.0
```

/etc/xen/dhcp.cfg:

```
kernel = '/boot/vmlinuz-2.6.18-4-xen-686'
ramdisk = '/boot/initrd.img-2.6.18-4-xen-686'

memory = '128'
root    = '/dev/hda1 ro'

disk = ['file:/home/xen/domains/dhcp/disk.img,hda1,w',\
        'file:/home/xen/domains/dhcp/swap.img,hda2,w']

name = 'dhcp'

vif = [ 'bridge=xenbr0' ]

on_poweroff = 'destroy'
on_reboot   = 'restart'
on_crash    = 'restart'
```

A.2.4 Test Client

The files, */etc/hosts* and */etc/fstab* are the same as for the RADIUS server described in Sect. A.2.1 above.
/etc/hostname:

```
client
```

/etc/network/interfaces:

```
iface lo inet loopback

# The primary network interface
auto eth0
iface eth0 inet static
  address 172.16.20.81
  network 172.16.20.0
  gateway 172.16.20.1
  netmask 255.255.255.0
```

/etc/xen/client.cfg:

```
kernel = '/boot/vmlinuz-2.6.18-4-xen-686'
ramdisk = '/boot/initrd.img-2.6.18-4-xen-686'
```

```
memory = '128'
root    = '/dev/hda1 ro'

disk
    = ['file:/home/xen/domains/client/disk.img,hda1,w',\
       'file:/home/xen/domains/client/swap.img,hda2,w']

name = 'client'

vif = [ 'bridge=xenbr0' ]

on_poweroff = 'destroy'
on_reboot   = 'restart'
on_crash    = 'restart'
```

Appendix B
Initial Configuration of Access-Point Controllers

The Alcalel-Lucent Omniaccess and Meru Network's wireless range is controller based. In this appendix, we show the initial configuration of the respective controllers.

B.1 Alcalel-Lucent Omniaccess Controller

Connect to the controller's console port with a terminal emulator application using the settings: 9600 baud, 8 bits, no parity, 1 stop bit and no flow control.

After a number of boot statements, the configuration sequence starts. Enter the name of the controller and IP address details. The switch-role needs to be set to "master":

```
Enter System name [OAW-4302]: controller1
Enter VLAN 1 interface IP address [172.16.0.254]:
172.16.50.101
Enter VLAN 1 interface subnet mask [255.255.255.0]:
255.255.255.0
Enter IP Default gateway [none]: 172.16.50.254
Enter Switch Role, (master|local) [master]: master
```

Select the appropriate country code. Do not select this option arbitrarily, as it configures the wireless channels pursuant to that country's regulations. Furthermore, if you select the country code "US", it cannot be changed[1] For the purpose of this example, we select "GB":

```
Enter Country code (ISO-3166), <ctrl-I> for supported
list: GB
```

Confirm your selection:

---

[1]This is a peculiarity of the Omniaccess controller.

A. Holt, C.-Y. Huang, *802.11 Wireless Networks*,
Computer Communications and Networks,
DOI 10.1007/978-1-84996-275-9, © Springer-Verlag London Limited 2010

```
You have chosen Country code GB for United Kingdom
(yes|no)?: yes
```

Configure the time and data and set the passwords:

```
Enter Time Zone [PST-8:0]:
Enter Time in GMT [10:05:01]: 10:13:00
Enter Date (MM/DD/YYYY) [3/12/2009]: 03//12/2009
Enter Password for admin login (up to 32 chars): admin
Re-type Password for admin login: admin
Enter Password for enable mode (up to 15 chars): admin
Re-type Password for enable mode: admin
Do you wish to shutdown all the ports (yes|no)? [no]:
yes
```

Note, the passwords are not echoed to the screen. The controller prompts you to confirm the configuration details:

```
Current choices are:

System name: controller1
VLAN 1 interface IP address: 172.16.50.101
VLAN 1 interface subnet mask: 255.255.255.0
IP Default gateway: 172.16.50.254
Switch Role: master
Country code: GB
Time Zone: PST-8:0
Ports shutdown: yes


If you accept the changes the switch will restart!
Type <ctrl-P> to go back and change answer for any
question
Do you wish to accept the changes (yes|no)
```

Answer "yes" if the details are correct. The controller will then reboot:

```
Creating configuration... Done.

System will now restart!
   :
   :
```

B.2 Meru Controller

The serial console settings for the Meru controller are 115200 baud, 8 bits, no parity, 1 stop bit and no flow control. When the controller starts up, displays the following output:

Controller startup:

```
CPU: Intel(R) Pentium(R) 4 CPU 2.00GHz stepping 09
PCI: Device 00:1f.1 not available because of resource
collisions
PCI_IDE: (ide_setup_pci_device:) Could not enable
device.
hda: 512MB CompactFlash Card,

 hda1 hda2 hda3
ICMP, UDP, TCP, IGMP
<6>EXT3-fs: INFO: recovery required on readonly
filesystem.
EXT3-fs: write access will be enabled during recovery.
kjournald starting.  Commit interval 5 seconds
EXT3-fs: recovery complete.
EXT3-fs: mounted filesystem with ordered data mode.
Your system appears to have shut down uncleanly
Checking root filesystem
[/sbin/fsck.ext2 (1) -- /] fsck.ext2 -a /dev/hda2
/: clean, 5032/228928 files, 277150/457728 blocks
EXT3 FS 2.4-0.9.17, 10 Jan 2002 on ide0(3,2), internal
journal
Mounting local filesystems ...

Accepting reset requests...

Intel(R) PRO/1000 Network Driver - version 6.1.16
Copyright (c) 1999-2005 Intel Corporation.
e1000: 01:0d.0: e1000_validate_option: Flow Control
Disabled
e1000: 01:0d.0: e1000_check_options: Interrupt
Throttling Rate (ints/sec) set te
e1000: eth0: e1000_probe: Intel(R) PRO/1000 Network
Connection
e1000: 01:0e.0: e1000_validate_option: Flow Control
Disabled
e1000: 01:0e.0: e1000_check_options: Interrupt
Throttling Rate (ints/sec) set te
e1000: eth1: e1000_probe: Intel(R) PRO/1000 Network
Connection
Using /lib/modules/2.4.18-3-meruenabled/kernel/drivers/
net/e1000_6_1_6/e1000.o
Setting hostname: default

...no longer accepting reset requests.
```

```
Starting Meru 3.4.2-135 wireless LAN services ...

ERROR : Cannot determine wireless subnet address.
System not fully operational.
Login as admin and use the "setup" command to correct
configuration errors.


default login:
```

Login as "admin" with password "admin" (the password is not echoed to the screen):

```
default login: admin
Password:
The system is not fully operational
```

Run the controller setup function:

```
default# setup

Begin system configuration ...
```

Set the region:

```
Set country code:


Country code configuration for this machine.


The country code is currently set to:   US
```

The default country code is "US", at this point we elect to change it:

```
Would you like to change it [yes/no/quit]?: y

The supported countries are:
    :
    :
GB (United Kingdom)
    :
    :
** WARNING: Once set to anything other than US, you
will not be able to change*
```

In this example, we select "GB":

```
Please enter a valid country code, or q to quit: GB
```

```
The system is configured for the following ISO country
code:    GB
Host Name configuration for this machine
```

We give the controller the hostname "controller":

```
Set host name:


Please enter host name, or q to quit: controller
Is controller correct [yes/no/quit]?: y
```

We keep the default password, but we strongly advise changing it:

```
Passwords (keep defaults):


Currently default password is used for admin
Would you like to change the password [yes/no/quit]?:
no

Currently default password is used for guest
Would you like to change the password [yes/no/quit]?:
no
```

Configure networking:

```
Networking:


IP configuration for this machine.

Would you like to configure networking [yes/no/quit]?:
yes

Would you like to use Dynamic IP configuration (DHCP)
[yes/no/quit]?: no

Please enter the IP configuration for this machine.
Each item should be entered as an IP version 4 style
address in dotted-decimal
notation (for example, 10.20.30.40)

Enter IP address, or q to quit: 172.16.11.50
Is 172.16.11.50 correct [yes/no/quit]?: yes
```

```
Enter netmask, or q to quit: 255.255.255.0
Is 255.255.255.0 correct [yes/no/quit]?: yes

Enter default gateway (IP), or q to quit: 172.16.11.1
Is 172.16.11.1 correct [yes/no/quit]?: yes


Would you like to configure a Domain Name Server
[yes/no/quit]?: no
```

Set the time:

```
Time:


The time is now Tue Aug 12 22:05:18 UTC 2008
Would you like to change the time zone for this machine
[yes/no/quit]?: yes
Please identify a location so that time zone rules can
be set correctly.
Please select a continent or ocean.
 1) Africa
 2) Americas
 3) Antarctica
 4) Arctic Ocean
 5) Asia
 6) Atlantic Ocean
 7) Australia
 8) Europe
 9) Indian Ocean
10) Pacific Ocean
11) none—I want to specify the time zone using the
Posix TZ format.
#? 8
Please select a country.
 1) Aaland Islands          25) Latvia
 2) Albania                 26) Liechtenstein
 3) Andorra                 27) Lithuania
 4) Austria                 28) Luxembourg
 5) Belarus                 29) Macedonia
 6) Belgium                 30) Malta
 7) Bosnia & Herzegovina    31) Moldova
 8) Britain (UK)            32) Monaco
 9) Bulgaria                33) Netherlands
10) Croatia                 34) Norway
11) Czech Republic          35) Poland
```

12) Denmark   36) Portugal
13) Estonia   37) Romania
14) Finland   38) Russia
15) France   39) San Marino
16) Germany   40) Serbia and Montenegro
17) Gibraltar   41) Slovakia
18) Greece   42) Slovenia
19) Guernsey   43) Spain
20) Hungary   44) Sweden
21) Ireland   45) Switzerland
22) Isle of Man   46) Turkey
23) Italy   47) Ukraine
24) Jersey   48) Vatican City
#? 8

The following information has been given:

        Britain (UK)

The name of the time zone is 'Europe/London'.
Is the above information OK?
#? 1

The following command is the alternative way of
selecting the same time zone

        timezone set Europe/London

Set system time for this machine.

Synchronize time with a Network Time Protocol (NTP)
server [yes/no/quit]?: yes

Please enter the name or IP address of an NTP server,
or q to quit: 130.88.203.2
Is 130.88.203.12 correct [yes/no/quit]?: yes

Upon completion, the controller reboots:

System configuration completed.
Do you want to commit your changes and reboot
[yes/no/quit]?: yes

Broadcast message from root (ttyS0) (Tue Aug 12
23:10:36 2008):

```
Now rebooting system...
The system is going down for reboot NOW!
flushing ide devices: hda
Restarting system.
```

References

1. N. Abramson. Development of the alohanet. In *IEEE Transactions on Information Theory*, volume 31.
2. Sam Bartels, John Monk, Alan Holt, and Chi-Yu Huang. Monitoring large management domains with mobile agents, volume 4, pages 13–19, 1 2008.
3. Christian Bettstetter, Christian Hartmann and Clemens Moser. How does randomized beamforming improve the connectivity of ad hoc networks? In *IEEE International Conference on Communications*, volume 5.
4. Vaduvur Bharghavan, Alan Demers, Scott Shenker and Lixia Zhang. MACAW: A media access protocol for wireless LANs. In *ACM SIGCOMM '94*, pages 212–225, 1994.
5. Jeffry B. Carruthers. In *Wiley Encyclopedia of Telecommunications*, pages 1–10. 2002.
6. Sayantan Choudhury and Jerry D. Gibson. Joint PHY/MAC based link adaptation for wireless LANs with multipath fading. In *IEEE Wireless Communications and Networking Conference*, volume 2, pages 757–762.
7. R.H. Coase. Federal Communications Commission. In *Journal of Law and Economics*, pages 1–40, 1959.
8. Jishu DasGupta, Karla Ziri-Castro, and Hajime Suzuki. Capacity analysis of MIMO-OFDM broadband channels in populated indoor environments. In *ISCIT '07. International Symposium on Communications and Information Technologies*, pages 273–278, 10 2007.
9. Federal Communications Commission. FCC makes additional spectrum available for unlicensed use, 11 2003. http://hraunfoss.fcc.gov/edocs_public/attachmatch/DOC-241220A1.doc.
10. Federal Communications Commission. Part 15—Radio Frequency Devices—of the Commission's Rules to Permit Unlicensed National Information Infrastructure (U NII) devices in the 5 GHz band, 2005.
11. Scott R. Fluhrer, Itsik Mantin, and AdiShamir. Weaknesses in the key scheduling algorithm of rc4. In *SAC '01: Revised Papers from the 8th Annual International Workshop on Selected Areas in Cryptography*, pages 1–24. Springer, London, 2001.
12. Behrouz A. Forouzan. *Introduction to Cryptography and Network Security*. McGraw–Hill, Berkeley, 2008.
13. P. Fuxjager, D. Valerio, and F. Ricciato. The myth of non-overlapping channels: interference measurements in IEEE 802.11. In *Wireless on Demand Network Systems and Services Conference, 2007*, pages 1–8, 2007.
14. Yoshinori K. Okuji. GNU Grub, 11 2009. http://www.gnu.org/software/grub/.
15. K. Halford, S. Halford, M. Webster, and C. Andren. Complementary code keying for rake-based indoor wireless communication. In *ISCAS 99. Proceedings of the 1999 IEEE International Symposium on Circuits and Systems*, volume 4, pages 427–430, 7 1999.

A. Holt, C.-Y. Huang, *802.11 Wireless Networks*,
Computer Communications and Networks,
DOI 10.1007/978-1-84996-275-9, © Springer-Verlag London Limited 2010

16. Lee Heeyoung, Kim Seongkwan, Lee Okhwan, Choi Sunghyun, and Lee Sung-Ju. Available bandwidth-based association in ieee 802.11 wireless lans. In *Proceedings of the 11th International Symposium on Modeling, Analysis and Simulation of Wireless and Mobile Systems*, page 132.

17. IEEE 802.11 WG. IEEE 802.11i Part 11: Wireless LAN Medium Access Control (MAC) and Physical Layer (PHY) Specifications. Amendment 6: Medium Access Control (MAC) Security Enhancements, 07 2004. Reference number ISO/IEC 8802-11-2004.

18. Intersil. HFA3861B direct sequence spread spectrum baseband processor, 2 2002. http://www.datasheetcatalog.org/datasheets/1150/76703_DS.pdf.

19. Institute of Electrical and Inc. Electronics Engineers. IEEE Standard for Information technology-Telecommunications and information exchange between systems-Local and metropolitan area networks-Specific requirements Part 11: Wireless LAN Medium Access Control (MAC) and Physical Layer (PHY) specifications. Amendment 5: Spectrum and Transmit Power Management Extensions in the 5 GHz band in Europe, 10 2003. IEEE Std 802.11h-2003.

20. Institute of Electrical and Inc. Electronics Engineers. IEEE Standard for Information technology-Telecommunications and information exchange between systems-Local and metropolitan area networks-Specific requirements Part 11: Wireless LAN Medium Access Control (MAC) and Physical Layer (PHY) specifications. Amendment 1: Radio Resource Measurement of Wireless LANs, 6 2008. IEEE Std 802.11k-2008.

21. Institute of Electrical and Inc. Electronics Engineers. IEEE Standard for Information technology-Telecommunications and information exchange between systems-Local and metropolitan area networks-Specific requirements Part 11: Wireless LAN Medium Access Control (MAC) and Physical Layer (PHY) Specifications, 06 2007. IEEE Std 802.11-2007.

22. Institute of Electrical and Inc. Electronics Engineers. IEEE Std 802.d-2004, ieee standard for Local and Metropolitan Area Networks: Medium Access control (MAC) Bridges, 06 2004.

23. P. Karn. MACA—a new channel access method for packet radio. In *ARRL/CRRL Amateur Radio 9th Computer Networking Conference*, 1990.

24. Greg Kroah-Hartman. *Linux Kernel in a Netshell*. O'Reilly, USA, 2007.

25. Mourad Melliti, Salem Hasnaoui, and Ridha Bouallegue. Analysis of frequency offsets and phase noise effects on an OFDM 802.11g transceiver. *International Journal of Computer Science and Network Security*, 5:87–91, 2007.

26. Meru Networks Inc. Meru System Director configuration guide, release 3.5, 2008. http://www.merunetworks.com/.

27. Metageek. Metageek, visualize your wireless landscape, 2009. http://www.metageek.net/.

28. Saikat Ray, Jeffrey B. Carruthers, and David Starobinski. RTS/CTS-induced congestion in ad hoc wireless LANs. *Wireless Communications and Networking*, 3:1516–1521, 2003.

29. Claude E. Shannon and Warren Weaver. *The Mathematical Theory of Communication*. University of Illinois Press, Chicago, 1963.

30. S. Salam Shumona, Sabrina Islam, Sabrina Ralman, Fakhrul Alam, and Forruk Almed. Performance of IEEE 802.11b wireless local area network. In *ICECE 2004, 3rd International Conference on Electrical & Computer Engineering*, pages 283–286, 12 2004.

31. Samuel Sotillo. Extensible Authentication Protocol (EAP) Security Issues, 11 2007. http://www.infosecwriters.com/text_resources/pdf/SSotillo_EAP.pdf.

32. William Stallings. *Handbook of Computer Communications Standards*, 2nd edition, volume 2. Howard W. Sams, Carmel, 1990.

33. Falko Timme. How to set up a load balanced MySQL cluster. 3 2006. http://www.howtoforge.com/loadbalanced_mysql_cluster_debian.

34. F.A. Tobagi and L. Kleinrock. Packet switching in radio channels: Part II—the hidden terminal problem in carrier sense multiple access modes and the busy-tone solution. In *IEEE Transactions on Communications*, 1975.

35. Ozan Tonguz and Gianluigi Ferrari. *Ad Hoc Wireless Networks: A Communication-Theoretic Perspective*. Wiley, USA, 2006.

36. Bruce Tuch. Development of waveLAN an ISM band wireless WAN. In *AT&T Technical Journal*, volume 72, pages 27–37, 07 1993.

37. Cabinet Official Committee on UK Spectrum Strategy. United Kingdom Frequency Allocation Table, 2008. http://www.ofcom.org.uk/radiocomms/isu/ukfat/ukfat08.pdf.
38. Bernhard H. Walke, Lars Berlemann, Guido Hertz, Christian Hoymann, and Ingo Forkel. Wireless communications—basics. In *IEEE 802 Wireless Systems*, pages 7–41. Wiley, New York, 2006.
39. Soekris Engineering Inc. Welcome to Soekris Engineering's website, 2008. http://www.soekris.com/.
40. Dominic Welsh. *Codes and Cryptography*. Oxford University Press, Oxford, 2004.
41. A. Zelst. Per-Antenna-Coded Schemes for MIMO OFDM, volume 4, pages 2032–2836, 05 2003.

Futher Reading

1. B. Aboda, L. Blunk, J. Vollbrecht, J. Carlson, and H. Levkowetz. RFC3738: Extensible Authentication Protocol (EAP), 2004. http://www.ietf.org/rfc/rfc3748.txt.
2. George Athanasiou, Thanasis Korakis, and Leandros Tassiulas. An 802.11k compliant framework for cooperative handoff in wireless networks. In *EURASIP Journal on Wireless Communications and Networking*, 7 2009.
3. Daniel J. Barrett and Richard E. Silverman. *SSH The Secure Shell*. O'Reilly, USA, 2001.
4. Stefano Basagni, Marco Conti, Silvia Giordano, and Ivan Stojmenovic. *Mobile Ad Hoc Networking*. Wiley, USA, 2004.
5. Mike Bauer. Securing your WLAN with WPA and FreeRadius, part I. *Linux Journal*, 48:36–38, 2005.
6. Mike Bauer. Securing your WLAN with WPA and FreeRadius, part II. *Linux Journal*, 49:32–36, 2005.
7. David M. Beazley. *Python Essential Reference*. New Riders, Indianapolis, 2000.
8. Christian Benvenuti. *Understanding Linux Network Internals*. O'Reilly, USA, 2006.
9. B. Boskovic and M. Markovic. On spread spectrum modulation techniques applied in IEEE 802.11 wireless LAN standard. In *EUROCOMM 2000. Information Systems for Enhanced Public Safety and Security*, pages 238–241, 2000.
10. Michael Elizabeth Chastain. Ioctl numbers. Linux kernel source, filename: Documentation-ioctl-numbers.txt, 10 1999.
11. D. Comer. *Internetworking With TCP/IP Volume 1: Principles Protocols, and Architecture*, 5 edition. Prentice Hall, Englewood Cliffs, 2006.
12. Carlton R. Davies. *IPSec Securing VPNs*. McGraw–Hill, Berkeley, 2001.
13. Angela Doufexi, Eustace Tameh, Andrew Nix, Simon Armou, and Araceli Molina. Hotspot wireless LANs to enhance the performance of 3G and beyond cellular networks. In *IEEE Communications Magazine*, volume 41.
14. Paul DuBois. *MySQL*, New Riders, Indianapolis, 2000.
15. Alan Flatman. Wireless lans: development in technology and standards, volume 5, pages 219–224, 10 1994.
16. Robert Flickenger. *Wireless Hacks*. O'Reilly, California, 2003.
17. M.S. Gast. *802.11 Wireless Networks*. O'Reilly, California, 2002.
18. Keith Haviland and Ben Salama. *Unix System Programming*. Addison–Wesley, Boston, 1987.
19. Carl W. Helstrom. *Probability and Stochastic Processes for Engineers*, 2nd edition. Macmillan, New York, 1984.
20. Guido Hertz, Erik Weiss, and Bernhard H. Walke. Ieee 802.11 wireless local area networks. In Bernhard H. Walke, Stefan Mangold, and Lars Berlemann, editors, *IEEE 802 Wireless Systems*, pages 7–41. Wiley, USA, 2006.
21. Raj Jain. *The Art of Computer Systems Performance Analysis*. Wiley, New York, 1991.
22. Christopher A. Jones and Fred L. Drake. *Python and XML*. O'Reilly, USA, 2002.

23. Oleg Kolesnikov and Brian Hatch. *Building Linux Virtual Private Networks (VPNs)*. New Riders, USA, 2002.
24. Mark Lutz. *Programming Python*, 3 edition. O'Reilly, Indianapolis, 2005.
25. S. Makridakis, S. Wheelwright, and R. Hyndman. *Forecasting Methods and Applications*, 3rd edition. Wiley, New York, 1998.
26. Alex Martelli and David Axcher. *Python Cookbook*. O'Reilly, USA, 2002.
27. Robert M. Metcalfe and David R. Boggs. Ethernet: Distributed packet switching for local computer networks. *Communications of the ACM*, 19(5):395–404, 1976.
28. Max Moser. Hotspotting. *Linux Magazine*, 56:22–24, 2005.
29. C. Siva Ram Murphy and B.S. Manoj. *Ad Hoc Wireless Networks, Architectures and Protocols*. Prentice Hall, New Jersey, 2004.
30. Thi Mai Trang Nguyen, Mohamed Ali Sfaxi, and Solange Ghernaouti-Heli. 802.11i encryption key distribution using quantum cryptography. *Journal of Networks*, 1(5):9–20, 2006.
31. Alessandro Rubini and Jonathan Corbet. *Linux Device Drivers*, O'Reilly, USA, 2001.
32. Michael Schwartzkopff. Shutting out strangers: Securing network access with 802.1X, RADIUS and ldap. *Linux Magazine*, 49:62–65, 2005.
33. Uwe Schwarz and Nils Magnus. Big mesh. *Linux Magazine*, 98:56–59, 2009.
34. W.R. Stevens. *Advanced Programming in the Unix Environment*. Addison–Wesley, Boston, 1992.
35. W.R. Stevens. *TCP/IP Illustrated Volume 1, The Protocols*. Addison–Wesley, Boston, 1994.
36. Andrew S. Tanenbaum. *Computer Networks*. Prentice Hall, New Jersey, 1989.
37. Mihalis Tsoukatos. Using a mysql database to store network data. *Sys Admin*, 16(6):6, 2007.
38. Srinivas Vegesna. *IP Quality of Service*. Ciscopress, Indianapolis, 2001.
39. John Viega, Matt Messier, and Chandra Pravir. *Network Security with OpenSSL*. O'Reilly, USA, 2002.
40. Roger Weeks, Edd Dumbill, and Brian Jepson. *Linux Unwired*. O'Reilly, USA, 2004.

Index

802.11
    Coordination functions, 39–50
802.11a, 61
802.11e, 46
802.11g, 61
    DSSS-OFDM, 61
    ERP-CCK/DSSS, 61
    ERP-OFDM, 61
    ERP-PBCC, 61
    Protection mechanism, 61
802.11i
    pre-RSNA, 99
802.11n, 51
    Channel bonding, 66
802.16, 58
802.3, 36, 121

A

Abstract syntax notation 1 (ASN.1), 85
AC, *see* Access category
Access category (AC), 47
Ad-hoc network, 36, 112
ADP, *see* Alcatel-Lucent discovery protocol
ADSL, *see* Asynchronous digital subscriber
    line
Advanced encryption system (AES), 80, 107
AES, *see* Advanced encryption system
Aircrack, 8
Aironet
    dot11 ssid command, 114
    interface Dot11Radio command, 114
AirSnort, 8
Alcatel-Lucent, 111

Alcatel-Lucent discovery protocol (ADP),
    115
Aloha
    Carrier-sense, 5
    Half duplex, 5
    Pure, 4
    Slotted, 4
American National Standards Institute
    (ANSI), 2
ANSI, *see* American National Standards
    Institute
ARQ, *see* Automatic repeat request
ASN.1, *see* Abstract syntax notation 1
Asymmetric key cryptography, 76
Asynchronous digital subscriber line
    (ADSL), 58
Automatic repeat request (ARQ), 44

B

Basic service set (BSS), 36
Beamforming, 66–71
BEB, *see* Binary exponential back-off
Berg model, 168
Binary exponential back-off (BEB), 43
Binary phase shift key (BPSK), 11
Binary phase shift keying (BPSK), 55
Bit error rates (BER), 11
Bluetooth, 3
BPSK, *see* Binary phase shift keying
Bridge priority tags, 47
BSS, *see* Basic service set
BTMA, *see* Busy tone multiple access
    protocol

A. Holt, C.-Y. Huang, *802.11 Wireless Networks,*
Computer Communications and Networks,
DOI 10.1007/978-1-84996-275-9, © Springer-Verlag London Limited 2010

Busy tone multiple access protocol
        (BTMA), 7

C

CA, *see* Certificate authority
Carrier sense multiple access (CSMA), 5
Carrier sense multiple access with collision
        avoidance (CSMA/CA), 40
Carrier sense multiple access with collision
        detect (CSMA/CD), 3
CBC-MAC, *see* Cipher-block chaining
        message authentication code
CCK, *see* Complimentary code keying
CCMP, *see* Counter-mode/CBC-MAC
        protocol, 107
Certificate authority, 84
Certificate authority (CA), 84, 87, 88
CFP, *see* Contention free period, *see*
        contention period
Channel bonding, 66
Cipher feedback (CFB), 74
Cipher-block chaining (CBC), 74
Cipher-block chaining message
        authentication code (CBC-MAC),
        107
Cisco, 111
Clause Shannon, 64
Clear-to-send (CTS), 7, 41, 61
Command
    bvi, 82
    chmod, 142
    chown, 142
    iwconfig, 112, 113
    iwpriv, 113
    wlanconfig, 113
Commands
    apt-get, 137, 140
    chroot, 127
    debootstrap, 126, 127
    dhclient, 153
    echo, 75
    fdisk, 133
    grub, 133
    iwlist, 151, 152
    md5sum, 82
    minicom, 115
    mkdir, 127
    mkfs.ext3, 133
    mount, 133
    mysql, 141

    mysqladmin, 140
    od, 79
    openssl, 92
    radclient, 138
    radtest, 138
    rcconf, 139
    ssh, 76
    tar, 133
    umount, 133
    wget, 79, 96
    yes, 92
Complimentary code keying (CCK), 56, 61
Configuration files
    /etc/fstab, 128
    /etc/hosts, 187
    /etc/inittab, 128
    /etc/network/interfaces, 187
    fstab, 187
Contention free period (CFP), 45
Contention period (CP), 45
Counter (CTR), 74
Counter-mode/CBC-MAC protol (CCMP),
        106
CRC, *see* Cyclic redundancy check
Cryptography, 73
    mode of operation, 74
    Public key, 76
    Symmetric key, 74
CSMA, *see* Carrier sense multiple access
CSMA/CA, *see* Carrier sense multiple
        access with collision avoidance
CSMA/CD, *see* Carrier sense multiple
        access with collision detect
CTS, *see* Clear-to-send
Cyclic redundancy check (CRC), 101

D

DAB, *see* Digital audio broadcasting
Data encryption system (DES), 80
DBPSK, *see* Differential binary phase shift
        keying
DCF, *see* Distributed coordination function
DES, *see* Data encryption system
Dictionary attacks, 104
Differential binary phase shift keying
        (DBPSK), 55
Differential quadrature phase shift keying
        (DQPSK), 55
DIFS, *see* Distributed inter-frame spaces

Digital audio broadcasting (DAB), 58
Digital certificates
  certificate authority, 88
Digital video broadcasting (DVB), 58
Direct sequence spread spectrum (DSSS),
      32, 51, 61
Distributed coordination function (DCF),
      39–44
Distributed inter-frame spaces (DIFS), 40
Distributed system (DS), 36
DNS, *see* Domain name system
Domain name system (DNS), 86
DQPSK, *see* Differential quadrature phase
      shift keying
DS, *see* Distributed system
DSSS, *see* Direct sequence spread spectrum
DVB, *see* Digital video broadcasting

E
EAP, *see* Extensible authentication protocol,
      146
EAP over LAN (EAPoL), 104
EAPOL, *see* Extensible authentication
      protocol over LANs
EAPoL, *see* EAP over LAN
Electronic codebook (ECB), 74
Encryption, 78
  asymmetric key, 76
  plaintext, 78
  symmetric key, 74
ESS, *see* Extended service set
Ethernet, 36, 121
Exposed terminal, 6
Extended service set (ESS), 36
Extensible authentication protocol
  EAP-LEAP, 104
  EAP-MD5, 104
  EAP-MSCHAPv2, 104
  EAP-PEAP, 104
  EAP-TLS, 105
  EAP-TTLS, 105
Extensible authentication protocol (EAP),
      104
Extensible Authentication Protocol (EAP),
      146
Extensible authentication protocol over
      LANs (EAPOL), 102

F
FCC, *see* Federal communications
      commission
Federal communications commission
      (FCC), 28
FHSS, *see* Frequency hopping spread
      spectrum
Free-space loss, 20
FreeRadius
  clients.conf, 138
  eap.conf, 148
  compile, 137
  MySQL, 140
Frequency hopping spread spectrum
      (FHSS), 32, 51–54

G
Gamma rays, 16
Gaussian frequency shift keying (GFSK), 53
GFSK, *see* Gaussian frequency shift keying
      (GFSK)
Global positioning system (GPS), 81
GPS, *see* Global positioning system
Group transient keys (GTK), 105
GTK, *see* Group transient keys

H
HA, *see* High-availability
HCCA, *see* HCF controlled channel access
HCF, *see* Hybrid coordination function
HCF controlled channel access (HCCA), 48
Hidden terminal, 6
High-availability, 135
Hybrid coordination function (HCF), 45–50
Hyperlan/2, 58

I
IBSS, *see* Independent basic service set
ICI, *see* Inter-carrier interference
ICV, *see* Integrity check value
IEEE, *see* Institute of Electrical and
      Electronic Engineers
IEEE 802.1D, 47
IEEE 802.1X, 102
  supplicant, 103
IFFT, *see* Inverse fast Fourier transform
Independent basic service set (IBSS), 36
Industrial. medical and scientific (ISM), 29
Infrared (IR), 51

Infrastructure mode, 36
Initialisation vector
    Collisions, 101
Initialisation vector (IV), 106
Institute of Electrical and Electronic
        Engineers (IEEE), 2
Integrity check value (ICV), 101
Inter-carrier interference (ICI), 60
International Organization
        for Standardization (ISO), 2
International Telecommunication Union
        (ITU), 84
Intersymbol interference (ISI), 60
Inverse fast Fourier transform (IFFT), 58
IR, *see* Infrared
ISI, *see* Intersymbol interference
ISM, *see* Industrial, scientific, medical
ISM, *see* Idustrial medical and scientific, 29
ISO, *see* International Organization for
        Standardization
Isotropic antenna, 15, 22
ITU, *see* International Telecommunication
        Union
IV, *see* Initialisation vector

K

KCK, *see* Key confirmation key
KEK, *see* Key encryption key
Key confirmation key (KCK), 105
Key encryption key (KEK), 105

L

LLC, *see* Logical link control
Logical link control (LLC), 2, 35

M

MAC, *see* Medium access control layer,
        see Medium access control
MACA, *see* Multiple access collision
        avoidance
MAN, *see* Metropolitan area networks
Man-in-the-middle attacks, 104
Master session key (MSK), 105
Maximum ratio combining (MRC), 62
Media access control (MAC), 4
Medium access control layer (MAC), 2
Medium access control (MAC), 35
Meru networks, 111
Message integrity check (MIC), 106

Metropolitan area networks (MAN), 3
MIC, *see* Message integrity check
Michael, 106
Microwaves, 16
MIMO, *see* Multiple input multiple output
MRC, *see* Maximum ratio combining
MSK, *see* Master session key
Multiple access collision avoidance
        (MACA), 7
Multiple input multiple output MIMO, 8
Multiple-input, multiple-output (MIMO), 66
Multiple-input multiple-output (MIMO), 62
MySQL, 137, 140
    /etc/mysql/my.cnf, 141
    FLUSH PRIVILEGES, 141
    SHOWS TABLES, 143

N

NAS, *see* Network authentication server
National Marine Electronics Association
        (NMEA), 81
National Telecommunications Information
        Administration (NTIA), 28
NAV, *see* Network allocation vector,
        see Network access vector
Network access vector (NAV), 61
Network allocation vector (NAV), 40
Network authentication server (NAS), 103
NMEA, *see* National Marine Electronics
        Association
Noise floor, 11
NTIA, *see* National Telecommunications
        Information Administration

O

OFCOM, 27
OFDM, *see* Orthogonal frequency division
        multiplexing
Omniaccess
    dot1x supplicant-info, 153
    show associations, 153
One-time pad cipher, 74
Open systems interconnection (OSI), 2
OpenSSL
    -subj option, 90
    ca command, 93
    dhparam, 142
    rand, 141
    req, 88
    req command, 88, 91

OpenSSL (*cont.*)
  x509 command, 90
Orthogonal frequency division multiplexing
    (OFDM), 58, 62
OSI, *see* Open systems interconnection
Output feedback (OFB), 74

P

Packet binary convolution coding (PBCC),
    56, 61
Pairwise master key (PMK), 105
Pairwise transient key (PTK), 105
PAN, *see* Personal area networks
PBCC, *see* Packet binary convolution coding
PC, *see* point coordinator
PCF, *see* Point coordination function
PCS, *see* Physical carrier sensing
Personal area networks (PAN), 3
Physical carrier sensing (PCS), 40
Physical layer convergence procedure
    (PLCP), 4, 35
Physical layer convergence procedure
    (PLCP) sub-layer, 51
Physical media dependent (PMD), 4
Physical medium dependent (PMD), 35
Physical medium dependent (PMD)
    sub-layer, 51
PLCP, *see* Physical layer convergence
    protocol, *see* Physical layer
    convergence procedure
PMD, *see* Physical media dependent, *see*
    Physical medium dependent, *see*
    Physical medium dependent
    sub-layer
PMK, *see* Pairwise master key
Point coordination function (PCF), 45
Point coordinator (PC), 45
Point-to-point protocol (PPP), 104
PPP, *see* Point-to-point protocol
Pre-RSNA, 99
Pre-shared key, 115, 124
Pre-shared key (PSK), 102
PRNG, *see* Pseudo-random number
    generator
Pseudo-random number generator (PRNG),
    101
PSK, *see* Pre-shared key
PTK, *see* Pairwise transient key
Public key cryptography, 76

Q

QAM, *see* Quadrature amplitude modulation
QPSK, *see* Quadrature phase shift keying
Quadrature amplitude modulation (QAM),
    58
Quadrature phase shift keying (QPSK), 55

R

Radio waves, 16
  ground waves, 17
Rayleigh distribution, 25
RC4, 79, 100, 106
Ready-to-send (RTS), 7
Receive sensitivity, 11
Request-to-send (RTS), 41, 61
Rice distribution, 25
Root certificate, 84
ROT13, 78
RTS, *see* Ready-to-send

S

Secure shell (SSH), 76
Short inter-frame space (SIFS), 41
Soekris, 126
Space-time codes (STC), 62
Spectral masks, 30
Split-channel reservation multiple access
    (SRMA), 7
SRMA, *see* Split-channel reservation
    multiple access
SSL
  Distinguished name, 88
STC, *see* Space-time code
Superframe, 45
Switched diversity, 62
Symmetric key cryptography, 74

T

Temporal key(TK), 105
Time-of-flight (TOF), 162
TK, *see* Temporal key
TKIP, *see* Temporal key integrity protocol
    countermeasures, 107
TKIP sequence counter (TSC), 106
TLS, *see* Transport layer security
TOF, *see* Time-of-flight
Traffic specification (TSPEC), 49
Tragedy of the commons, 34
Transmit opportunity (TXOP), 46

Transport layer security (TLS), 148, 149
TSC, *see* TKIP sequence counter
TSPEC, *see* Traffic specification
TXOP, *see* Transmit opportunity

U
ULA, *see* Uniform linear array
Ultraviolet, 16
Uniform linear array (ULA), 68
UNII, *see* Unlicensed National Information
        Infrastructure
Unlicensed National Information
        Infrastructure (UNII), 30

V
VCS, *see* Virtual carrier sensing
Vernam cipher, 74
Virtual carrier sensing (VCS), 40
Virtual LAN (VLAN), 115
VLAN, *see* Virtual LAN

W
Walffish-Ikegami model, 167
WDS, *see* Wireless distributions system

WEP, *see* Wired equivalent privacy
Wi-Fi Alliance, 8
WiMAX, *see* 802.16
Wired equivalent privacy, 114
Wired equivalent privacy (WEP), 7, 99
Wireless bridge, 123
Wireless distributions system (WDS), 121
WPA
    Pre-shared key, 124
WPA-PSK, 115

X
X-rays, 16
X.500
    Distinguished name (DN), 85
X.509, 84–86, 90

Z
Zigbee, 3